Wisdom from

the World's Religions

Wisdom from the World's Religions

A Guide to Basic Human Questions

Peter Feldmeier

ORBIS ★ BOOKS
Maryknoll, New York 10545

ORBIS BOOKS
Maryknoll, New York 10545

Fathers and Brothers
MARYKNOLL

Founded in 1970, Orbis Books endeavors to publish works that enlighten the mind, nourish the spirit, and challenge the conscience. The publishing arm of the Maryknoll Fathers and Brothers, Orbis seeks to explore the global dimensions of the Christian faith and mission, to invite dialogue with diverse cultures and religious traditions, and to serve the cause of reconciliation and peace. The books published reflect the views of their authors and do not represent the official position of the Maryknoll Society. To learn more about Orbis Books, please visit our website at www.orbisbooks.com.

Library of Congress Cataloging-in-Publication Data

Names: Feldmeier, Peter, author.
Title: Wisdom from the world's religions : a guide to basic human questions / Peter Feldmeier.
Description: Maryknoll, NY : Orbis Books, [2022] | Includes bibliographical references and index. | Summary: "Offers a unique and inspiring way to think about religions—even one's own—in light of the religious plurality that exists today"— Provided by publisher.
Identifiers: LCCN 2022015947 (print) | LCCN 2022015948 (ebook) | ISBN 9781626984851 (trade paperback) | ISBN 9781608339471 (epub)
Subjects: LCSH: Religion—Comparative studies.
Classification: LCC BL41 .F455 2022 (print) | LCC BL41 (ebook) | DDC 200.71—dc23/eng20220718
LC record available at https://lccn.loc.gov/2022015947
LC ebook record available at https://lccn.loc.gov/2022015948

I would like to dedicate this book to

my colleague Dr. John Sarnecki, the chair of my department.

John has been nothing but pure support for me

and my work over the past decade,

and I owe him more thanks than I can give.

Contents

Introduction

In 1971, John Lennon released *Imagine*, a song of peace in the midst of the Vietnam War. What would the world look like, he asked us to imagine, if there were no countries *to kill and die for*, if there were *no possessions* and *no need for greed or hunger*, but rather a universal *brotherhood of man*? We were also invited to *Imagine there's no heaven, it's easy if you try. No hell below us. Above us, only sky*, and ultimately *no religion too*.

These realities—countries, possessions, and religion—were imagined to be the very things that divide us, that create hatred, greed, and impoverishment. Indeed, it is not hard to find examples where patriotism, consumerism, and religious bigotry have caused considerable human suffering. According to a British poll, the belief that religion itself is divisive and causes violence was over 80 percent. In 2019, scholars representing the British Psychological Society, in an attempt to make sense of widely divergent results from modern studies, noted that "the literature is clearly a hodgepodge."[1] But the assumptions about religions and violence is widespread in Europe and the United States. In fact, the belief that religion divides and harms is so common, it would not be unusual to see defenders of religion accepting it as fact and trying to explain it away, such as by saying that moderates are not violent—only fanatics are. But what if the belief is fundamentally false?

Some of the most up-to-date studies on religion in America are correlated in Robert Putnam and David Campbell's *American Grace: How Religion Divides and Unites Us*.[2] Among their findings was a high correlation between religious observance and what they call "good neighborliness." They found that religiously observant Americans volunteer more, are more civically active, and are more generous with their time and money, and that this is true for secular causes as well as religious ones. They also found a high correlation between religious observance and religious tolerance. Among the most religiously dedicated, 89 percent believe that members of other religions can go to heaven. In other words, the more religious you are, the more likely you are to be particularly sympathetic to religious others.

But can we go further? Can religions actually *unite* us in some ways? Could we go beyond mere acceptance and tolerance to seeing other religions as repositories of wisdom that we ourselves could use? I believe that exposure to other religions and their deep insights into the spiritual condition of humanity can be a boon for all of us, even if one is purely secular and even atheistic. When I was interviewing for my job at the University of Toledo, a secular state school, I taught a class as an example of the kind of teacher I would be. In my presentation, I shared a version of a bodhisattva vow to the class. *Bodhisattva* means "enlightened being," and the vow to become one has everything to do with service to others. The very reason one wants to be enlightened is to use that enlightenment solely for the purpose of helping release others from their suffering. This is what I shared:

> The bodhisattva resolves: I take upon myself the burden of all suffering. . . . At all costs I must bear the burdens of all living beings. . . . All beings I must set free. . . . I must not cheat all beings out of my store of merit. . . . It

is surely better that I alone should be in pain then that
all these should fall into the states of woe . . . and with
this my own body I must experience, for the sake of
all beings, the whole mass of all painful feelings. . . .
In reward for all this righteousness that I have won by
my works . . . may I be balm to the sick, their healer
and servitor . . . may I be in the famine of the ages' end
their drink and meat; may I become an unfailing store
for the poor.[3]

Attending the lecture was the chair of my department,
a philosopher who is an atheist. He later told me that he was
so inspired by the heroism of the bodhisattva vow that he was
teary-eyed the rest of the class period. What would life look like if
everyone were this humbly devoted to service? If one shared one's
own good karma with others that they may flourish and took on
the bad karma of others, personally enduring their pain, to free
them from future suffering? *Imagine*, John Lennon asked us in
1971. Maybe insights from other religions would help us imagine
our lives differently, having been exposed to a very different vision
of humanity and spiritual pursuits. Certainly, it would encourage
a deeper respect and even honor for those who have embraced
other paths.

One might be concerned by such a project, particularly if one
is decidedly religious. A devout Muslim, for example, believes the
Qur'an represents the fullness of revelation and that the Prophet
Muhammad is the singular example of faithfulness. The teachings of the Qur'an and the examples and sayings of the Prophet
make for the surest expression of how to live an authentic spiritual life. Likewise, a Christian holds that Jesus himself is the absolute expression of the divine. St. Paul writes, "He is the image of
the invisible God, the firstborn of all creation. . . . For in him, all
the fullness of God was pleased to dwell, and through him God
was pleased to reconcile to himself all things" (Col 1:15–20). One

might argue that if I have the fullest revelation, even if other religions have interesting beliefs or practices, those beliefs can only be less than the fullness I already have.

There is another problem: If two claims about reality contradict each other, then at best only one of them could be right. So entertaining religious claims that contradict my religion could compromise it with falsehoods (presuming mine is right). And there is still another problem: Religious claims are not islands unto themselves, but are part of a web of understanding of the nature of the universe, the human condition, and the Divine. Taking a given claim or insight out of its context, as though that context did not matter, can undermine the integrity of that religion or one's own. It can even lead to the problem of syncretism, the amalgamation of different religions into one. This amounts to metaphysical mush.

This book is decidedly opposed to syncretism, which ultimately fails to respect religious traditions in themselves. I have been studying religions of the world for thirty years, particularly Christian and Buddhist traditions, and see large problems in blurring differences or making all-too-easy equivalences where they should not be made. I tell my students, "A great way to insult a Buddhist is to tell them: 'I know what you mean by Nirvana; it's what we call heaven.'" A Buddhist ought to think: "You've just co-opted my religion and shoved it into yours!"

None of these pitfalls has to be one's fate. With prudence, exposure to the wisdom and experience of religious others can expand our minds and hearts. We can actually become more spiritually mature in our own religion. We can learn to apply the insights we encounter in ways that do not undermine what we believe but may help us see ourselves differently and engage our lives more fully.

Here is an example I have used many times. Much of Buddhist thought is concentrated on the quality of one's consciousness and what proceeds from it. As the Buddha taught:

> All phenomena are preceded by the mind, created
> by the mind, and have the mind as their master. If
> one speaks or acts from a corrupted mind, suffering
> follows as a cartwheel follows the ox's foot. . . . All
> phenomena are preceded by the mind, created by the
> mind, and have the mind as their master. If one speaks
> or acts from a pure mind, happiness follows as a never-
> departing shadow.[4]

Buddhism particularly emphasizes that life is dissatisfying because
we have a grasping, craving mind. To the degree that we grasp
and crave, we are suffering, even if we are not directly aware of
this. We are our own worst enemies. Another saying of the Buddha: "Whatever an enemy would do to an enemy, a hater to one
hated, worse than that is the harm a wrongly directed mind can
do to oneself."[5] Taking the Buddha's teachings seriously, let us
consider a famous parable given by Jesus:

> Two men went up to the temple to pray, one a Pharisee
> and the other a tax-collector. The Pharisee, standing by
> himself, was praying thus, "God, I thank you that I am
> not like other people: thieves, rogues, adulterers, or even
> like this tax-collector. I fast twice a week; I give a tenth
> of all my income." But the tax-collector, standing far off,
> would not even look up to heaven, but was beating his
> breast and saying, "God be merciful to me, a sinner!"
> I tell you, this man went down to his home justified
> rather than the other; for all who exalt themselves will
> be humbled, but all who humble themselves will be
> exalted. (Lk 18:10–14)

It is obvious that Jesus contrasts here the posture of pride with
that of humility and challenges his hearers to embrace the latter. A
Buddhist sensibility, however, invites an additional analysis, that is,
it sees that the Pharisee is suffering—not only will his ego-inflated

pride condition a wretched afterlife, it also creates suffering in the moment. Of course, the Pharisee does not realize his situation, and his delusion makes him all the more tragic.

Buddhist awareness of the burden of a toxic mind does not stop here. Without deep mindfulness, such as that fostered by Buddhism, the reader can easily and unwittingly take on the very mental state of the Pharisee. One can proudly imagine oneself superior for not being like that judgmental Pharisee, whom one is of course now judging! Buddhist wisdom constantly brings us back to the quality of our own minds and the relationship we have with our experience. What is our mental state as we appropriate the insights of the parable?

One could go further here. Buddhism insists that our thoughts, like everything else, are ultimately empty of any permanent substance. One might be tempted to see one's own judgmentalism as something to condemn oneself with: I'm just like the Pharisee! Given Buddhism's regular practice of mindfulness, however, we realize that we do not have to identify with those thoughts. They arise and dissipate on their own. Thus, we realize we do not have to judge either the Pharisee or ourselves. Rather, we find an invitation to embrace the parable more fully and to cultivate compassion toward all who suffer delusion—the Pharisee, ourselves, everyone. In short, Buddhism does not hinder our understanding of the parable, but lets us appropriate its message more deeply.

Throughout this book, I intend to provide wisdom, insight, and inspiration drawn from various religious traditions, from the great Abrahamic traditions to Native American to Hindu and Buddhist thought to the Daoist understanding of wise living. In doing so, I hope to show how one's own religious categories might be enlarged or even reimagined. One does not have to believe each and every claim made here, some of which may directly challenge one's own religious sensibilities (not that this is a bad thing). But we can use these insights to better understand both ourselves and others. Pondering religious wisdom that has fed millions for millennia can only help us appreciate and be inspired by other paths.

This book will be broken up into large questions or issues that are themselves divided into two exemplars. In chapter 1, we address the very nature of God using Hindu ideas of *Brahman* and the Christian claims about God as Trinity. In chapter 2, we consider what is called "theological anthropology," that is, how humans are understood from a theological perspective. Here we will draw on the Islamic perspective on the simultaneously exalted position humans are placed in as well as the extraordinarily humble posture they must have. Then we will look into the enigmatic teachings of Buddhism, which hold that there is in fact no intrinsic self and yet that very *no self* is capable of attaining enlightenment. Chapter 3 investigates possibilities of finding and serving God. We will consider different *yogas* from the Hindu tradition and explore how they can be mutually supportive, drawing from the teachings of the Bhagavad-Gita. Then we will return to Islamic sources and their "Five Pillars of Islam." These represent a very concrete way to find and serve God that is surprisingly many layered and potentially extremely transformative. In chapter 4, we will consider how one might skillfully live as a religious person. This chapter will be entirely devoted to the Jewish tradition, but under two forms. First, we will look at the standard Jewish understanding of following God's *Torah* (guidance or law) and the sacred deeds and commandments (*mitzvot*) that go with this. Then we will see how the Hasidic community endeavors to infuse daily life with a kind of mystical ecstasy.

Chapter 5 explores the possibility of rethinking how the universe works and how we might live profoundly in these different worldviews. First, we will consider the Daoist tradition and its way of working with the relationships and energies around us. Next, we will look into the Buddhist expression of a bodhisattva's life and why Nirvana is by definition a way of service and compassion. In chapter 6, we investigate how we might cultivate a life of spiritual balance. Here we are led to a Jewish understanding that life ought to be robustly embraced and that one can hold together both selfless and self-interested concerns. Balance is understood quite differently for Buddhists, and we will look at a form of Buddhist meditation that unites love, compassion, joy, and equanimity to collectively live wholesomely in this world and the next. Chapter 7 considers how one might imagine living more harmoniously in the natural world. In the context of global warming, we will hear from the Christian tradition's understanding of caring for the world, particularly as it is reflected in the writing of Pope Francis. Next, we will look at three examples of Native American spirituality, all of which see the world as a spiritually united reality. Here, there is no relationship *with* the natural world. We *are* the natural world.

Chapter 8 asks us to think about how we might "see" God. As God is beyond the visual or conceptual possibilities of humans, can it still be possible to *see* the Divine? Here we will exclusively consider the Christian tradition, which makes a bold and unique claim: to see Jesus is to see God. Chapter 9 investigates the process of death and what is beyond death. We will see how Tibetan Buddhism imagines the *bardo* or "between" state from dying to rebirth and the practices Tibetan Buddhists engage in to prepare for this potent moment. We will also look at strikingly similar proclamations in many religions that understand the end game to be union with God. Our final chapter (10) returns to the question of the plurality of religions and what to make of them. There are no easy answers here, but we will consider responsible ways of thinking about this question. The second part of the chapter describes qualities of spiritual maturity that seem to cross the spiritual imaginations of many world religions.

A final word regarding sources. Where I have drawn on insights from others, I have been attentive to citing these sources. In only a few cases have I provided my own translation of primary texts. Typically, I have relied on trusted translations by experts, some of whom do not cite a specific manuscript they are relying on, and thus neither do I. In the bibliography, I cite the direct translations I am using, and only use specific endnotes when these sources vary. For the Bible I am relying on the New

Revised Standard Version (NRSV). Mostly, I have striven to limit my endnotes so as not to burden the reader. This book is intended to be less a work of critical, independent scholarship on specific texts and their interpretations and more an opportunity to appreciate the breadth and depth of our fellow spiritual travelers from around the world.

Notes

1. Jesse Singal, "Does Religion Really Cause Violence?" *BPS Research Digest*, May 10, 2019, https://digest.bps.org.uk/2019/05/10/does-religion-really-cause-violence-a-new-review-suggests-any-link-is-far-from-straight-forward/.

2. Robert Putman and David Campbell, *American Grace: How Religion Divides and Unites Us* (New York: Simon & Schuster, 2010).

3. E. A. Burtt, ed., *The Teachings of the Compassionate Buddha: Early Discourses, the Dhammapada, and Later Basic Writings* (New York: New American Library, 2000), 109–18.

4. *Dhammapada*, 1–2. Translation is mine.

5. *Dhammapada*, 42. Translation is mine.

1

Who Is God?

What do we mean when we use the term *God*? Many, wittingly or not, imagine God much like a great and perfect human, with a similar kind of consciousness and inner life, albeit infinitely greater. This need not actually be a serious problem, but we ought to know where we are starting from. Philosophers regularly posit God as having three characteristics: All-Knowing; All-Loving; and All-Powerful. These are the "omnis" (omniscient, omnibenevolent, and omnipotent). I was once in a public debate with an atheist philosopher on the question of God, and the moderator of the debate began by asking, "Can we all agree to what we are talking about? Can we posit God with the *omnis*?" Both my debate opponent and I agreed.

Given these qualities, my opponent began with a typical challenge: the problem of evil or suffering. The challenge looks like this: There cannot be a God who is all knowing, loving, and powerful if there is such vast suffering. Either God doesn't know or really care about God's creatures or God is powerless to do anything about it. And if God is omniscient, why did God create the world knowing the depths of suffering that would emerge? Theistic responses often lean on issues of the cost of free will or perhaps a positive value in suffering. Others have responded that

1

the very status of being a creature and not the Creator necessarily means limitations and forms of brokenness.

The Greek philosopher Plato understood God as the source and ground of the Good, the True, and the Beautiful. These reside in God as something of God's nature, and the created world participates in these *transcendentals*. Thus, when we are pursuing and living out goodness or truth we are participating in the life of God. To recognize beauty is implicitly to see veiled expressions of the Divine. The Platonic tradition saw God as emanating outward as a creative act, so that the physical world is associated with God through the transcendentals. For Plato, we are, in this sense, an extension of God's essential life.

Hindu Wisdom: Brahman

Striving to understand God, who or what God is, and how God is related to the created world is hardly isolated to the West. Ancient Hindus also strove to understand the nature of the Divine. Hindus are known for their many gods. Today, one of the most popular is Ganesha, who is thought to be the son of the great god Shiva and his consort Parvati. Ganesha is considered the god of good fortune and the remover of obstacles. The earliest Hindu scripture, the *Rig Veda*, reveals many details about the gods and their powers and responsibilities. Over a quarter of the hymns are devoted to Indra, a god of storm, war, and the master of all the heavenly gods. Varuna is the god of cosmic order, and Agni is the god of fire. It was Agni's job to bring the sacrifice to the gods from the priest's fire altar. This task was so important in ancient India that we even find Agni being identified with other gods and even with the power underlying their own power. "You, O Agni, are Indra, the Bull of all that exists; you are the wide-striding Vishnu. . . . [Y]ou control sustenance" (II.I.3, 4, 6). The reason for Agni's importance is that Agni represents the actual and potential power inherent in reality. In some texts, the gods even appear to obtain their power from Agni (VI.7).

But these lower-case "g" gods are not God. Their creation and their underlying life sustenance are dependent on a greater transcendent source called *Brahman*. The term "Brahman" is derived from the verbal root *brh-*, meaning to grow or become great. In early Vedas, the word *brahman* referred to sacred utterances through which the gods became great. In some later Vedic texts, it came to denote sacred rituals and the priests who were in charge of them. One Vedic text, the *Shatapatha Brahmana*, describes how creation happened. "This universe was nonexistent in the beginning."[1] The text then describes how there were only the *breaths* or vital powers of life. These vital breaths created seven separate beings or realities, which combined to make one Person or being. This person was given the title *Prajapati*, Lord of the Generation. The now unified Prajapati exerted itself through its own inner heat and created the universe, including the gods and mortal creatures. Then Prajapati started to become "disjointed" as the vital breaths had departed from him. He called on Agni to restore him.

Although this is mythically and not scientifically framed, what one sees here is that the underlying power of the universe has something to do with essential heat. Prajapati loses his heat in creation and it must be restored by Agni. And, since Agni is heat itself, one can see the connections the text is trying to make. Agni, who is fire, is both the source of the heat and its early manifestation in the Hindu sacrifice. In this sense, the fire of the sacrifice is identical with the underlying reality of the universe, and the creation and ongoing continuation of the universe depend on the continual performance of priestly rituals around fire.

The Upanishads, most of which were written between 800 BCE and 300 BCE, are canonical texts that follow the Vedas. These writings were devoted to a deeper understanding of the nature of Ultimate Reality. Although they did not directly dismiss what the Vedas taught, they advanced their own philosophical inquiries. They used the term *Brahman* to refer to Ultimate Reality and the essence that underlies all reality.[2] Some references in the Upanishads seem to identify Brahman in ways that sound like God as understood in the West. Brahman is periodically denoted as Creator, Sustainer, Benign Giver, and Omnipresent Being. Brahman is also not like other beings. One of the most typical descriptions of Brahman is *neti neti* (not this, not that), for Brahman is transcendent and indescribable.[3]

One thing is clear: Brahman is the underlying source of all reality, and that source is imbued in all reality. In the *Brahadaranyka Upanishad* we read, "As a spider moves along the thread, as small sparks come forth from the fire, even so from this Self [Brahman] comes forth all breaths, all worlds, all divinities, all beings. Its secret meaning is the truth of truth. Vital breaths are the truth and their truth is It" (2.1.20). This Upanishad also has a brief note on creation: "In the beginning this [world] was only the Self, in the shape of a person. Looking around he saw nothing else. He first said 'I am.'" Later in the text we find, "In the beginning Brahman indeed was this [world]. It knows itself as 'I am Brahman'" (5.5.4).[4] Everything begins and ends with Brahman. Brahman is the ultimate referent that underlies any meaning. In the *Taittiriya Bhasya* we find a chant that is fascinating:

> I am food, I am food, I am food; I am the eater of food, I am the eater of food, I am the eater of food; I am the synthesizer [digester], I am the synthesizer, I am the synthesizer; I am the firstborn of world-order, prior to the gods, in the navel of immortality. Whoso gives me, he verily saves. I am the food that eats the eater of food. I have overwhelmed the universe; [I am] the many-hued light.[5]

If we can put all this together, Brahman is the sustaining power of reality in the universe, the essence of life that grounds all life. The *Atharva Veda* says, "All things come from Brahman and are supported by Brahman; to know Brahman is to know all, since Brahman is this All, this universe" (10.8.44).

Is Brahman then merely an impersonal spiritual essence that existed eternally and through which the universe was created? Does Brahman have a *personality*? Many Hindus argue no. To personalize Brahman is to imagine a "being" and not Being itself. They refer to this impersonal expression of Brahman as *Nirguna-Brahman*, Brahman without qualities. Yet even here Brahman is not without some descriptives. The *Brihadaranyaka Upanishad* characterizes Brahman as *satchitananda* (*sat*-being, *chit*-consciousness, *ananda*-bliss) (2.4, 3.9, 4.3). In the later *Tejobindu Upanishad*, satchitananda is more fully explained:

> I am of the nature of consciousness.
> I am made of consciousness and bliss.
> I am nondual, devoid of desire or anger, I am detached.
> I am One Essence, unlimitedness, utter consciousness.
> I am boundless Bliss, existence and transcendent Bliss.
> I am the Self that reveals itself.
> I am the Satchitananda that is eternal, enlightened and pure. (3.1–3.12).[6]

All this represents a significant development in the Hindu understanding of the Divine—from Brahman needing the essential heat of the fire worship and its associated god Agni, to Brahman as pure, eternal existence, whose essence is absolute being, consciousness, and bliss. But even with these descriptives, Brahman is wholly impersonal. Brahman does not care about creation or human liberation. Brahman simply is. Not all Hindus, however, think that Brahman is at its core *nirguna* (without qualities). Many consider Brahman as very personal, one who intervenes in the created world and who positively desires our liberation; one who in essence loves us. This is known as *Saguna-Brahman*.

The relationship between the gods and Brahman is complex. Many Hindus believe the gods—particularly Shiva, Vishnu, and Shakti—represent access to, or even the face of, Brahman. There is an interesting conversation in the *Brihadaranyaka Upanishad* between Vidagdha Shakalya and the wiser Yajnavalkya. Vidagdha asks him how many gods there are, and Yajnavalkya replies, "As many as are mentioned in the *nivid* [invocation of the gods] of the hymn of praise of the Vishve-devas, namely, three hundred and three, and three thousand and three [3,306]." Vidagdha seems unsatisfied and repeats the question: "Yes," he says, "but how many gods are there, Yajnavalkya?" Yajnavalkya's answer is then thirty-three. Vidagdha asks the same question five more times to receive the answers of six, three, two, one and a half, and finally one. After explaining that these gods are all manifestations of divinity itself, Yajnavalkya finally declares, "Which is the one God? . . . He is Brahman, they call him that" (III.9.–19).

The great eighth-century philosopher and mystic Shankara, who for much of his life had a devotion to Shiva, taught that the worship of the Divine as personal was highly spiritually skillful. But if one wanted to be liberated, one would have to eventually shed any sense that the Divine had personal qualities or was in any way personal. While Shankara's position is highly respected, it is not the majority opinion, even among scholars. Many Hindus believe that one of the gods is actually the fullness of Brahman. In modern Hinduism the vast majority of these represent Shaivites who worship Shiva, Vaishnavites who worship Vishnu, or Shaktas who worship Shakti the Mother God. For each, they believe that Absolute Brahman is exactly their God.

Thus, we have a philosophical conflict among Hindu scholars themselves and lay people alike. Is the Divine ultimately impersonal or personal, nirguna or saguna? Could the Divine be both at the same time? One way to consider this question is through the experience of one of Hinduism's greatest mystics of the modern period, Sri Ramakrishna (1836–1886). Ramakrishna's biography is fascinating. He was born in a small village of Kamarpukur in Bengal to a Brahmin family. His father died when he was around seven, and his brother Ramakumar, thirty years his senior, took responsibility for the family. Bengali worship of Vishnu was widespread, and Ramakrishna's family would have considered themselves Vaishnavites. They did also, however, participate in the veneration of other deities of devotional Hindu religion, such as Shiva and the goddess Durga. Ramakrishna was intensely interested in God. He was something of a natural mystic, and regularly entered into deep, overwhelming consciousness of divine things. His first mystical experience was when he was ten years old. He described it like this:

> One morning I took parched rice in a small basket and was eating it while walking. . . . In one part of the sky there appeared a beautiful black cloud charged with rain. I was looking at it while eating the rice. Very soon, the cloud covered almost the whole sky, when a flock of milk-white cranes flew against that black cloud. It looked so beautiful that I became very soon absorbed in an extraordinary mood. Such a state came on me that my external consciousness was lost. I fell down and the rice got scattered. . . . People saw it and carried me home. This was the first time that I lost external consciousness in ecstasy.[7]

From an early age, Ramakrishna had the habit of striking up conversations about the spiritual life from anyone he deemed wise, including various wandering *sadhus* or holy renunciants who passed through his village. He regularly experimented with their diverse spiritual practices.

In order to improve the family's financial situation, his brother Ramakumar moved to the city of Calcutta and opened a Sanskrit school there. In 1852, he brought Ramakrishna, then in his late teens, to the city. In 1855, a wealthy woman named Rani Rasmani, who was devoted to Shakti, the Divine power conceived of as the Great Goddess, built a new temple to the Divine Mother in her fierce form of Kali along the banks of the Ganges. Ramakumar, who was trained as a priest and had undergone the initiation qualifying him to perform ritual worship of Kali, was appointed chief priest of the temple. Ramakrishna was appointed priest of a shrine in the temple precinct that was devoted to the spiritual union of the divine Krishna and human Radha. Within a year, Ramkumar's health had seriously deteriorated and Ramakrishna was prevailed upon to seek training and initiation in Shakta ritual and become the temple's chief priest to Kali.

Kali is known as a fierce and intimidating God, but Ramakrishna understood her as "my eternal Mother." One of his favorite hymns to her, written by the Bengali poet Ramprasad, goes: *My mind is overwhelmed with wonder, pondering my Mother's mystery. Her very name removes the fear of Kala, death himself. Beneath her feet lies Maha-Kala* [Shiva].[8]

Ramakrishna experienced the presence of the Divine Mother often. He also, however, experienced times in which it seemed as though she were utterly absent from him, in what is sometimes referred to as a dark night of the soul. He declared to his disciples, "Oh what days of suffering I passed through! You can't imagine my agony at separation from Mother. . . . I became mad for her."[9] He also described the climax of his crises and its mystical resolution:

> There was an intolerable anguish in my heart because I could not have Her vision. . . . Greatly afflicted with the thought that I might never have Mother's vision, I was dying of despair. . . . My eyes suddenly fell upon the sword that was there in the Mother's temple. I made up my mind to put an end to my life with it that very moment. Like one mad, I ran and caught hold of it, when suddenly I had the wonderful vision of the Mother and fell down unconscious. I did not know what happened then in the external world. . . . But in my heart of hearts, there was flowing a current of intense bliss, never experienced before, and I had the immediate knowledge

of the light that was Mother . . . what I saw was a boundless infinite conscious sea of light! However far and in whatever direction I looked, I found a continuous succession of effulgent waves coming forward, raging and storming from all sides with great speed. Very soon, they fell on me and made me sink into the unknown bottom. I panted, struggled and fell unconscious.[10]

Later, Ramakrishna recounted that during this early period he would sometimes see "that form of the Mother with hands that give boons and freedom from fear—the form that smiled, spoke and consoled and taught me in endless ways!"[11]

In 1860, he returned to his hometown and the Dakshineswar temple, awash with "divine madness and inebriation." He entered extraordinary states of consciousness regularly. In 1861, a holy woman (*sadhvi*) named Yogashvari arrived at Dakshineswar. She was an accomplished master in the Tantric form of spiritual discipline and became Ramakrishna's first formal guru. She helped him subject his religious struggles to a more systematic, long-term discipline. Under her tutelage, he came to realize "that the whole world was filled with God alone," and to see that all deities were really forms of the Divine Mother.[12]

In around 1864, a holy man (*sadhu*) named Totapuri came through town. He was a guru of the school that taught that there was ultimately only Nirguna-Brahman. Through Totapuri's instructions, Ramakrishna learned to meditate with a consciousness devoid of all conceptual forms (*nirvikalpa samadhi*). On his very first attempt, Ramakrishna remained in that deep meditative state for three days. Ramakrishna became convinced that the Divine was both absolutely impersonal and absolutely personal at the same time. He told his disciples, "A vijnani [one with full knowledge] isn't afraid of anything. He has realized both aspects of God: Personal and Impersonal. He has talked with God. He has enjoyed the Bliss of God."[13]

What Can We Learn?

What we have seen so far is that there has been quite a bit of speculation about the Divine in Hinduism. At first, it was speculation aligned with fire-sacrifice—God created through God's own inner heat, and that inner heat had to be sustained through sacrifice. Further, sentient life has within it that same heat. The *vital breaths* that represent God's essence are our vital breath as well. But spiritual practice is just that: practice. We need to learn how to develop and open up our own inner life. The meditation mantra of OM or AUM was identified as that sacred syllable capable of calling forth our own interior dimension and uniting that core self to God. In the Svetashvatara Upanishad we find:

> As the form of fire when latent in its source is not seen and yet its seed is not destroyed, but may be seized again and again in its source by means of the drill [friction], so it is in both cases. The self has to be seized in the body by means of the syllable *aum*. By making one's body the lower friction stick and the syllable *aum* the upper friction stick, by practicing the drill [friction] of meditation one may see God [Brahman] hidden as it were. (I.13–14)

What we see here is that our essence and the Divine essence unite, and our essence comes from and participates in the Divine Essence. Participating in the universal Divine is really possible, they claim. Such a possibility might strike some readers as wrongheaded and impossible. But there are soundings from other traditions that suggest much the same thing. Christianity, for example, seems to dramatically distinguish the Divine from everything else. Blurring these lines is a philosophical category mistake: There is the Creator who exists outside of the created world, and then there are creatures who are assuredly not God! And yet its biblical and theological tradition actually points to certain kinds of creaturely identification with the Divine. Genesis tells us that humans were made in the image and likeness of God (1:26), and that Adam was created out of the earth and God's very breath (2:7), that is, from materiality and God's Spirit. Here one is certainly not God, which is something Adam and Eve strove to attain. Still, there is a transcendence in the human condition, one that seems to have ultimate possibilities.

The New Testament is filled with images and outright teachings on sharing God's life and in some ways sharing in God's divinity. Consider the following:

- "Beloved, we are God's children now; what we will be has not been revealed. What we do know is this: when he is revealed, we will be like him, for we will see him as he is" (1 Jn 3:2);
- "For all who are led by the Spirit of God are children of God. . . . When we cry, 'Abba! Father!' it is that very Spirit bearing witness with our spirit that we are children of God . . . heirs of God and joint heirs with Christ . . . so that we may also be glorified with him" (Rom 8:14–17);
- "His divine power has given us everything needed for life and godliness . . . so that through them you may escape from the corruption that is in the world because of lust and become participants in the divine nature" (2 Pet 1:3–4);
- "But he disciplines us for our good, in order that we may share his holiness" (Heb 12:10);
- "Love has been perfected among us . . . because as he is, so we are in the world" (1 Jn 4:17).[14]

This kind of language is not only found in the Bible but is part of widespread Christian teaching, formally in the Roman Catholic, Eastern Orthodox, Anglican, and many Protestant Churches. The following texts come from Catholicism's Second Vatican Council:

- "For God has called man, and still calls him, to cleave with all his being to him in sharing forever a life that is divine and free from all decay" (*Church in the Modern World*, no. 18);
- "In his wisdom and goodness the eternal Father . . . decreed that men would be raised up to share in the divine nature" (*Constitution on the Church*, no. 16);
- "God's will was that men should have access to the Father through Christ, in the Holy Spirit, and thus become sharers in the divine nature" (*Constitution on Divine Revelation*, no. 2);
- "The Son of God entered the world by means of a true incarnation that he might make us sharers in the divine nature" (*Church's Missionary Activity*, no. 3).[15]

Thomas Aquinas taught that God as God is Absolute Mystery. Our language, our concepts, all are part of a natural brain trying to negotiate the created world. And God transcends creation. So how can we know or say anything about God? Aquinas and so many others argued that our language about God is analogous. To say "God is good" and to say "Mary is good" is not to use the word "good" in exactly the same way. God is good *as God* and Mary is good *as a human*, but "goodness" does analogously refer to both. The challenge is not to anthropomorphize God, to make God like a human or equate God's qualities to similar human qualities. Still, if our words about God mean anything, then they are related to how we know these concepts in our own existence.

The *principle of non-contradiction* is a philosophical axiom that insists that two opposed claims cannot be true at the same time. So, which is it? Is God ultimately impersonal or ultimately personal? It cannot be both. Or can it? Perhaps what we learn here is that God transcends linear logic, which itself is only valuable in negotiating the created world. The impersonal God makes us recognize that God is inscrutable, beyond our concepts, beyond any human comparative. The personal God moves us to see that God really does purposefully and lovingly engage the world and beings in that world. God is personal and impersonal and that which transcends those categories altogether. One thing is for sure: Hindu wisdom insists that you cannot capture or contain God. God is beyond and beyond and beyond.

Christian Wisdom: Trinity

One of the most challenging conceptions of God is the Christian one. Christians assure themselves and others that they are monotheists whose God is also the God of Abraham, Isaac, and Jacob, the God of Moses and the prophets, the God whose kingdom Jesus of Nazareth preached, and to whom Jesus prayed. And yet Jesus's followers also experienced the Divine presence and action in him. He is the savior who forgives sins and establishes the new divine covenant on his own authority. These certainly appear to be divine prerogatives. To add to the problem, there is the Holy Spirit:

- Jesus is both led by and filled with the Holy Spirit (Lk 4:1–2);
- Jesus promises the Holy Spirit to his faithful followers; the Holy Spirit speaks through believers (Mk 13:11) and guides them (Jn 16:13);
- St. Paul declares that "all who are led by the Spirit of God are children of God" (Rom 8:14), and one can know that one is filled with and guided by the spirit by the quality of one's heart: "The fruit of the Spirit is love, joy, peace, patience, kindness, generosity, faithfulness, gentleness, and self-control" (Gal 5:22);
- In other places, Paul seems to even identify Christ with the Holy Spirit: "Now the Lord is the Spirit" (2 Cor 3:17).

The biblical witness is, quite frankly, sometimes confusing. Consider the following passage:

> But you are not in the flesh, you are in the Spirit, since the Spirit of God dwells in you. Anyone who does not have the Spirit of Christ does not belong to him. But if Christ is in you, though the body is dead because of sin, the Spirit is life because of righteousness. If the Spirit of him who raised Jesus from the dead dwells in you, he who raised Christ from the dead will give life to your mortal bodies also through his Spirit who dwells in you. (Rom 8:9–11)

Here we see what looks like a complete blurring of Father, Son, and Holy Spirit. In the beginning of the passage the Spirit is the Spirit of God (Father). In the next sentence, the Spirit is identified with Christ. This same Spirit then seems to be identified either with the Father who raised Jesus from the dead or as distinct from the Father. Finally, the same Spirit resides in believers, but is identified as Christ within.

One thing is certain: the early church worshipped the Father, the Son, and the Holy Spirit, which they distinguished as three "persons" while still claiming to be monotheists. Conceptualizing the nature and mission of Jesus is also quite challenging. He was clearly a human being, and yet seemed to be more. In order to understand Jesus's identity, St. Paul drew on two principal streams of Jewish thought. The first comes from the Wisdom tradition. Wisdom appears personified in the books of Proverbs (1:20–33; 8:1–9:18) and Baruch (3:9–4:4) as a woman who is the messenger of truth. In Sirach, Wisdom is someone who dwells with God (Sir 24:1–4). In the Wisdom of Solomon, Wisdom appears as a personification of God's grace: "Therefore I prayed, and understanding was given me; I called on God, and the spirit of wisdom came to me. . . . All good things came to me along with her, and in her hands uncounted wealth" (Wis 7:7,

10–11). She is also the "breath of the power of God, and a pure emanation of the glory of the Almighty" (Wis 7:25). Proverbs even suggests that God created through wisdom: "The Lord created me at the beginning of his work, the first of his acts of long ago. . . . I was beside him, like a master worker" (Prov 8:22, 30). Paul seems to make a direct association between Wisdom and Christ: "There is one God, the Father, from whom are all things and for whom we exist, and one Lord, Jesus Christ, through whom are all things and through whom we exist" (1 Cor 8:6). To Paul, Jesus "is the image of the invisible God, the firstborn of all creation; for in him all things in heaven and on earth were created. . . . [A]ll things have been created through him and for him" (Col 1:15–16). While he is not the Father (God), still "in him the wholeness of deity dwells bodily" (Col 2:9).

A second stream of Jewish thought was that of an anticipated preexistent messiah who would come to save God's people. As St. Paul wrote, "But when the fullness of time had come, God sent his Son, born of a woman, born under the law, in order to redeem those who were under the law" (Gal 4:4–5). God sent Christ as redeemer "to gather up all things in him, things in heaven and on earth" (Eph 1:10). Paul's vision is cosmic: "[W]hen all things are subjected to him, then the Son himself will also be subjected to the one who put all things in subjection under him, so that God may be all in all" (1 Cor 15:28). It seems that the "Father," whom Paul simply calls God, has the ultimate priority, while Christ works to carry out God's cosmic plan of salvation. Christ is not, however, merely a human being; he is an expression of God and God's saving presence.[16]

Through four ecumenical councils in the fourth and fifth centuries, the church came up with dogmas that attempted to bring some clarity to their understanding of the nature of God and the status of Jesus Christ. Here we find that God is a singularity of three relations: the Father, Son, and Holy Spirit. From eternity, the Father begot the Son and the Holy Spirit proceeded from the Father. In this sense, the Father relation has a kind of priority. But there was never a Father without a Son or Holy Spirit. Rather, they mutually imply each other. In the monumental treatise *The Trinity*, St. Augustine (354–430) offers two analogies in trying to make sense of it. One is Mind-Thinking-Thought. Augustine assumed that an active mind always thinks, and it always thinks thoughts. These can be distinguished, and thinking and thoughts both come from the mind. But, they must always be there together. His second analogy is Love-Beloved-Love Shared. For love (Father) to be active, it must have a beloved (Son), and together they necessarily share love (Holy Spirit) in communion with each other. There can never be one without the other two. Theologically, the Trinity as love gained influence in the Christian imagination.

The thirteenth-century theologian St. Bonaventure understood the Trinity as the very nature of divine love. The Father is the font of all goodness and love, and the infinite depth of the Father's goodness and love is necessarily inexhaustible and perfectly self-diffusive. To exist in this goodness and love, that same goodness and love had to be communicated to another Person within the Godhead, and that Person had to be capable of receiving the infinite gift of love and mirror it back to the Father. This Son then had to have equal divinity as the Father, so that the love between the Father and the Son reaches its total self-diffusion. Together they must generate a Person who is the shared object of their love, the Holy Spirit. This Holy Spirit flows from the depths of their being and represents the love of the Father and the Son.[17] Some of my philosopher colleagues have shaken their heads at the belief that God could be both singular and intra-relational at the same time. It does stretch the imagination.

And what about Jesus? The council fathers argued that Jesus was a singular being, but that being had two natures, human and divine. These did not mix, and Jesus is surely not a hybrid of both. Rather, the Son relation in the Trinity *intrinsically identified* with the human person Jesus of Nazareth from the moment of his conception. The Son relation of the Trinity did not *become* human, but from the moment of Jesus's conception, the Son relation could not be other than Jesus as well. None of this exactly looks like what St. Paul taught, but the council fathers strove to insist that God in God's absolute divinity does not change and yet that Jesus really was Divine as well as human. The council fathers also insisted that language about God is analogical and not literally descriptive. At the end of the day, God remains a mystery to the conceptualizing mind.

What Can We Learn?

That God remains a mystery does not suggest that one cannot find great depth in the Christian formulation. Even as some of my colleagues find the conception of God as Trinity something that does not seem to make sense to them, I actually find it inspiring. For Christians, the very nature of divinity is relationality. God seeks a loving relationship with us because the divine nature is intrinsically love. Even before creation, God expresses the Divine Life as love. This means, among other things, that knowledge of God is less about knowing the dogmas of the Trinity than it is about love. "God is love," proclaims the First Letter of John (4:16). As the twelfth-century theologian and mystic William of St. Thierry writes in his exposition of the Song of Songs, "Love of God is knowledge of him; unless he is loved, he is not known, and unless he is known, he is not loved." William teaches that the intimate union of knowledge and love actually reflects the indwelling of the Divine persons of the Trinity.[18]

When we love, we actually instantiate God's love. We become sacraments of the very inner life of God. The First Letter of John makes this explicit:

> Beloved, let us love one another, because love is from God; everyone who loves is born of God and knows God. . . . No one has ever seen God; if we love one another, God lives in us and his love is perfected in us. . . .

Whoever does not love does not know God, for God is love. . . . God is love, and those who abide in love abide in God and God abides in them. . . . The commandment we have from him is this: those who love God must love their brothers and sisters also. (1 Jn 4:7–21)

Karl Rahner, Catholicism's most influential modern theologian, had little interest in extraordinary spiritual experiences and what they might reveal. Rather, Rahner strove to highlight God's constant presence in our lives as the ground from which we exist. We make sense and meaning in our experience precisely because God's presence as the source and ultimate horizon of meaning creates the conditions for our authentic engagement in life. Rahner referred to this as the *supernatural existential*. By "existential" he meant something about us that is core to our existence. God's presence (the "supernatural") is a constant, and operates as part of the core of our lived existence. Rahner writes:

When the fragmentary experience of love, beauty, and joy is experienced and accepted purely and simply as the promise of love, beauty and joy, without their being understood in ultimate skepticism as a cheap form of consolation for some final deception; where the bitter, deceptive, and vanishing everyday world is withstood until the accepted end, and accepted out of a force whose ultimate source is still unknown to us but can be tapped by us . . . where one lets oneself go unconditionally and experiences this capitulation as true victory . . . there is God and his liberating grace.[19]

This is a dense citation. What Rahner is presenting is that even in seemingly normal experiences, when we engage them fully for the sake of their truth and goodness alone, we participate in God's very life working within us. With a heart and mind truly open then, to love a spouse, to experience real compassion for a stranger suffering, to witness a sunset—all of it—is to know the loving presence of God who is the source of it all and the horizon of it all.

I recall one event while volunteering for a mission supporting the homeless that was particularly moving and for me insightful. The particular ministry I was involved with was guiding guests toward gaining their GED and helping them get vocational instruction. One of the men I served was Ralph, a homeless resident who was very, very difficult. Ralph responded to direction dismissively and always seemed to have a bad attitude. Renee was my supervisor. She and I had a meeting with Ralph. He rarely made eye contact, and Renee had to ask him repeatedly to stay "with" her. Ralph ended up telling us something of his story—about an absent father and a mother who moved him around following one failed romantic relationship after another, caring little for Ralph. I felt for Ralph's plight. And I could honestly say that I loved him in the sense that I wanted and supported the possibility of Ralph living a productive and happy life. Renee went much deeper. She told him, "Ralph, I love you." Ralph looked away. Again, "Ralph, look at me. I love you, and I want you to be whole and happy. You have to work with us to support you. I love you Ralph, will you do this?"

There was a real contrast between my love for Ralph and Renee's. She didn't love him as an object in need of her support; she simply loved him. This love is God's grace, and Renee's heart was filled with this grace. The synergy of God's love and Renee's love made distinguishing between God's and Renee's love impossible. It was just love, loving. This is how being a sacrament really works in life. Humans were made by love for love.

Earlier, when we were looking at Hindu notions of unifying traits between the deepest self and Brahman, I noted that Christianity also had biblical resources that suggested real participation with the Divine. This is particularly important regarding the dogmas about Christ and about life in heaven. One of the arguments that the church fathers used to insist that Jesus Christ has a fully divine nature as well as a human one is that they believed heaven was an existence whereby souls lived God's life as God lives God's life. Later this came to be called *theosis*, which literally means in Greek, "becoming God." In the West, it came to be known as *deification* or *divinization*. The church fathers certainly did distinguish between the divine nature and human nature, and maintained that humans never stop being creatures to the Creator. But they also believed that, by God's grace, we had the capacity to participate in God's existence with God. Consider several early witnesses of eminent church authorities who predated any of the ecumenical councils:

- Justin Martyr (100–165): "And we have learned that those only are deified who have lived near to God in holiness and virtue" (*First Apology* XXI);
- Irenaeus of Lyons (130–202): "That faith of men to be placed in God has increased . . . that man might too become a partaker of God" (*Against Heresies* 5.28.2);
- Clement of Alexandria (150–215): "Logos, the Word of God, became man in order that you can learn through the intercession of Man how many can become God by grace" (*Protreptikos* 1.8);
- Hippolytus of Rome (170–235): "Friends of God and coheirs with Christ . . . we shall have become divine" (*Refutation of All Heresies*);
- Origen (185–253): "Let us pray unceasingly with that disposition of soul with which the word may make us divine" (*Notebook on Prayer*).

Thus, for full salvation to be achieved, they argued, Jesus Christ would have to be fully human, saving the whole human condition, and fully Divine, raising humans to his divine life. What seems like a philosophical category mistake—a God/Man—is for Christianity a proclamation of the fullest possibilities for salvation. It may be the oddest claim in Christianity, and certainly one of the most contentious among other monotheists. And yet for Christians it is exactly the necessary condition to be fully saved.

I mentioned earlier that Paul's theology of Christ followed two Jewish streams, that of Wisdom incarnate and that of a preexistent messiah. And I said that Christian dogma did not exactly follow these. But this doesn't mean they are not important. Imagine the Divine Son who has received the fullness of the Father's love, truth, and goodness. Everything redounds to the Father, but only through the Son. For Christians, he really is the Wisdom of the Divine and it is only through this Divine Wisdom that we can know the Father's primordial love. Christian wisdom says that to be truly alive, we must exist in and through this love, and it is through this love that we know the Triune life of love. In striving to look to the Father, we can do this only through the Son and by the Holy Spirit. In an earlier publication I suggested the following:

> The Holy Spirit is the spiritual context through which the risen Lord is known. Christian spirituality is a manifestation of life in the Spirit. The Father represents the eternal source of the Son and Holy Spirit. The Holy Spirit is the life of the church because the Spirit is the common good of the Father and the Son. The Spirit infuses believers with God's love. The Son, now incarnate, is the very access to the Father, even as intimacy with the Word is conditioned by the Spirit.[20]

Notes

1. Thomas Hopkins, *The Hindu Religious Tradition* (Encino, CA: Dickenson, 1971), 32.

2. Klaus Klostermaier, *A Survey of Hinduism*, 2nd ed. (Albany: State University of New York, 1994), 205.

3. Krishna Sivaraman, ed., *Hindu Spirituality: Vedas through Vedanta* (Delhi: Motilal Banarsidass, 1995), 72–73.

4. Ibid., 70.

5. Ibid., 67.

6. T. R. Srinivasa Ayyangar, *The Yoga Upanishads* (Madrass: Vedanta Press, 1938), 42–43.

7. Swami Saradananda, *Sri Ramakrishna the Great Master*, 3rd ed., trans. Swami Jagadananda (Madras: Sri Ramakrishna Math, 1963), 101.

8. Sri Ramakrishna, *The Gospel of Sri Ramakrishna*, intro. and trans. Swami Nikhilananda (New York: Ramakrishna-Vivekanada Center, 1952).

9. *Life of Ramakrishna Compiled from Various Authentic Sources*, 2nd rev. ed. (Calcutta: Advaita Ashrama, 1964), 68.

10. Saradananda, *Sri Ramakrishna the Great Master*, 140–41.

11. Ibid., 141.

12. Ramakrishna, *Gospel of Sri Ramakrishna*, 544, 667.

13. Ibid., 478–79.

14. See also Jn 1:12–13; 1 Cor 15:8, 49; 2 Cor 3:17–18, 5:15, 21; Eph 1:22, 4:24; Col 3:10.

15. All Vatican texts from Austin Flannery, ed., *Vatican Council II: The Conciliar and Post Conciliar Documents*, rev. ed. (Northport, NY: Costello, 1975).

16. See Peter Feldmeier, *The Christian Tradition: A Historical and Theological Introduction* (New York: Oxford University Press, 2017), 57–78.

17. Rik Van Nieuwenhove and William Crozier, "The Trinity," in *The Oxford Handbook of Mystical Theology*, ed. Edward Howells and Mark McIntosh (Oxford: Oxford University Press, 2020), 470–71.

18. Ibid., 467.

19. Karl Rahner, *The Spirit in the Church* (New York: Seabury, 1979), 21–22, as cited in Rik Van Nieuwenhove, "Trinitarian Indwelling" in *The Oxford Handbook of Mystical Theology*, ed. Howells and McIntosh, 388–403.

20. Peter Feldmeier, *Christian Spirituality: Lived Expressions in the Life of the Church* (Winona: MN: Anselm Academic, 2015), 17.

2

Who Am I?

How does one conceive of oneself or the human condition? It is not as obvious as one might think. In today's relatively secular society, locating truth, meaning, and value are less grounded in religious sensibilities than they are in secular assumptions. The sciences have been excellent in understanding the workings of the body and, increasingly, the chemical and neural dynamics of the brain. The social sciences too are excellent in analyzing how various conditions support or cause people's behavior or even what and how they think. In a secular culture, many stop there, implicitly taking on a materialistic view, that is, only physical things exist. As philosopher of religion John Hick has argued:

> In our Western World, beginning around the seventeenth century, the earlier pervasive religious outlook has increasingly been replaced by an equally pervasive naturalistic outlook, and during the twentieth century this replacement has become almost complete. Naturalism has created a consensus reality of our culture. It has become so ingrained that we no longer see it, but see everything through it.[1]

Philosopher John Lucas recognized the same thing in terms of scholarly discourse: "Philosophical naturalism is now the orthodoxy of the Western intellectual world."[2] Naturalism posits that nothing exists other than physical things that operate through natural laws. To hold this position, as some of my colleagues do, not only dismisses the possibility of God, but also of any actual independent agency. Trevor Harley, a leading figure in consciousness research, notes that "many consciousness researchers argue that the self is an illusion."[3] There we have it; there is no independent consciousness, no free will, no soul, and, at the end of the day, no objective morality or truth.

One of the limits of the scientific method is that it is geared exclusively to understanding physical properties and their causes and correlations among other physical properties. It simply is not equipped to look for or understand that which is not physical. Religions certainly need to be respectful of the extraordinary advances of the sciences, but their interest goes beyond the scope of what science can do. Human flourishing and self-agency are real, religions claim, but only make sense when you understand that they represent something more than merely neurons being neurons.

Islamic Wisdom: Dyed in the Dye of God

Among the Abrahamic religions of Judaism, Christianity, and Islam, it is the Islamic tradition that is the most optimistic about the human condition. There is no *original sin*. Even though Islam holds that Adam and Eve were indeed led astray by Satan (also known as Iblis), this did not curse the human condition. Humans are born pure, although not outside of the consequences of history. So we will always have to deal with a compromised humanity and be affected by it. Yet if someone is especially sinful, a typical Islamic response might be, "What happened in his (or her) childhood to corrupt this pure child?"[4]

Actually, for Muslims, the history of the human race and its spiritual dignity and destiny began before creation itself. Before the physical creation of the world, human souls existed with God, who asked of them: "'Am I not your Lord?' They replied: 'We bear witness that You are.' Thus He did, lest you should say on the Day or Resurrection: 'We had no knowledge of that'" (Qur'an 7:172). Commenting on this classic verse, Maria Massi Dakake writes:

> This verse is in many ways the cornerstone of Islamic sacred history and anthropology and establishes that the fundamental relationship between God and all human beings is premised on the simple, unmediated recognition of His Lordship at the moment of their pretemporal creation. . . . Even though human beings do not remember the pretemporal covenant, their testimony to God's Lordship is understood to have left an indelible imprint upon their souls and to have established moral responsibility for them.[5]

We know God and God's majesty and Lordship in the very core of our souls. Our fundamental problem is that we forgot this central truth of the universe. There is a myth in Islam that says that when we are actually being born, an angel touches us just above the lip and below the nose and says, "forget." This give us the challenge to dig deep into our souls and draw out the fundamental truth of our existence. And it is why we have a crease between our nose and lip.

Among God's creatures, only three types of beings have spiritual self-agency: angels, Jinn (whom we have called in the West genies), and humans. In one sense, humans are on the low end of the spectrum, being seemingly the weakest. But there is something about us that has the capacity for God that angels and Jinn do not. Angels are imagined in Islam to be rather simple beings, so it is not difficult for them to follow God. The Jinn are made of fire and are spiritual beings with more complicated personal agency, much like humans. Some are faithful and will end up in heaven, while others are not and will find themselves damned.

The Christian tradition holds that Satan was a great arch-angel named Lucifer (light bearer) who refused to bow to God. He and his followers were then banished from heaven. In the Islamic telling, Satan (Iblis) was commanded by God to bow to Adam. But, he thought, I'm made of fire and this being is made of dirt. I'm not bowing down to him! What Satan did not recognize was the spiritual capacity of the human race. God declares, "We have created humanity of the best stature" (Qur'an 95:4). A favorite rendering of one saying in the Qur'an is that we are "dyed in the dye of God" (2:138). After God created Adam he said:

> Now remember My favors to you, for I have made you the masterpiece of My creation, fashioned you a man according to My will, breathed into you of My spirit, made My angels do obeisance to you and carry you on their shoulders, made you a preacher to them, loosened your tongue to all languages. . . . All this I have done for you as glory and honor.[6]

According to the Islamic tradition, in 619 CE Muhammad was swept away from Mecca and carried to the Temple Mount in Jerusalem. There the angel Gabriel led him through the seven levels of heaven where he met prophets such as Moses and Jesus. Finally, he is led to the Divine Throne. And tradition has it that he was "two bows length from God." What is particularly inter-esting about this encounter is that Gabriel had to withdraw, for he did not have the capacity for such nearness with God. But, by God's mercy, Muhammad was able to enter that level of commu-nion with the Divine. In seeking and finding the face of the Lord, Muhammad expresses humanity's highest possibilities, which are to see and know God intimately. Al-Suyuti's famous account of Muhammad's encounter describes one traditional telling of Muhammad's ascent.

Now when I was brought on my Night Journey to the place of the Throne and drew near to it . . . [m]y sight was so dazzled by it that I feared blindness. Therefore, I shut my eyes, which was by Allah's good favor. When I thus veiled my sight, Allah shifted my sight to my heart, so with my heart I began to look at what I had been looking at with my eyes. . . . There he was, when the veil had been lifted from Him, seated on His Throne, in His dignity, His might, His glory, His exaltedness, but beyond that is not permitted me to describe Him to you.[7]

Muhammad stands out as the perfect exemplar of how to be human. Even Muhammad's name points to his status. In Arabic, HaMaDo means *to praise*. HaMMaDa brings an intensifier: *to highly praise*. And, MuHaMMaD is *the highly praised one*. For Muslims, God loves those who love the Prophet. Muhammad is something of a "living Qur'an," whose witness and words reveal God's will, and who models the human response to God. Islamic scholar Charles Le Gai Eaton notes, "The key to the Muslim view of Man is to be found in the person of the Prophet of Islam. He has many titles of glory, but the first, which even precedes the designation *messenger* in the confession of faith, is *slave* or *servant* (*'abd*)."[8] Indeed the word *Islam* means *surrender* or *submission*.

Muhammad's holiness, faithfulness, and obedience to God models for Muslims how humans ought to live. His life examples and teachings, called *sunnah* ("trodden path" or "example"), are extraordinarily influential. Muslims follow Muhammad's examples, or the principles that underlie them, and apply them analogically to their own lives and society. These have become precedents that fortify Islamic law and custom (*shari'a*).

Most of what we know about Muhammad's life comes from the Qur'an and from biographies based on oral tradition. His biography by Muhammad Ibn Ishaq (d. 768) is the most authoritative. Muhammad seemed to do everything well. He lived boldly and in long-suffering in the midst of many years of rejection and persecution. He was a brave and just warrior. As a statesman, he succeeded in uniting contentious tribes in Yathrib, also known as Medina al-Nabi (City of the Prophet) and creating a well-functioning city. As the administrator of Yathrib, he showed himself a tireless servant who lived modestly and made himself available night and day to those who sought his guidance. From his leadership, the corrupt city of Mecca was transformed into a center of pilgrimage for the worship and service of the one God.

Most important, Muhammad was a deeply religious man, and his life of prayer is perhaps his greatest witness to his vocation. As a child and adolescent, Muhammad minded his uncle's flocks. This gave him a great deal of time to be alone and thoughtful. When he reached adulthood, a widow named Khadijah employed him as head of her caravan business. She later became his wife. His life of trading and travel gave him the opportunity to meet religiously serious Jews and Christians, particularly monks who led lives of contemplation. When Muhammad was home, he spent many solitary nights in prayer. His favorite spot to pray was on the top of Jabal Nur (Mountain of Light), just a few miles north of Mecca.

In 610, on the "Night of Power and Excellence" Muhammad was in a cave on Jabal Nur when the angel Gabriel appeared to him and demanded, "Proclaim in the name of your Lord who created! Created man from a clot of blood. Proclaim: Your Lord is Most Generous, Who teaches by the pen; teaches man what he knew not" (Qur'an 96:1–3). Muhammad received messages from Gabriel for the next twenty-three years. These represent the Qur'an. At times, receiving these messages was very difficult. He was often seized with violent shuddering, and the event would leave him covered with sweat and exhausted. Progressively, they became less taxing. One of the most remarkable aspects of his receiving and reciting God's revelations was that he could remember them infallibly for the rest of his life. Muslims accept the divine source of these revelations, and the vast majority of Muslims believe that he received and reported them with no internal filter. That is, the messages had nothing to do with his own consciousness or subjectivity. He simply received and conveyed the revelation.

What Can We Learn?

I once heard a debate between an atheist and a devout Muslim. The atheist argued that religious belief *infantilizes* us; it keeps us as if we are children who cannot take responsibility for ourselves. For the atheist, religious faith prevents having authority over our own lives. The Muslim, on the other hand, had been speaking about how his religious faith had transformed him in adulthood. As a young man, he sneered at Islam, the religion he was raised in. But his life seemed to be going nowhere, and he said that he abused alcohol throughout his twenties. Now, he said, he had purpose, an ordered life, and deep joy. Why, he asked, would he want to renounce his faith? The atheist said that then he could truly be free. "Free to be a drunk narcissist?" he retorted. "No thanks!"

I was very inspired by his response. We could even go deeper. Consider: if God is the ground of all that is good and true, and if God is the transcendent horizon of all goodness and truth, then utter servitude to God is total dedication to goodness and truth and a participation in them. We humans actualize our glory—our goodness and truth—but only insofar as we pursue it to its utter end, which is God. This *servitude* is actually freedom, freedom from any bondage that would hinder our truest selves living out our deepest truth, our fullest goodness.

Islam asks us to consider our lives as a kind of creative tension. On the one hand, because of Islam's optimism about the human race, we have great possibilities, including intimacy with the Divine. God has even designated humans to be the Divine's vicegerent on the earth. That is to say, humans are delegated by

God with the power of sovereignty on behalf of the Divine Sovereign.[9] On the other hand, Islam sees humanity as a creature of dust or clay. We are nothingness before the Almighty, who is Everything. Eaton wisely reflects, "Mastery—that is to say, the quality of vicegerency—is intimately linked to *slavehood*, and *slavehood* as such is neither more nor less than the excellence of a clear mirror that reflects the higher realities and could not reflect them if it were less than clear."[10] There is an Islamic saying, *A slave to Allah is free from any other servitude*. The great theological and mystical master al-Gazzali (d. 1111) noted that a human being has "a face of its own and a face of its Lord; in respect of its own face it is nothingness, and in respect of the face of the Lord it is Being."[11]

I am from Minnesota, and was living there when Jesse Ventura, the former professional wrestler, inexplicably became the thirty-eighth governor of the state from 1999 to 2003. He was a populist, with no real governing aptitude. He rarely seemed to fully understand the legislation he either supported or derided, and he frequently abruptly left interviews when challenged. The press, he argued, was the enemy of the people; he called them "jackals." He also struck many as extremely narcissistic. (We have seen this kind of leadership style on a national level as well.) During a 2001 interview, Ventura not only declared that he was not religious but that he thought religion was for "weak" people and he was strong. He just didn't need it. His wife, he mentioned on the other hand, did need religion when she felt weak and needed to be told she was lovable and valuable.

There was the expected outrage from religious leaders, including an editorial that proclaimed that yes indeed we are all weak and we all need God. A better answer comes from Islamic wisdom. Islam calls its believers to utter faith in God, that is, entrusting ourselves only to God. The opposite of faith is not exactly faithlessness, but *jahl*, the behavior of one who is arrogant, quick-tempered, who surrenders oneself to the control of one's passions.

This is the person who is actually weak. I considered Jesse Ventura an extremely weak man, one enslaved by his self-absorption, his easily bruised ego, and his passions.

A fully authentic person, one who lives with full strength and the original dignity that is ours, is one who lives the truth about oneself and the universe. Islam teaches that we actually know this. In Arabic, what is translated as "unbelief" is *kuffa*, which has the etymology of "covering over." We cover over the truth—but if we hadn't done so, it would have naturally revealed itself. This directly corresponds to the Islamic imperative that from our very prehistory we have always known that God is the true Lord. We know the truth deep in our souls, but have covered it up. Even the Arabic terms for right and wrong lead us to this conclusion. Right (*al-ma'ruf*) is "known" and wrong (*al-munkar*) is "unknown." Right is what people should already know if they are listening to themselves. In one Qur'anic verse we read, "You are indeed the best community that has ever been brought forth for the good of mankind: you enjoy what is right [*al-ma'ruf*—known] and you forbid the doing of what is wrong [*al-munkar*—unknown], and you believe in God" (Qur'an 3:110).

In St. Augustine's *Confessions*, he addresses the issue of memory and God. My gloss is this: If you do not know something but are looking to discover it, how will you know when you find it? And if you know something already, why are you looking for it? With regard to God, Augustine realized that he already knew God because God was present in his soul from the beginning. "I have found you not outside my memory, but in my memory" (10:24). "Where did I find you to be able to learn of you were you not already in my memory before I learned of you?" (10:26).[12] Augustine anticipates Islam's great insight, which is that deep down God has already drawn humanity to himself. The deeper one enters into one's consciousness, the closer one comes to recognizing a presence that is already abiding and a voice that has already spoken.

Buddhist Wisdom: I Am No Self

From the Upanishads onward, the vast majority of Hindus believe that not only do they undergo a seemingly interminable number of lifetimes, but that these lives are rather pointless at the end. Even the greatest of births, such as those of the gods, are subject to decay. Further, even the most excellent of rebirths, upon deep scrutiny, are less excellent than they appear on the surface. They never really satisfy the soul in an ultimate way. Hindus call the cycle of rebirths *samsara*, which can be translated as "wandering." What they ultimately sought then was liberation from rebirth, or *moksha*.

We saw in chapter 1 that Hinduism understands the Divine as Brahman, the grounding essence of all that exists. In the Upanishads, Brahman is identified in some way with one's very self (*atman*). In the *advaita* or *non-dual* philosophy of Shankara, Atman and Brahman are two words for the same reality. The deepest self is exactly the Universal Absolute. The majority of Hindu philosophers and theologians do not think that Atman and Brahman are exactly the same. Some hold that, upon liberation from rebirth, the self attains unity with Brahman. Others maintain that the liberated self takes on the form of Brahman or the state of existence of Brahman (being-consciousness-bliss). One thing they all agree on is that there is an Absolute Reality and that the very nature of the deepest self participates in that Reality and identifies (in some way) with that Reality. Thus, the great spiritual quest is discovering one's deepest self as one discovers the Divine.

In a nutshell, here is how it all works. Until one discovers their true and ultimate identity—the deepest self (atman)—one will constantly self-identify with one's superficial self, that self that has a body, emotions, and thoughts. When we act, we cling to those actions with this conventional or superficial self. The Sanskrit word for action is *karma*, and the word for the result of that action is *karma-vipaka* (literally, "ripening of action"). Karma is the glue that binds the conventional self to its actions, and it acts as the energy that spins us into our future lives. Good actions create good karma, which condition good future lives, just as immoral actions lead to woeful future lives. In order to stop the karma, we need to stop identifying with that conventional self. The only possible way is to realize that underneath our superficial selves is our true self, unsullied by our actions. This is the atman.

The Buddha (c. 563–483 BCE) agreed with much of his Hindu heritage, including how karma works and how necessary it is to stop identifying with or being attached to our body, thoughts, emotions, and so on. But he also taught that there was no atman, no enduring or eternal self underneath our superficial selves. To seek some kind of eternal soul is a fool's errand. Further, to strive to identify with this nonexistent self continues to create an attachment that leads to more rebirths. There is no self, he taught, to identify with. Rather, our minds and bodies are made up of five impersonal aggregates of physical, perceptual, and cognitive operations. Unless one realizes that there is no underlying atman or self, one cannot become free. This is a great contrast to the Hindu belief that one needed to discover one's ultimate self and associate it with Brahman. The Buddha taught about Nirvana, which had nothing to do with atman or Brahman.

The Buddha's biography is part historical fact and part legend, but there is certainly general agreement that he (Siddhartha Gautama) was the son of a local king of the Shakya clan in northern India, now Nepal. At the age of twenty-nine, he left the palace in search of spiritual liberation. The story goes that sages predicted that Siddhartha, the future Buddha, would become either a great king or a universal spiritual master, and his father strove to ensure that he would be the former. Thus, he kept his son in luxury so that he would not see the trials of life and seek liberation from them. But on four separate occasions he left the palace and saw "four sights." The first was a sick man, then an old man, then a corpse, and finally a mendicant seeker of holiness. Thus, he encountered sickness, old age, death, and the possibility of escaping them. One night he stealthily left the palace, never to return.

Of course, it would be impossible to be twenty-nine years of age without knowing about all of these things. In one famous rendering by the first-century poet Ashvaghosha, we find a sensible interpretation: "When he thus gained insight into the fact that the blemishes of disease, old age, and death vitiate the very core of this world, he lost at the same moment all self-intoxication, which normally arises with pride in one's own strength, youth, and vitality."[13] Everyone knows that death is universal, but ironically most people live as though this isn't the case for them personally. Adolescents and young adults are famous for taking risks, implicitly thinking that nothing bad could happen to them. Others cling to projects as though they were creating something of lasting significance. Many get alarmed when they see themselves aging in midlife. Ashvaghosha calls it "self-intoxication."

Coming to terms with our mortality is a critical moment in the spiritual life. This is not merely conceding the fact of aging and death, but incorporating that truth into our own lives, living in the context of that truth. To *see* sickness, aging, and death in this case is to fully realize their implications. To *see* a holy man seeking liberation is to recognize eternal possibilities.

The Buddha spent years training in the deepest forms of Hindu meditation and ascetical practices, only to discover that they did not ultimately lead to liberation. Finally, he sat under a fig tree and determined not to leave until he was enlightened. After great torrents of intimidation and temptations by the god Mara, the Buddha became enlightened one night. On the first watch of the night he recollected his past lives. In the second watch he surveyed the entire universe and all beings in it. In doing so, he discovered that nothing exists that is substantial. Thus, he discovered that all things are impermanent and without a self. In the third watch he saw the conditions that lead to death and rebirth and the Four Noble Truths. Finally, as dawn approached he attained all knowledge. From this moment on, Siddhartha was known as the Buddha (awakened one). He spent the next forty-five years tirelessly teaching the means to awaken and escape sam-sara, which he called Nirvana.

Who or what am I if not a *self*? The Buddha's answer is noth-ing other than a collection of impermanent, impersonal aggregates (materiality, feeling, perception, mental formations, and conscious-ness). And if one deeply assessed them, one would find no self underneath. Of course, like Hindus, he understood that there is a "conventional" self; the aggregates do unite to form a real sen-tient being. But there is no center that is an "ultimate" self. In a famous dialogue between the monk Nagasena and King Melinda, the king is utterly doubtful. That he is (or has) a self is obvious to him. Nagasena challenges him to explain a chariot, to which the king replied that it consists of an axle, wheels, a carriage, and so on. Nagasena presses to know what the essence of a chariot is, to which the king replies that it has no essence; "chariot" refers to the collection of the parts. So it is, Nagasena argues, with the self; the conventional term is useful in describing the collection, but there is no essence underneath it.

Here is the conundrum: Who is the self that can liberate the self to see that there is no self and thus attain Nirvana, the place of ultimate refuge for the *self*? Who or what gets liberated? A typical Buddhist answer is that there are two kinds of truth; one is conventional and relative (*samvriti-satya*), and the other is ulti-mate (*paramartha-satya*). The relative truth is really true, but only in terms of the phenomenal world and only on this side of Nir-vana. Nirvana is a real referent, but it is beyond the reality of the phenomenal world, beyond reference points. The teaching of "no self" is part of *samvriti-sacca*.

A second Buddhist answer is that these kinds of questions are not skillful. Once the Buddha encountered a disgruntled monk named Malunkyaputta, who was frustrated that the Buddha refused to address many philosophical questions. The Buddha responded, "Because it is unbeneficial, it does not belong to the fundamentals of the holy life, it does not lead . . . to direct knowl-edge, to enlightenment, to Nirvana." The Buddha continued,

Suppose Malunkyaputta, a man were wounded by an arrow thickly smeared with poison, and his friends and companions, his kinsmen and relatives, brought a surgeon to treat him. The man would say: "I will not let the surgeon pull this arrow until I know whether the man who wounded me was a noble or a brahmin, or a merchant or a worker. . . ."

The Buddha goes on to say that this man now demands to discover first the clan, then the attacker's size, then his skin tone, and then his lifestyle. Finally, the victim insists on discovering the kind of bow used, then the type of feather on the arrow, then the wrapping. The Buddha concludes, "All this would still not be known to that man and meanwhile he would die" (*Majjhima Nikaya*, 63.4–5).

Doctrine is taken seriously by Buddhists, but it is tricky. In one teaching, the Buddha uses two similes regarding holding on to doctrine. The first involves a poisonous snake. One must hold the snake firmly, but if one squeezes too tightly the snake would bite. The second is that of a raft. One must rely on the raft to cross the river. Once across, one does not keep carrying the raft, but must let it go. "The dharma is similar to the raft, being for the purpose of crossing over, not for the purpose of clinging" (*Majjhima Nikaya*, 22.11–14). Nirvana is inaccessible to thought (*atakkavacara*) and beyond conceptual range (*avisayasmim*). What is fascinating then is that the Buddha knew he had attained Nirvana, and anticipated Final-Nirvana (*pari-nirvana*) after death. But he did not actually understand it.

What Can We Learn?

One way for me to understand where I am spiritually is by looking at my emotional life when I have an important talk to give or a professional paper to deliver. Am I nervous? Is there a lot of adrenaline in my veins? If so, this tells me that I'm attached to what others may think of me. Am I valuable, worthy of respect among my peers? Will they like me? Be impressed by me? I do not ask myself these questions explicitly, but implicitly they must be there. Why else would I be nervous? What if I fail or my presentation is regarded as just another boring talk? This is something we all have endured and probably judge others for in ways that we fear being judged ourselves.

Ironically, the more concerned I am about such things the more likely I will perform poorly. These obsessions get in the way. Still, shouldn't my importance be valued by me? Buddha's answer is, assuredly no! Once a famous Buddhist teacher and I were talking, and he asked me what I thought was the most important teaching of the *Buddhadharma* [Buddha's teaching]. I replied that it had to be Buddha's teaching of no self. He laughed and agreed, "No self, no problem."

Nagasena's dialogue with King Melinda not only tells us that what we call a chariot is only conventionally so, that there is no *chariot essence* there; it also tells us that the conventional designation can be useful, even if only up to a point. It is useful for me to locate myself socially, professionally, and in terms of personal agency. Buddhism does not say that there is no sentient being there or that there is no one with personal freedom who is morally responsible and has valued relationships. We surely do exist. The point is to hold on to this reality lightly, to keep from clinging to it.

In teaching Buddhism to my students, I often ask them to consider why we tend to hang on to resentments, which seem to do little but create a toxic and painful mental state. As the saying goes, "Resentments are like drinking poison and waiting for the other person to die." The answer is that resentments inflate my ego, my sense of my own self, my importance. So-and-so did this to ME. Horrible things are happening to people around the world and certainly even locally, but I'm obsessed with the person who told me off. Perhaps I might even have suffered something more significant. Still, ought I to cultivate a resentment toward that?

To what end? Consider the following exaggerated scenario: Fred
maliciously cuts my hand. I want to show others, "Look what
Fred did to me." They may encourage me to get that treated as it
looks like it's starting to get infected. Why would I want to have
it healed? The uglier the better, to show everyone what Fred did
to me! I refuse to get it properly treated and it eventually turns
gangrenous. Now my hand has to be cut off to prevent further
infection. "Perfect," I think, "then everyone can see just how hor-
ribly Fred treated me!" Absurd of course, but we perform small
versions of this kind of self-harm all the time.

Let us consider another scenario, also exaggerated. Jane
and John are married and love each other. But to Jane, one of
the annoying things about John is that he is often running late.
Tonight, they were to go to an important social event, but John
was late and she was mad. He finally arrives home, and Jane finds
out why he was late. It started with him going to a bar after work
and then getting into an accident on the way home. He also had
to wait for the police to arrive. Now she is irate. She has every
"right" to be. But then she learns that it was the boss's birthday
and there was an after-work party at this bar. John felt he had to
go, but he ordered club soda and left quickly and with plenty of
time to get home. Now Jane's anger is lessened, as she has lost
the right to be irate. On John's way home, a small child escaped
from his mother's grasp and ran into the middle of the street,
right in front of his car. John adroitly swerved to avoid the child
and hit a tree. When the police officer came, the young mother
was in grateful tears, profusely thanking him. She called him a
hero for saving her child, and the officer nodded in agreement.
Now Jane's attitude has completely changed. She lost the right to
be angry and took on the right to be proud of her husband. My
point here is *not* that it is bad to have legitimate expectations, or
to be concerned when they are not met and pleased when they
are exceeded. The problem is that we consider it our "right" to
have a given emotion or reaction when these correspond to the
rather arbitrary assumptions we've made about life. Jane's initial

response to John's lateness could have been one of equanimity: I have to accept my husband as he is. Or perhaps it could have provoked another concern: John and I need counseling to see why he always keeps me waiting. Or perhaps humor: What a crazy world this is!

An enlarged sense of "self" constricts us and makes us cling to things. Virtually everything the Buddha taught related to the Four Noble Truths he discovered on his night of enlightenment. They are: (1) Life is suffering or dissatisfying; (2) We suffer because we crave or are attached; (3) To end the suffering, we must end the craving—this is Nirvana; and (4) The way to end craving is the Eight-fold Path. The Buddha phrased the First Noble Truth as the following: "This is the Noble Truth of suffering: birth is suffering, aging is suffering, illness is suffering, death is suffering, union with what is displeasing is suffering, separation from what is pleasing is suffering, not to get what one wants is suffering" (*Samyutta Nikaya* 5:56.11). In the above scenario, Jane's suffering was caused by her clinging to the assumptions she had made about what she felt was due to her. This clinging is a trap, the Buddha taught.

One typical Buddhist simile for the dynamics of clinging has to do with a way to catch monkeys in Southeast Asia. One puts a sweet in a trap and hangs it in a tree. The opening to the trap is rather small, but not so small that it prevents a monkey from slipping its "hand" through. It then grabs the sweet and tries to remove its hand. But with a fist, the hand is too big to get through the opening. The monkey flails and flails, to no avail. All it has to do is let go of the sweet and slide the empty hand out. But it won't, or more accurately can't, because this does not occur to it. The monkey stays trapped by its own clinging.

There can be a wonderful spaciousness of mind and heart when one lets go of one's clinging, grasping ego. What would life look like if we did not cling in an absolute way to a self-identity? If we had no ego to protect or advance? If we lived with no artifice, no pretensions, no affectations? If we lived instead in pure freedom and spaciousness? Paradoxically, without a big sense of "self" we actually become more self-aware and have more self-possession. This is because without the reactivity and the restrictive mental state that it causes, we understand ourselves better. And we have less fear of change and can grow as we should. With no big "self" we have nothing to fear. We are also better able to experience surprising gifts from life—a closed fist is not open to receive them.

In an earlier publication, I told the following story: In 1996, the Monastic Interreligious Dialogue group sponsored their first Gethsemani Encounter, a weeklong conference at Thomas Merton's historical monastery outside of Louisville. One of the participants I got to know during that week was Zenkei Blanche Hartman, the co-abbot of the San Francisco Zen Center. I found her profoundly authentic, utterly transparent, and free. During lunch on our last day, I asked Blanche to give me a teaching. She demurred, saying that she did not have any great wisdom to offer, and we ended up talking seemingly casually until I had a realization that dramatically affected my interior life. A button was pushed, or something hidden emerged. How did that happen? The conversation ended this way: I said to her, "You know, Blanche, you are so ordinary, such an obvious nothing." Blanche hugged me. She said, "Thank you for such gracious words, for this is my life's goal."[14]

Notes

1. John Hick, *The Fifth Dimension* (Oxford: Oneworld, 1999), 14.

2. As cited in Alvin Plantinga, "Dennett's Dangerous Idea: Evolution and the Meanings of Life," *Books and Culture* 2 (May/June 1996): 16–18.

3. Trevor Harley, *The Science of Consciousness: Waking, Sleeping, and Dreaming* (Cambridge: Cambridge University Press, 2021), 5.

4. Muhammad's third wife, Aisha, claims she heard the Prophet say, "Let none of you say 'My soul is corrupted.'" See Farid Esack, *On Being a Muslim: Finding a Religious Path in the World Today* (Oxford: Oneworld, 1999), 55.

5. Maria Massi Dakake, Commentary on "The Heights," in *The Study Quran: A New Translation and Commentary*, ed. Seyyed Hossein Nasr et al. (New York: HarperOne, 2015), 466–67.

6. Arthur Jeffery, ed., *A Reader on Islam: Passages from Standard Arabic Writing Illustrative of the Beliefs and Practices of Muslims* (The Hague: Mouton, 1962), 187.

7. Ja'far Qasimi, Commentary on "The Life, Traditions, and Sayings of the Prophet," in *Islamic Spirituality: Foundations*, ed. Seyyed Hossein Nasr (New York: Crossroad, 1987), 78–80.

8. Charles Le Gai Eaton, "Man," in Nasr, *Islamic Spirituality*, 262.

9. Ibid., 358.

10. Ibid., 359.

11. Ibid.

12. Augustine, *The Confessions*, trans. Henry Chadwick (Oxford: Oxford University Press, 1991).

13. Edward Conze, ed., *Buddhist Scriptures* (New York: Penguin, 1959), 43.

14. I originally published this brief conversation in Peter Feldmeier, *Experiments in Buddhist-Christian Encounter: From Buddha-Nature to the Divine Nature* (Maryknoll, NY: Orbis Books, 2019), 186.

3

How Might I Find and Serve God?

There is a Hindu story of a holy woman, a *sadhvi*, who spent her later years wandering. She spent many days and nights in the forest, communing with the Divine. When she needed food or other provisions, she would enter a town to obtain what she needed and often to engage in spiritual conversations with others. One day, she entered a town but had no money for food, as was often the case. Instead of begging, she took the clay water jar she carried and went into the town square. There she put dirt from the road into it along with some water and began to stir. Periodically, she put her hand in the jar and removed a small piece of gold. She set it down and continued stirring until again and again she would remove small pieces of gold. A curious merchant watched all this. Finally, when she thought she had enough to buy provisions and to make a donation to the local temple, she got up. The merchant came to her amazed. "How did you come to have that magical jar?" he asked. "It is not magical," she replied. "It's just a jar." He asked, "Then what mantras or incantations do you use to get the gold?" She answered, "There is no magic, no prayers, no incantations. I just put in dirt and water, stir, and when I have a sense that gold has emerged, I remove it." The merchant offered to buy the jar for a large amount of money. She replied that he could have it as long as he would give her another jar in exchange—she needed some kind of water jar.

After she left, he spent hours upon hours over the next several weeks putting in dirt and water and stirring until his arms were sore. But whenever he put his hand in the jar, he only found mud. Months went by when by happenstance she was traveling through that same town. He accosted her and accused her of making a fool of him. "There must be some kind of magic that you did not tell me about." She demurred, saying, "No, no magic. But there is one thing I may have forgotten to tell you. In order to obtain the gold, you have to be without any greed."

Therein lies the problem. The reason for his wanting the gold was to be rich. If he had no greed, he would have no use for the jar. There was no way to get out of it. Of course, since this is a story about a holy person, the gold is a metaphor for spiritual wealth. Desiring spiritual riches as a personal acquisition or because they would be attractive to the ego is exactly the very posture that keeps one from those riches. To say that I love God because God will give me blessings is really to say that I love myself and my desires, and then acknowledge that God has the goods I want. God becomes a satellite revolving around the planet of my narcissism. Surely, it is not bad to desire the end to which we were created. But if that end is conceived wrongly, as only about ME, then it cannot be obtained. Jesus taught a similar paradox: "Those who want to save their life will lose it, and those who lose their life for my sake will find it" (Mt 16:25). This presents the same problem. If all I want is to save my life, then I will lose my life *in order to save it*. But then I haven't really lost it or given it away. I'm just strategically striving to save it in the first place.

Many years ago I was in the ministry, and I happened to preside over the funeral of a woman in a neighboring parish. Her husband had lived a wretched life. For years, he had been a raging alcoholic, and he regularly beat both his wife and children. Weeks after the funeral, he came to see me. He was worried about the state of his soul and asked me what I thought his chances were of getting into heaven. In Christian terms, this is not well framed. It is not a matter of odds, but of God's grace and our committed life in that grace. But I stayed in his framework. I asked him if he belonged to that church I helped out at. He replied that he didn't think much of church and hadn't been in one for decades. I asked him if he prayed. "I never really got into that," he said. I asked him, now that he was recovered from active alcoholism, if he strived to follow God's will in his life as well he could. His reply again was rather casual: "You know how it is, Father, sometimes you do and sometimes you don't." I ended up telling him that I thought his soul was in grave danger. He had a lot of repair work to do with his adult children and a lot of penance for the kind of life he had lived. I told him that I thought it was imperative for him to return to the church and strive to engage God and God's mercy. He left seemingly unhappy. What I wanted to say was, "Why do you want to go to heaven? Heaven is all God all the time, and you're not interested in God." Clearly, what he wanted was not God, but some kind of heavenly bliss for himself. It was still all about him.

This chapter looks at two ways of knowing and serving God. We will look at the Bhagavad-Gita, the classic Hindu text, and the Five Pillars of Islam. In very different ways, they will serve to help us understand the main obstacles of life, especially our narcissism, and how God has an answer.

Hindu Wisdom: God and the Bhagavad-Gita

Early Vedic cosmology understood the created universe in terms of karma—action and the results of that action. When sacrifices were properly made to the gods, they responded by giving the boon for which the sacrifice was designed. In a sense, they had to give the boon. They too were bound by cosmic order and the laws of karma. In later Vedic texts, these same laws of karma were understood as capable of affecting one's rebirth. Good deeds redounded to a good rebirth and bad deeds to a woeful state.

Consider the laws of karma as part of the natural law. Karma does not reward good deeds or punish bad ones, it is simply that the results of our deeds have consequences. By the time of the Upanishads, there was a shift in this thinking. The belief in rebirth was not challenged, but the thought that one continued to wander from one rebirth to another seemed ultimately pointless. There arose a desire to escape the unending wandering (*samsara*) of rebirths altogether. Now, for the spiritual virtuoso, the path led to the unmoving center of the wheel of samsara. This center was Brahman.

The great religious quest, therefore, was to escape the transient and illusory world, and enter into the eternal Brahman. Accomplishing this requires austerity, meditation, and knowledge. The only reality that was not considered transient and illusory was the *atman*, the soul or inner self that is not touched by the phenomenal world. As we saw in chapter 1, there were many versions of what that could mean, from identifying the atman as Brahman to forms of uniting with Brahman or taking on Brahman's mode of existence.

The Hindu tradition highlights three *yogas* (disciplines) as particularly prominent. *Karma-yoga* is focused on good works and performing in accordance with the expectations of one's caste and position. This certainly guarantees a good rebirth, but the highest expression of karma-yoga is to strive to be detached from karmic consequences. One does the right and moral thing simply because it is right, without concern for its outcome or karmic rewards. *Bhakti-yoga* focuses on one's love for God, whom we called Saguna-Brahman in chapter 1. There are two classical texts called Bhakti-sutras. One, by Sandilya, describes bhakti as "passionate longing for the Lord from one's whole heart." The other, by Narada, frames bhakti as *parama prema*, the highest affection for the Lord, desiring nothing but the Lord.[1] *Jnana-yoga* is focused on spiritual knowledge, particularly knowledge about one's truest inner self, the atman. Jnana-yoga is the obsession of the Upanishads. One has to search beyond the reactive self and the self that has desires or ambitions to that eternal unmoved-moving center, the true self.

All this provides the background of the Bhagavad-Gita. The Gita is a small portion of a larger saga called the Mahabharata, the "Great Epic of the Bharata Dynasty," which was produced orally over many centuries between 400 BCE and 200 CE. It tells the story of the struggle for sovereignty between two groups of cousins, the Kauravas and the Pandavas. Having come to rightfully claim the throne, the Pandavas are rejected by the Kauravas, who are ruling in their stead. Thus, a war is about to ensue. As neighboring states choose sides, Krishna arrives on the scene, disguised as a prince from the neighboring Yadava kingdom. Krishna is an incarnation (*avatara*) of Vishnu, and he only appears in the world when the cosmic order is being disrupted. Here, it is the Kauravas who are disrupting it, and the Pandavas are setting it back in order. The third Pandava brother is Arjuna, the general of their troops. Krishna offers to be his charioteer in the battle that would settle the conflict. The Bhagavad-Gita is the lengthy dialogue that Arjuna and Krishna have just before the battle. It will take time for Arjuna to realize who Krishna really is, though he is sure that Krishna is more than just a mere human.

The Gita's narrative begins with each army poised for battle, each surveying the other on opposing hills with a valley in between where the battle would ensue. As Arjuna thinks about the seemingly inevitable slaughter, he sees on the opposing side some of his teachers, uncles, cousins, and old friends, and he tells Krishna, "I see no good in killing my kinsmen in battle. . . . What joy is there for us, Krishna. . . . How can we know happiness if we kill our own kinsmen? . . . I lament the great sin we commit when our greed for kingship and pleasures drives us to kill our kinsmen" (1.26, 36–37, 45). Arjuna's point is well made on two fronts: first, he recognizes that the motive for the battle is egotistical (greed for kingship and pleasures); second, he fears the karmic consequences for killing.

Krishna's initial response is dismissive: "Why this cowardice?" (2.2). His larger argument is richer, as he reminds Arjuna of his duty. Arjuna's *dharma* (here, "duty") is as a warrior, and this is a just cause. "Your own duty, done imperfectly is better than another man's done well. It is better to die in one's own duty; [taking] another man's duty is perilous" (3.35). Throughout the Gita, Krishna will suggest other ways of considering the issue. One is that their bodies are not their true selves, their atman. So, killing a body is not really killing anything truly valuable. Another is that, as the Divine, Krishna transcends time. Thus, for him, all the warriors on both sides have already been killed and reborn again and again. More important, we see that the war is really a metaphor for something much greater. On the one hand, it is a microcosm of the universe. When cosmic order is disturbed, it must be regained. This is why Krishna has come: "Though unborn, undying, the Lord of all creatures, I fashion nature, which is mine, and I come into being through my own magic. Whenever sacred duty decays and chaos prevails, I create myself, Arjuna" (4.6–7). On the other hand, it is a macrocosm of the real war, the inner war of human passions that must be subdued. But how?

Arjuna and Krishna continue to discuss ethical and spiritual questions, but Arjuna comes to find that all of his logic fails within Krishna's cosmic truth. The solution lies where oppositions coexist within Krishna's cosmic knowledge. Freedom lies not in the renunciation of the world, but in disciplined action, that is, action performed without attachment to the fruit (karma) of the action. This is karma-yoga. But how might one do such a thing? How can you intend something and then do that thing, and not be attached to its results? Krishna tells Arjuna that he needs to dedicate the fruit of his action to Krishna (Vishnu/God) personally. It is as though all one's actions become a loving sacrifice to God. Thus, bhakti-yoga is crucial. But this is not all. Arjuna also has to train himself, to meditate unbound by his passions and desires. And in deep concentration he will realize that his truest self (atman) is not his body or his thoughts or emotions. This is jnana-yoga. Krishna assures him:

Knowing nature and the spirit of man, as well as the
qualities of nature, one is not born again—no matter
how one now exists. By meditating on the self (atman),
some men see the self through the self. . . . Beginningless,
without qualities, the supreme self is unchanging; even
abiding in a body, Arjuna, it does not act, nor is it
defiled. (13.23–24, 31)

Thus, being attached to one's actions is to fail to see that it is the
body—not the atman—that performs them.

Arjuna can dedicate himself to Krishna only after his delusions about the nature of life and death have been dispelled and
he has the power to see Krishna in his cosmic form. Krishna gives
him the divine eye with which to see Krishna's universal majesty.
It is only later that Krishna defines the battlefield as the human
body, the material realm in which one struggles to know oneself.
Krishna identifies the real enemy as desire, which is due to attachment. This can be overcome by arming oneself with discipline and
acting to transcend the narrow limits of individual desire. On the
one hand, Krishna advocates the life of action and moral duty. On
the other hand, he insists that we need to transcend our experiences in search of liberation.

There are eighteen chapters in the Gita. In chapter 9, Krishna
tells Arjuna that he has a secret teaching, which is that he (as a
form of Vishnu) and not Brahman is the true object of worship and
source of salvation: "Arjuna, know that no one devoted to me is
lost. . . . Keep me in your mind and devotion, sacrifice to me, bow
to me, discipline your self toward me, and you will reach me" (9.31,
34). In the last chapter, Krishna tells him that he has even a greater
secret: he positively loves Arjuna and desires communion with him.
"Listen to my profound words, the deepest mystery of all, for you
are precious to me and I tell you for your good. Keep your mind on
me, be my devotee, sacrificing, bow to me—you will come to me, I
promise, for you are dear to me" (18.64–65).

Let us try to put this all together. Since one must act, one should do so according to one's duties, according to morality and the natural law. But every action creates karmic energy that jettisons us into the next life, and we remain prisoners of samsara. Karma, as we recall from chapter 2, is the glue that binds us to our actions and the energy that pushes us forward into another rebirth. We create the glue and energy not by the action itself, but by identifying ourselves with that action. We cling to it: I did this, I strove for that. The only way to free us from the karmic consequences is to be detached from them, to realize that the deepest self (atman) is disconnected from them. So Krishna is saying, "Dedicate the fruits of your actions (the karma) to me. This is how you can be detached. As God, it is all about me anyway." So far, we have integrated karma-yoga and bhakti-yoga.

Still, strive to do this, and see how far it goes. There will always be some part of our psyche that thinks, "I've got merit, and I'm the one offering it to Krishna." Here I haven't really stopped identifying with the actions. Thus, another piece needs to be added. I need jnana-yoga, that deep meditative life that progressively sees the difference between my deepest free self and my psychic and physical self. Jnana-yoga will ultimately free me from this confusion of selves. But for jnana-yoga to be successful, I need to bring down the temperature of my psyche, to practice detachment in all I do (karma-yoga), and the best kind of detachment is to constantly offer what I do and am to God (bhakti-yoga). They work together to progressively allow my inner freedom and my bonding to God.

None of this happens overnight. The path is progressive. I become less attached when I'm devoting myself to God. The less attached I am, the better I can see beyond the conventional self. The better I start seeing this, the more detached I can be, and the more detached I am, the easier it is to actually offer all that I am and do to God.

What Can We Learn?

Every religious tradition I have encountered has a strong sense that narcissism is a fundamental problem in the human condition. As noted above, unwittingly, we see reality as though its meaning and value are judged insofar as it is meaningful and valuable to ourselves. Everyone is a satellite revolving around the planet ME. In some ways, it would be difficult not to be like this. We have a center of consciousness and experience the world through it. We see the world as it relates to ourselves. Consider driving on the freeway and slowing down to let another car into your lane, or holding a door for someone behind you, or giving up your place in line at a grocery store to someone who has just an item or two while you have a full cart. You want recognition; you want a wave, a smile, a thanks. I did something for you; where's the nod? All this is trivial, and we know it. But if this is true on the trivial level, think of how much more so it is throughout our day with things more substantive.

The ego gets in the way all the time. I know that I want my students to like me, to respect me, to think that I am intelligent and capable, and to appreciate my personality. Why? Because it inflates my ego. I'm not neurotic about this. Mostly, I want them to learn, to be inspired by religious traditions they may not know about, and to grow as persons. Shouldn't this be enough? If I purely loved my students, then their growth and empowerment would be the *only* thing I cared about. So if they learned more and grew better in the context of disliking me, wouldn't this be a better scenario? Seemingly so. Of course, it rarely works that way (thank God). Students perform best when they know they are respected and cared about and when they have confidence in the competence of their professor. But not caring exactly what they think allows me to act in ways that I judge would be in their best interest. Ironically, being free from the enslavement of "What do they think of me?" allows me greater interior spaciousness to be attentive to them and their needs. I would also likely be more natural in the classroom and probably be all the more respected. Still, if "being more respected" is my goal, then I'm operating in the kind of artificiality that compromises literally everything.

What about my spiritual life? Do I want God, or do I want blessings from God, stuff from God? Is God my spiritual Santa Claus, where if I'm on the "nice" list I *deserve* blessings, happiness, an easier life? Or can I love God for God's sake? Hindu wisdom teaches us that it is a long haul to leave our narcissistic self and gain a fully free self that sees life as truly about God and not about me. But this effort, this pilgrimage, has to be intentional. Striving to be unattached from the results of our moral actions is difficult; it can only be realized insofar as we recognize that there is a deeper self than my narcissistic self, a soul that is made for God and has God as its truest end. And yet knowing this truth can come only when we realize that everything we do really should be, at the end of the day, for God. This was the prayer my family prayed daily at breakfast when I was growing up:

> O *Jesus of the Immaculate Heart of Mary,*
> *I offer you my prayers, works, joys, and sufferings of this day,*
> *in union with the Holy Sacrifice of the Mass throughout*
> the world,
> *in reparation for my sins, for the intentions of all my*
> associates,
> *in communion with the holy church throughout the world,*
> *for the intensions of Thy Sacred Heart,*
> *and for the special intentions of the Holy Father.*

This is quite a loaded prayer. Like devotion to Krishna, the incarnation of Vishnu, we prayed to Jesus, the incarnation of the Divine Son. Everything that we do and everything that happens to us, we offer to Jesus. And the Eucharist, which for Catholics is the source and summit of our spiritual lives, is the ritual that reengages the original sacrifice of Jesus all the while ritualizing our joining Jesus in offering ourselves to the Father. I offer all that I am and do in penance for my sins, in communion with the needs of my family, friends, and co-workers. I offer everything in communion with the whole body of Christ, the church, which is aligned with the mercy of Jesus (the Sacred Heart) and joined with our universal pastor, the pope.

In offering ourselves to God, we actually free ourselves to be our authentic selves, which brings us both closer to God and gives us a deeper understanding of our souls. This, then, allows us to act more honestly, with more self-possession, and without the tyranny of the ego. I have taught the Bhagavad-Gita many times over the years. Most of my students self-identify as religious believers. The majority are Christians, but they also include Muslims, Jews, Buddhists, Pagans, and so on. Very few are Hindus. I have asked all of them if this message could be applicable to their own lives in their own religion. In twenty-five years as a professor, not one student voiced the thought that she or he was unable to apply this message personally in their own faith. My shorthand for the Bhagavad-Gita's message is: *Perform your dharma, renounce the fruit of your karma.* The following was printed on a sign on the wall of Shishu Vhavan, Mother Teresa's home in Calcutta:

ANYWAY

People are often self-centered and loving them can hurt you.
LOVE THEM ANYWAY

If you care, you will be exploited or even accused of selfish motives.
CARE ANYWAY

The good that you do may be forgotten tomorrow.
DO GOOD ANYWAY

Honesty and frankness make you vulnerable.
BE HONEST AND FRANK ANYWAY

What you spent years building may be destroyed overnight.
BUILD ANYWAY

> *The people you help may not thank you.*
> *HELP THEM ANYWAY*

> *Give the world the best and it may not care.*
> *GIVE THE WORLD YOUR BEST ANYWAY*

> *For all that you do is ultimately done for God.*
> *And this makes everything you do and are eternally meaningful.*
> *IT IS REALLY ABOUT GOD ANYWAY*

Islamic Wisdom: The Five Pillars

The Bhagavad-Gita and its spiritual message may seem a bit abstract to some, and perhaps even impossible to actually realize. It is one way to think about finding and serving God. Islam has another way, a lifestyle that at least on the surface seems very concrete.

> *In the name of God the Compassionate, the Merciful,*
> *Praise be to God, Lord of the Universe,*
> *The Compassionate, the Merciful,*
> *Sovereign of the Day of Judgment!*
> *You alone we worship, and to You alone we turn for help.*
> *Guide us to the straight path,*
> *The path of those whom you have favored,*
> *Not of those who have incurred Your wrath,*
> *Nor of those who have gone astray. (Qur'an, Sura 1)*

This text is the first chapter of the Qur'an, known as the *Al-Fatihah* (The Opening). Muslims recite it in every one of their five daily formal prayer periods. The *Al-Fatihah* grounds the souls of devout Muslims. Who is God? God is the Compassionate, the Merciful, the Sovereign. What does a Muslim seek from God? A Muslim seeks the grace to follow the straight path, the one God has already laid out. Islam provides a structure for the devout soul in this life and assures a happy destiny in the next.

The straight path has Five Pillars: (1) Confession of Faith; (2) Prayer; (3) Almsgiving; (4) Fasting; and (5) Pilgrimage to Mecca.

The Confession of Faith is straightforward. It declares: "There is no God but God and Muhammad is His prophet." In the Arabian world of Muhammad, some were monotheists (*Allah* is simply the Arabic word for God); others were polytheists who worshipped their own tribe's god(s); and still others were henotheists, that is, those who believe in an absolute God but still worship lower gods whom they believe could give them blessings they thought they needed. Arabs, and particularly Muhammad, were also well aware of Christians, whom they thought odd for believing that God had a son. Thus Confession of Faith is crucial for Muslims. It not only declares the singular God, but it also ratifies that Muhammad is his prophet—and as we saw in chapter 2, Muhammad is the final prophet and utter exemplar of faithfulness. In the Islamic tradition, this declaration is a "witness with words." But it is not enough. If God is indeed the Sovereign, then one has to witness this Pillar with one's life, that is, with acts of justice and mercy. This is the "witness with the body." Finally, there is the "witness of the heart," representing the fullest expression of the Confession of Faith. One does not simply act justly, but one must have a heart that has become truly compassionate.

Prayer is likewise multilayered, and I would like to spend much more time on it because it represents the key component of the five Pillars. On the surface, it represents praising God five times a day (morning, midday, midafternoon, sunset, and night) in a rather invariant manner. The only variation is in the number of "units" or *rak'ah'* that are required. Muslims also ritualistically wash before every prayer period. This involves washing one's hands three times, rinsing one's mouth, sniffing water into one's nostrils, washing one's face three times, one's arms to the elbow, one's ears, the nape of the neck, and one's feet three times. A rak'ah is the following:

Standing, facing Mecca, and placing one's hands around one's ears:

God is greater.

Standing, one proclaims the first chapter of the Qur'an, the *Al-Fatihah*:

In the name of God the Compassionate, the Merciful,
Praise be to God, Lord of the Universe,
The Compassionate, the Merciful,
Sovereign of the Day of Judgment!
You alone we worship, and to You alone we turn for help.
Guide us to the straight path,
The path of those whom you have favored,
Not of those who have incurred Your wrath,
Nor of those who have gone astray. Amen.

Standing, one recites at least three verses from the Qur'an, ending with:

God is greater.

Bending and placing one's hands to one's knees:

Glorify my Magnificent Lord.
Glorify my Magnificent Lord.
Glorify my Magnificent Lord.

Standing straight:

God is greater.
God Listens to one who praises God.
Our Lord, praise be for You only.

Kneeling prostrate with head and hands on the ground:

Glorify my Highest Lord.
Glorify my Highest Lord.
Glorify my Highest Lord.

Sitting on one's knees:

> *God is greater.*

Kneeling prostrate with head and hands on the ground:

> *Glorify my Lord the Highest.*
> *Glorify my Lord the Highest.*
> *Glorify my Lord the Highest.*

The above is repeated, depending on the number of units required for that time of prayer. Prayer ends with the believer sitting on one's knees and saying:

> *All Greeting to Allah and prayers and good will. [omitted by Shi'ites]*
> *Peace be on you Prophet as well as mercy and blessing of Allah be on you.*
> *May peace be upon us and on the devout worshipper of Allah.*
> *I testify that there is no God but Allah and*
> *I testify that Muhammad is His slave and messenger.*
> *O God, send Your mercy on Muhammad and his posterity,*
> *As you sent your mercy on Abraham and his posterity.*
> *O God, send Your blessings on Muhammad and his posterity,*
> *As you have blessed Abraham and his posterity.*
> *You are the Most Praised, the Most Glorious.*

Moving one's head to the right and addressing all in this direction:

> *The peace and mercy of Allah be on you.*

Moving one's head to the left and addressing all in this direction:

> *The peace and mercy of Allah be on you.*

It would be good, I think, to see what is or ought to be going on at a deeper level. The pre-prayer ablution is meant to be itself a kind of prayer even as it is also a preparation for prayer. Muslims ask God to forgive their sins with their hands and cleanse their mouth of any evil. Filling their nostrils invokes the desire to know the sweet scent of paradise, and washing their face seeks to purify it from any stains and illuminate it with the light of divine wisdom. In washing their right foot, they pray to stay on the straight path; in washing the left foot, they pray to be free from temptations. Islamic scholar Syed Ali Ashraf notes, "The purification of the outer limbs is accompanied by an inner purification and an intensive prayer for forgiveness, mercy, and guidance."[2]

The same interior dynamism ought to be part of the whole prayer. In the *Hadith Qudsi* (no. 8), Muhammad explains God's own engagement to the beginning of the prayer:

Muslim:	In the name of God the Compassionate, the Merciful,
God:	*My Servant mentions Me.*
Muslim:	Praise be to God, Lord of the Universe,
God:	*My servant lends Me grace.*
Muslim:	The Compassionate, the Merciful,
God:	*My servant praises Me.*
Muslim:	Sovereign of the Day of Judgment!
God:	*My servant glorifies Me and submits himself to Me.*
Muslim:	You alone we worship, and to You alone we turn for help.
God:	*This is shared between Me and My servant, and My servant will receive what he asks.*
Muslim:	Guide us to the straight path, The path of those whom you have favored, Not of those who have incurred Your wrath, Nor of those who have gone astray.
God:	*All that comes back to My servant, and My servant will receive that for which he asks.*

Prayer, as we see, is a forum for intimacy with God. It pleases God to hear God's attributes venerated. In the second half of the *Al-Fatihah*, the believer pleads with God for the grace to be led on the straight path, and God's response is to assure God's servant that this grace is given lovingly. In praying, Muslims become a kind of Muhammad. In reciting verses from the Qur'an, they experience and recite the original revelation of God to Muhammad. And in standing, kneeling, and prostrating before God, they replicate in some fashion Muhammad's own ascent to the Divine Throne. Prayer becomes a practice on earth to behold the Face of God and to anticipate with a foretaste the beatific vision of God for eternity. Islamic scholar Allahbakhsh Brohi notes, "The supreme opportunity that life provides is to turn to God consciously and purposively and to contemplate the beauty of His Face and His manifold Attributes. This helps man to secure the transformation of his being and to make a fit vehicle upon which God's light and grace may descend."[3]

The third Pillar of the straight path is almsgiving. The Arabic term for it is *zakat*, which literally means "cleansing" or "purification." The saying goes that one has not fulfilled *zakat* until one's heart is purified from greed. The Qur'an teaches, "You shall never be truly righteous until you give in alms what you dearly cherish" (3.92). Muslims are charged with giving 2.5 percent of their net worth to those in need. This is a tax, and it relies on an honest disclosure of all of one's assets. It would be typical for officials of one's local mosque to handle the funds and to assure that these go to the poor, though it also supports the regular efforts of the mosque itself. This is a yearly task, but Muslim generosity is hardly expected to stop here. A related term to *zakat* is *sadaqat*, which means "donation," as one is obliged to support family, friends in need, and those one meets in need. It also covers volunteerism. The great Persian mystic and poet Rumi wrote: "When you become a true servant of service, the Light graces you. You radiate! You become a divine lamp. You do not worry whether you are placed high or low."[4]

Fasting is the fourth Pillar, and it extends through the month of Ramadan. Muhammad's first revelations came during the month of Ramadan and it was during this month many years later that he made his historical flight (*hijrah*) from Mecca to Yathrib (Medina). Muslims observe this month with rigid fasting, even from water, during daylight hours. It is an opportunity to identify with Muhammad's plight on behalf of God's mission and represents a kind of month-long retreat that promotes greater devotion. The discipline required is daunting enough, but the underlying motivation is restraint from the tyranny of one's passions and the addiction we have to our levels of comfort.

Finally, the fifth Pillar is pilgrimage (*hajj*), whereby every healthy Muslim who has the means is charged with making a pilgrimage to Mecca during Dhu al-Hijjah, the last month of the lunar calendar. There are a number of rituals required for a full experience of the *hajj*. They include circling seven times the holy Ka'bah, a cube-shaped building within the Grand Mosque. Muslims believe that this was built by Abraham and is the site of Adam's original temple. Pilgrims then visit the plain of Arafat and pray for forgiveness. They cast stones at a pillar that marks the place where the devil tempted Abraham. They sacrifice an animal at Mina, just outside Mecca, to commemorate Abraham's sacrifice, and then arrange for the meat to be given to the poor. And last, they complete their pilgrimage with a farewell circling of the Ka'bah. In all of this, they attempt to ritually engage in their sacred history and hope for their future. For example, circling the Ka'bah mirrors doing so around the Divine House in the Seventh Heaven, beyond which stands the glorified Throne of God. The pilgrim participates with the angels circling the Divine Throne.[5]

What Can We Learn?

The clearest thing one can draw on here is that a deeply holy life does not have to be highly abstract or complex. There can be a concrete agenda of spiritual practices that can guide us. It is as though Muslims can assure us: do this and be saved! The Christian tradition is rife with methods and stages of spiritual progress: John of the Cross describes various active and passive nights to be endured; Teresa of Ávila details seven levels; John Ruysbroeck describes a spiritual ladder that must be ascended; Richard of St. Victor details fourteen stages for spiritual growth; and John Climacus provides no fewer than forty stages. The Islamic mystical tradition likewise is filled with esoteric material. But it does not have to be so complicated. Obviously, the Five Pillars do not represent the whole of Islamic piety, but their fundamental framework is: DO THIS—this is what God wants of you, and it works.

We also learn that holiness is still hard work. The point of the Five Pillars is to guide the soul to ever deeper levels of appropriation. Anyone with a modicum of discipline can *perform* the Five Pillars. But it takes an earnest soul, an increasingly sensitive soul, a soul that really does seek God (and not just obedience to outward forms) to interiorize them. That is the work. The deeper point of the Confession of Faith is recognizing God as *my* God, *my* master, the Lord of *my life*. And it is an ever-deepening reverence for his Prophet who ought to be my mentor and exemplar. The deeper realization of almsgiving is to develop a heart of mercy, compassion, justice, and freedom from greed and acquisitiveness in my soul. This refers to material things, but also to everything that I cling to that brings me a cheap and false sense of security. The more profound fast is disciplining my mind and body to conquer my predilections to everything that inhibits my freedom to be God's servant. Pilgrimage to Mecca is not about seeing the sights and doing the rituals, but about absorbing my faith's history, essence, and future. And as should be obvious from what I have said, the Pillar of prayer is about intimacy and communion with the living God. The kind of intentionality and purity of mind and heart that this calls for is daunting. But its possibilities are endlessly transforming and gratifying.

I began this chapter with paradoxes. The way to find and know God is possible, but it cannot be as an acquisition of the ego. The Five Pillars guide us from obedience to opportunity, from doing rote things or demanded things to absorbing the very essence that they participate in. Islam tells us that we have the capacity for true and deep union with the Divine. It is a message of great optimism and hope. In the Hadith Qudsi, God says this:

> *I cannot be contained in the space of earth.*
> *I cannot be contained in the space of the heavens.*
> *But I can be contained in the heart of my loving servant.*[6]

Notes

1. Klaus Klostermaier, *A Survey of Hinduism*, 2nd ed. (Albany: State University of New York, 1994), 222.

2. Syed Ali Ashraf, "The Inner Meaning of Islamic Rites," in *Islamic Spirituality: Foundations*, ed. Seyyed Hossein Nasr (New York: Crossroad, 1987), 112.

3. Allahbakhsh K. Brohi, "The Spiritual Dimension of Prayer," in Nasr, *Islamic Spirituality*, 138–39.

4. Jalalu'ddin Jam, *Jewels of Remembrance*, ed. Camille Helminski and Kabir Helminski (Putney, VT: Threshold Books, 1996), 90.

5. Ashraf, "The Inner Meaning of Islamic Rites," 122.

6. As cited in Jamal Rahman, *The Fragrance of Faith: The Enlightened Heart of Islam* (Bath, UK: Book Foundation, 2004), 104.

4

How Might I Live?

We saw in chapter 3's reflection on Islam's Five Pillars that being deeply involved in the pursuit of holiness does not need to be complicated. It turns out that these simple precepts have a profound capacity to provide one with an integrated life, a life lived justly, compassionately, and with divine intimacy. Real transformation requires hard inner work, but one's framing can be rather straightforward. Jewish spirituality corroborates this essential message, but it is a bit more challenging in terms of procedure. All religions require both *orthodoxy* (right belief) and *orthopraxy* (right action). Judaism leans heavily on the latter. Here, spiritual depth has less to do with what one believes and more with how and why one acts.

I was once on a panel with a Reform Jewish rabbi and an Islamic scholar. The rabbi noted that Christians and Muslims seem to think a lot about the afterlife, heaven and hell, and how to attain the former and avoid the latter. We nodded our heads in vigorous agreement. It is certainly a big-ticket item in our religions. We understand a human life as that one precious existence, one where we determine the kind of person we want to be. Although no one lives and dies as a morally pure soul or as an utterly evil one, life is certainly about whether one desires and pursues God and God's will in one's life or rejects God. Catholic moral thought calls this the *fundamental option*: Do you align your life with God or are you opposed to God?

Surely both traditions also believe that salvation is a matter of God's grace, and not something that can be earned. But both also think that God's grace is operating within the human soul, calling it to its truest self, which is nothing less than the pursuit of God. Catholic doctrine is particularly open about how this might personally play out: we would have implicit faith when we follow the dictates of our conscience, and we presume God is moving that conscience to seek the good and the true. Judaism also aligns itself to these intuitions. But what struck me was that the rabbi said that neither she nor the members of her congregation ever talk about the afterlife. "It just never comes up," she said. "We focus utterly on what needs to be done in this life, with little interest in what God intends after that." It turns out that many observant Jews have a wide variety of opinions about the afterlife but do not give it great significance. It would be very possible for three Jewish friends in the same Reform synagogue to legitimately believe wildly different things: one might anticipate heaven, another reincarnation, and still another no afterlife at all. In Judaism, the focus is on orthopraxy.

Like all the other chapters, this chapter considers two ways of being religious, but here both ways come from Jewish resources. I look at the Jewish understanding of God's *Torah* as a skillful guide in being religious and at life as a mystical celebration that Jews participate in from the Hasidic tradition. The quality of one's life here on earth is the dominating interest in Judaism.

Jewish Wisdom: *Torah and Mitzvot*

The Jewish word *Torah* has many meanings. A literal transla-tion could be "guidance," "instruction," or "law," and generally Torah includes all three. It is a term that can also refer to the first five books of the Hebrew Bible, known as the Pentateuch. Jewish tradition has it that these first five books were written by Moses and that collectively they represent God's covenant with the people of Israel. According to tradition, there are 613 laws in these five books. But rather than being a simple total of a list of laws, this number has something of a symbolic function. Rabbi Hammuna of the third century CE argued that 613 represented the numerology associated with the word *Torah*: *tav* = 400; *vov* = 6; *resh* = 200; and *hay* = 5, producing 611. The remaining two laws are represented by the statements: "I am the Lord, your God" and "You shall not have other gods before me." Rabbi Simlai, a contemporary of Hammuna, arrived at 613 by adding together the 365 days in the solar year and the number of parts of the human body, which were believed to be 248. Further, these numbers aligned with the 365 prohibitions in the Torah and the 248 positive commands.

Torah is such an important reference that it has even taken on cosmic significance in the tradition. According to a *midrash* (story) by Rabbi Eliezer, God was initially not successful in creating a stable world because the universe kept collapsing. The problem was that God lacked a design. So God thought, "I need an overall plan for My world. I want it to be One as I am One." God then created Torah as a blueprint for creation and declared, "In that way, I and my Torah will be within everything."[1]

Following God's commands and seeing the world through the eyes of the Torah dominate Jewish consciousness. It is, however, more complicated than that, because striving to understand the divine will regarding the commandments is not easy. The Talmud is a compendium of commentary on the Torah, and was produced over the first several centuries of the Common Era. There are actually two Talmuds, the Palestinian and Babylonian, with the latter being the most authoritative. These early rabbis strove to produce a vision of what Jewish life should be. They learned how to make religious arguments, to attend to varying interpretations, and to master a great deal of received teaching. In case after case, the careful study of Talmudic legal discussion reveals that there was no *real* law until the rabbinic authorities decided what the law is to be, that is, how it is to be understood. For example, the Torah commands that Israel is to *keep holy the Sabbath day*. The Talmud devotes two whole tractates (260 pages in my English translation), to articulate in detail what this meant and how it was to be observed.

Psalm 119 is the longest Psalm in the Hebrew Bible (176 verses). It is a beautiful meditation on the meaning of Torah for Jews. It begins, "Happy are those whose way is blameless, who walk in the law [Torah] of the Lord. Happy are those who keep his decrees, who seek him with their whole heart" (vv. 1–2). "Oh, how I love your law!" the Psalmist declares. "How sweet are your words to my taste, sweeter than honey to my mouth. . . . Your word is a lamp to my feet and a light to my path. . . . Your decrees are righteous forever" (vv. 97, 103, 105, 144). In some Christian circles, Jewish law is contrasted with grace. This simply misreads a true Jewish understanding of Torah. For Jews, God's Torah is the premier expression of God's grace. In Leviticus, God commands: "You shall be holy, for I am holy" (11:45). The Torah is a road map to that holiness.

Just as Torah is a complex word, so is *mitzvot*, a term that means "commandments" as well as "sacred deeds." Devout Jews obey the commandments as understood by their particular tradition (typically Orthodox, Conservative, and Reform), and thus commit themselves to engaging the world in a sacred manner. Such obedience is not mere performance of ancient religious laws, however. Rabbi Kushner, reflecting on the work of German Jewish philosopher Franz Rosenzweig, distinguishes "legislation, which is simply a law written on the books, and commandment, which is something we feel is addressed to us personally. We do *mitzvot* because we believe God calls on us personally to do them."[2] Some commandments strike the outsider as minutiae and hardly worth considering. Does God really care about not eating shellfish or avoiding mixing dairy and meat? Or about how soap is manufactured? A Jewish response would be: Yes! Everything matters. As the great American Jewish scholar Abraham Joshua Heschel noted, "The predominant feature of the biblical pattern of life is unassuming, unheroic, inconspicuous piety, the sanctification of trifles, attentiveness to detail."[3] "Moses," he argued, "was not concerned with initiating a new cult [religious practice], but with creating a new people. In the center of Jewish living is not a cult but observance . . . [which] comprises all of life."[4] For Heschel, "God asks for the heart, and we must spell our answer in terms of deeds. . . . Faith is a symphony of internal and external deeds, of bodily acts done with spirit."[5]

The central creation story in the Jewish mystical tradition (Kabbalah) holds that when God decided to create the universe, God had to personally contract in order to make space that was not Divinity itself. God then emanated the divine light that grounded God's presence in the created world. This light filled ten vessels that would create the world. This is the *sefirot* pattern in Jewish Kabbalah. The first three of these vessels, Crown, Wisdom, and Understanding, remained intact. The next six, Love, Power, Beauty, Endurance, Majesty, and Foundation, could not contain the radiance of the divine light and burst with divine sparks. The final vessel, Presence, representing the physical world, cracked but did not break. Most of the divine sparks returned to their point of origin in God, but some were trapped in the fragments of the burst vessels. The very order of creation as well as the possibility for life and love come from these sparks. The bursting of these vessels, however, also created the conditions for disorder in the world, particularly the moral disorder of human beings.

What then is the human challenge in all this? It is to repair the vessels and return the divine sparks to their intended placement. When humans sin, the errant sparks become increasingly lost and chaotic. This, according to the tradition, provides the energy for evil. (One might liken it to the Dark Side of the Force in *Star Wars*.) But when humans act compassionately, they repair the broken vessels so as to allow the sparks to re-enter them, thus bringing spiritual order to the world. For some Jews, the great task of all humanity is to restore the divine sparks to their appropriate place in the divine realm. The process will come to final fruition in the Messianic Age. What is the great charge? Perhaps it can be reduced to this essential thing: *tikkun olam*, "repair the world." If something is broken, fix it. If something is lost, return it to the owner. If something is disfigured, restore its beauty.

Repairing the world has its most important expression in compassion toward others. Compassion, justice, and attending to those who are marginalized may represent Judaism's greatest collective theme, and certainly these issues represent a central concern in the Hebrew Bible, in which the cry (*ztaaq, shava*) of the oppressed particularly moves God. Consider a contribution to the Talmud by Rabbi Simlai. Rabbi Simlai preached:

> Six hundred and thirteen commandments were revealed through Moses. Then David came, and found their basis in eleven commandments, as it is said in the fifteenth Psalm: Lord, who may stay in your Tent? Who may reside on Your holy mountain? (1) He who lives without blame, (2) who does what is right, (3) and in his heart acknowledges the truth, (4) who has no slander upon his tongue, (5) who has never done harm to his fellow. (6) or borne reproach for his acts toward his neighbor, (7) for whom a contemptible man is abhorrent, (8) but who honors those who fear the Lord, (9) who stands by his oath even to his heart, (10) who has never lent money on interest, (11) or accepted a bribe against the innocent—The man who acts thus shall never be shaken.
>
> Then Isaiah came, and found the basis in six commandments, as it is said in Isaiah 35:15–16: (1) he who walks in righteousness, (2) speaks uprightly, (3) spurns profit from fraudulent dealings, (4) waves away a bribe instead of grasping it, (5) stops his ears against

listening to infamy, (6) shuts his eyes against looking at evil—Such a one shall dwell in lofty security.

Then Micah came, and found the basis in three commandments, as it is said in Micah 6:8: He has told you, O man, what is good, and what the Lord requires of you: (1) only to do justice, (2) and to love goodness, (3) and to walk humbly with your God.

Then Isaiah returned, and found the basis in two commandments, as it is said in Isaiah 56:1: Thus said the Lord: (1) observe what is right, (2) and do what is just.

Then Amos came, and found the basis in one single commandment, as it is said in Amos 5:4: Thus said the Lord to the House of Israel: (1) Seek Me, and you will live![6]

One of the most fascinating aspects of kabbalistic cosmology is that once God created anything, including the *sefirot* pattern with the divine vessels, then God became vulnerable in some sense to what happens to them. Kabbalists are careful to say that God *as* God transcends the universe and cannot be immediately approached, known, or even affected. But once God emanated the Divine Self, God's manifestation cannot be completely divorced from God's very being. In this sense, God was affected by creation, its disordered qualities, and humanity's life in this complex spiritual reality. Consider it this way: the process of repairing the broken vessels and returning the sparks to their rightful order matters to God and God's own *personal* existence. It is not as though performing *mitzvot* heals a bleeding God, but rather that God and God's manifestation are affected by our deeds. Heschel declares,

God does not stand outside the range of human suffering and sorrow. He is personally involved in, even stirred by, the conduct and fate of man. History is often the record of human misery, and since God is concerned for human beings and involved in their history, God must be involved in their suffering. God's participation in human history . . . finds its deepest expression in the fact that God can actually suffer.[7]

Likewise, God is *actually* blessed when humans perform *mitzvot*, sacred deeds. And humans can be expressions of the divine activity here on earth. Adin Steinsaltz, who is perhaps one of the greatest Talmudic scholars of the last generation, expresses this dynamic beautifully:

Man may therefore be viewed as a symbol or a model of the divine essence, his entire outer and inner structure manifesting relationships and different aspects existing in that supreme essence. The secret of the positive *mitzvot*, the commandments to perform certain actions, lies, in a manner of speaking, in the activization of the limbs of the body, in certain movements and certain ways of doing things which are congruous with higher realities and higher relationships in other worlds. In fact, every movement, every gesture, every habitual pattern, and every isolated act that man does with his body has an effect in whole systems of essences in other dimensions with and against one another.[8]

What Can We Learn?

I noted earlier that some Christians think of Judaism as purely focused on laws, as though it is a legalistic religion based on works righteousness and not on grace. But did Jesus think this? Each of the synoptic gospels tells the story of a rich young man who approaches Jesus and wants to know what he must do to attain eternal life. Jesus's response is, "If you wish to enter into life, keep the commandments." Jesus will also tell him, "If you wish to be perfect, go, sell your possessions, and give the money to the poor, and you will have treasure in heaven; then come, follow me" (Mt 19:16, 21). Given the apocalyptic framework of Jesus's ministry, this last radical act makes great sense. But one shouldn't miss his foundational imperative: "If you wish to enter into life, keep the commandments." So crucial was Torah obedience to Jesus that he proclaims in his Sermon on the Mount:

> Do not think that I have come to abolish the law or the prophets; I have come not to abolish but to fulfill. For truly I tell you, until heaven and earth pass away, not one letter, not one strike of a letter, will pass from the law until all is accomplished. Therefore, whoever breaks one of the least of these commandments, and teaches others to do the same will be called least in the kingdom of heaven; but whoever does them and teaches them will be called great in the kingdom of heaven. (Mt 5:17–19)

When I was in college, I spent a Sabbath day with my Jewish friend Moshe and his family. Here, the dictates of Sabbath were rigorously observed. They had their lights on a timer so as not to have to manually turn them on that day, and a neighbor came over to start their oven for lunch. We went to a long synagogue service, and then came home and had lunch. In the afternoon we read, he the Torah and I my New Testament. We chatted, we went for a walk, we hung out with other family members. The day closed with a solemn blessing at twilight.

Regardless of one's religious identity, what would our life look like if we spent a full day every week close to family and focused on our spiritual lives? What if weekly we went on retreat? I cannot imagine it would result in anything but deep spiritual growth throughout the years of my life. I am a Christian, and my Sunday generally looks like this: I pray in the morning and then go to Mass. I come home to watch some football, take a nap, and do the weekly shopping and laundry. But since I go to Mass daily, there is really nothing much that distinguishes Sunday from any other day, except that it is a day off from university work (and sometimes not even that). Judaism insists on much greater intentionality in the spiritual life.

What if we imagined that following every dictate from God not only had moral significance but, on a subtle level, cosmic significance? Then the commandments would not only be personally valuable, but in following them I would participate in a universal restoration of the world. Life would be weightier, for sure. Life would also be far more sacramental. Sacraments are rites where the symbols of those rites participate in the very thing they symbolize. How might our lives be different if we understood the multitude of day-to-day activities as instantiating spiritual energy and truth, as sacraments? A typical way religious children are brought up morally is to be reminded that "God is watching." Thus, you can get away with nothing, even if your parents do not catch you stealing or fibbing or saying mean things to your siblings. From a Jewish point of view, the focus would be less "God is watching" than it would be "What I do actually matters to God's own self." I can bless God in what I do, and God is *literally* blessed. I can also rebel against God, against truth and goodness, and know that God is participating in the suffering that I cause, both to myself and to others.

What would life be like if I actually saw my hands as instruments of God's activity in this world? There is an ancient story from the land of Israel about a wealthy man who was dozing in the synagogue. He heard the chanting of verses from Leviticus where God tells Israel to place twelve loaves of challah on a table of the ancient tabernacle in Sinai. A bit confused, he thought that God had commanded him to do this. So he went home, baked the bread, and placed the loaves next to the Torah scrolls in the synagogue. As soon as he left, a very poor man entered the synagogue to plead to God. "O Lord," he moaned, "my family is starving. Unless you perform some miracle, we will perish." Then he noticed the loaves next to the Torah scrolls. The miracle happened. Minutes later the rich man returned to the synagogue and saw the loaves gone. He thought that God had taken them and perhaps consumed them personally. So he was intent on doing this weekly, and weekly the poor man discovered bread for his family. It became their practice for the next twenty years. One day the rabbi was detained longer than usual and saw the rich man leaving the loaves and later the poor man taking them. Speaking to them together, he discovered their intentions. "Shame on you both," he said. "God is pure spirit. God does not eat *challah* and God does not bake *challah*." They both agreed that it did seem silly to imagine this and thought they should stop. "No," said the rabbi. To the rich man he said, "Yours are the hands of God giving food to the poor." And to the poor man he said, "Yours are the hands of God receiving gifts from the rich." And then to them both, "Continue, your hands are the hands of God."[9]

Jewish Wisdom: The Ecstasy of the Hasidim

In the middle of the eighteenth century, in the Polish-Lithuanian Commonwealth, small circles of Jewish pietists attached themselves to rabbis who were believed to be particularly spiritually charged. They would come to be called *tsaddikim* (righteous ones), or in Yiddish, *rebbes*. It was from this small beginning that the movement eventually called Hasidism would emerge.[10] *Hasidut* means "piety" and the *Hasidim* were the "pious ones," the rebbe being the most pious among the pious. The Hasidic movement was principally a lay movement of devotees following spiritual masters. Some of these masters were learned scholars of Torah and respected rabbis, but others were far less lettered. Their authority was the spiritual gravitas they exuded—they were believed to be able to mediate intimacy with God. According to Elie Wiesel, Jews "had good reason to doubt the absolute power of rationalism. So they turned inward and became mystical."[11] They signified their relationship to God with such kabbalistic terms as *devekut* (ecstatic union) and *ha'alat nitzotzot* (raising the divine sparks). Thus for the Hasidim, Jewish life circled not around the intellect, but around the *divine spark*. "They turned to the rebbe, for only he knew how to comfort them, how to impart to them a sense of sacredness."[12]

By tradition, Hasidism began with the genius of Israel ben Eli'ezer (ca. 1700–1760), also known as the Ba'al Shem Tov, or Master of the [Divine] Name. Ba'al Shem Tov was a title that others held as well. They were something like Jewish shamans who could use spiritual techniques from the kabbalistic tradition (prayers, incantations, and rituals) to invoke divine forces.[13] Eli'ezer, if not exactly the founder of the movement, was its model. Jewish philosopher Martin Buber describes him thus: "He takes unto himself the quality of fervor. He arises from sleep with fervor, for he is hallowed . . . and is worthy to create and become like the Holy One."[14] Wiesel notes, "He would intercede on people's behalf and heaven would submit to his will."[15]

This was the power believed to be held by many rebbes, who know all the answers and hold supreme authority. It was said that in the presence of Rebbe Sternfeld of Lublin, "The weak forget their weakness, the old are unaware of their age . . . the poor are less poor, the sick forget their illnesses. . . . He carries them far away. They trust him. They do not know the outcome or the purpose of his [God's] secret plan; *he does*, and that should be enough."[16] Accounts of the power of rebbes are legion. Some were clairvoyant; others could see the past or future. Most important, they had power in heaven. It was said about Rebbe Israel Maggid of Kozhenitz that his prayers were always *obeyed* by heaven, except for on one night. Israel Maggid was shocked and demanded an explanation from heaven. When he received it, he understood and *forgave* God. It turns out that another rebbe, Naphtali of Ropshitz, was engaged in rescuing a wedding party that, due to a family tragedy, was sad. Naphtali entered the gathering, charmed and amused them, and led them in songs of love. By Naphtali's own charismatic presence, he healed the entire wedding party. And like the wedding guests, the angels in heaven were completely under his spell; thus, they were not paying attention to Rebbe Israel's prayers at the time.[17]

Hasidism is probably most known for its ethos of ecstatic joy. In the Hasidic literature, we find episodes again and again of great, joyous exuberance. This one takes place in 1814 in Lublin, in a celebration of Israel's reception of the Torah:

> Surrounding their Master, people sing and dance with frenzy. Like him, with him, they lift the Holy Scrolls higher and higher, as if to follow them—and follow *him*—and they do. He carries them away, far away. . . . They all feel it now: this celebration is unlike any other. Every word reverberates in higher palaces up there, in heaven, where Israel's fate is being determined—and mankind's too. . . . And to his own community, gathered from all over his kingdom, he repeated over and over again: "Drink and celebrate—it's an order. And if your ecstasy is pure enough, contagious enough, it will last forever—I promise you that." In spite of his age and his fatigue, he himself leads the assembly with astonishing vigor. It's as though his intention is to move the entire creation from darkness to redemption.[18]

Hasidism is a culture where the spiritual and even mystical life is grounded in experiences of the world. They seek to spiritualize their material existence. Rebbe Barukh of Kosov relates:

> I was once listening to a humble man bemoan the fact that sexual union naturally entails physical pleasure. He preferred that there be no physical pleasure at all, so that he could engage in union solely to fulfill the command of his creator. . . . Sometime later, however, God favored me with a gift of grace, granting me understanding of the true meaning of sanctification

during sexual intercourse: the sanctification derives precisely from feeling physical pleasure. This secret is wondrous, deep, and awesome.[19]

Here we see that the physical is not contrasted with the spiritual, but a potential mediation of a higher spiritual level. Perhaps the agenda could be framed that the material can be transformed into the spiritual, as a way of raising the divine sparks back to their source, known as *avodah be-gashmiyut*. An excellent example is the Hasidic practice of smoking, typically with a long pipe. The *Zohar*, a thirteenth-century magnum opus of kabbalistic theology, speaks of the smoke from incense as mediating between the lower worlds and the *sefirot*. The Hasidim applied this to tobacco smoke.[20]

Another example is the *tish*, the third meal of the Sabbath, which is eaten after midafternoon prayers by the rebbe and devotees. If a rebbe was not present in the city, they would gather at the home of a prominent member of the community. There, they ate, drank wine, sang, and danced. When the rebbe was present, he would end the meal with a sermon. One Hasidic story about the Ba'al Shem Tov goes like this: In a village he was visiting, a wealthy Hasidic farmer gathered many Jews from nearby farms where they ate and drank together in song and celebration. The Ba'al Shem Tov perceived that this practice found great favor in heaven. He called the farmer after the meal and asked him why he had devoted so much attention to the third meal. The farmer answered:

I have heard that people say, Let my soul depart [while I am] among my people Israel; and I have heard furthermore that on the Sabbath each Jew possesses an additional soul (*neshama yetera*) which departs from him at the termination of the Sabbath. So I said: Let my additional soul also depart while I am in the company of the people of Israel. This is why I gather these Jews together.[21]

Eating at the *tish* was believed to affect a connection in the *sefirot* that causes a flow to earth of divine abundance, something that cannot be achieved when eating alone.[22]

Hasidism emphasized the role of music and dance far more than mainstream Judaism had. In the court of Maggid of Mezritsh, when the Sabbath meal was finished the Maggid began to sing a *niggun* (wordless melody). While singing, he began to recite the names of all those present, even the names of people he had never met or been introduced to. The *niggun* acted as a prelude to his sermon. It was a meditative expression intended to elevate the community to another spiritual level. The *niggun* was also believed to be important in the Hasidic quest for union with God (*devekut*). Indeed, the *niggun* became a central practice everywhere, during prayer, public events, family gatherings, and so on.[23]

But it wasn't merely the *niggun* that Hasidism practiced. The Hasidim drew on the melodies and even words of a variety of European sources, from sacred Jewish songs to Austrian waltzes, Polish marches, and Russian and Hungarian folk songs. Nahman of Braslav taught that such borrowing was something of a magical practice: "When, God forbid, there is an evil decree by idolaters [Gentiles] against Israel, it is good to sing the melody of those same idolaters who are oppressing them, God forbid." Other Hasidim understood adopting foreign songs as a *mitzvah* (sacred deed) since they harbored a spark of divinity. And thus, appropriating these songs restored these sparks to the *sefirot*.[24]

Finally, Hasidic Judaism is famous for its love of dance, which like music has the potential to lead to higher states of consciousness. According to tradition, the Ba'al Shem Tov and his disciples would regularly erupt into ecstatic dance. Once during the fall festival of *Simhat Torah*, the Ba'al Shem Tov and his followers spontaneously started to dance, and those watching saw a vision of the divine presence: "They were dancing in a circle and flames of fire were burning around them like a canopy."[25] Nahman of Braslav believed that the physical movements of the dancer affected the *sefirot* of *netsah* (endurance) and *hod* (majesty), the "legs" of God's manifestation.[26]

What Can We Learn?

The Hasidic imagination is particularly significant in relation to the Jewish mysticism of Kabbalah, which was preserved and advanced the most in the Hasidic movement. Principally, through Martin Buber, Hasidic stories, doctrine, and kabbalistic insights have become integral to mainstream Judaism. Buber is, however, not without his critics. Gershom Scholem, perhaps the most important contributor to studies in Jewish mysticism in the modern period, has demonstrated serious bias in Buber's account of Hasidism. Among Scholem's criticisms is that Buber downplays Hasidism's firm grounding in Jewish law and interpretation while overemphasizing its ecstatic religiosity. Buber also ignores problems in Hasidic culture, including autocratic rebbes and historically exaggerated claims of their spiritual power. The most up-to-date studies support Scholem's assertions. Buber's slant is very romantic, a charge he might well have accepted. He wanted to present the ethos of a profound religious imagination in such a way as to allow it to be appropriated within mainstream Judaism and beyond. He describes his intent as one of mediating the experience of Hasidism as it transformed his own consciousness as well as the existential stance to which Hasidism as a whole points.[27]

Buber's message to us, through the medium of Hasidism, is that the world is far more mystical and spiritually charged than we might think. Buber did not want us to retreat into a medieval or even eighteenth-century culture, but to enrich our modern worldview with extraordinary divine possibilities. The infusion of Jewish Hasidic mysticism into our religious imagination can lead us to see that the physical world has a supernatural ground, and that the spiritual life involves learning how to negotiate the physical and spiritual at the same time. Further, Buber reminds us how important it is that our religious leaders also be spiritual masters. Masters do not merely announce the sacred, they communicate it; and this necessitates being in profound communion with it. A master cannot simply be a good and earnest person, but must also have great spiritual depth.

The Kabbalah is not the only inspiration of Hasidism, which is intense, mystical, and a bit magical in its framework. Hasidism's joyous piety and intense integration with the physical world has a Jewish medieval pedigree, even if not direct influence. The medieval golden age of Spain saw a tremendous output of prayers, poems, and songs that celebrated life on earth as a divine gift. Here is one such poem by Moses Ibn Ezra:

> The garden wears a colored coat,
>   The lawn has on embroidered robes,
> The trees are wearing checkered shifts,
>   They show their wonders to every eye,
> And every bud renewed by spring
>   Comes smiling forth to greet his lord.
> See! Before them marches a rose,
>   Kingly, his throne above them borne,
> Freed of the leaves that had guarded him,
>   No more to wear his prison clothes.
> Who will refuse to toast him there?
>   Such a man his sin will bear.[28]

Raymond Scheindlin notes that such a garden scene is "revisited in poem after poem: It is spring, and the poet summons the world to drink in celebration of the revival of nature."[29] This is not merely a celebration of nature, but is religiously infused and filled with dense biblical metaphors: "His throne above them borne" alludes to a saying by King David (2 Sam 23:1); "No more to wear his prison clothes" is a quotation from the release of King Jehoiachin from Babylonian imprisonment (2 Kings 25:29); Joseph also changed his prison clothes before serving Pharaoh as second in command of Egypt (Gen 41:14, 39–43); and if the rose is king, the flowers, trees, and grass are courtiers in the "colored coat," an allusion to King David's daughters (2 Sam 13:18).[30] Here is one more by Samuel the Nagid:

> The days of cold are past and days
>> Of spring have buried winter's rains.
> The doves are sighted in our land;
>> They flock to every lofty bough.
> So friends, be true, and keep your word.
>> Come quickly, do not disappoint a friend,
> But come into my garden—There are
>> Roses scented as with myrrh to pluck—
> And drink with me, amid the buds and birds
>> Assembled there to sing the summer's praise,
> Wine, red as my tears for loss
>> Of friends, or red as the blush on lovers' cheeks.[31]

As I noted earlier, the Jewish imagination considers God very much a part of our lives. It is, however, a philosophical challenge to think so. If God acts in time, this suggests that God has become part of the causal world, an actor among other actors, albeit a big one. Greek philosophers such as Plato and Aristotle did not think God *could* act in time. God's eternity excludes engagement with temporality. God *seems* to us to be part of our lives in time, but this is not the actual case. Thomas Aquinas taught that, since we are in time, *we* experience God in time. But God *as* God does not enter time personally. For God, everything and all time is present immediately and God stands outside it. But from God's eternal foreknowledge, God (as first cause) created the universe with God's blessings already there to be experienced by us in time.

Is this compelling? I have a hard time thinking it is the actual state of affairs. We saw this problem played out in the first chapter regarding the creative tension between *Nirguna-Brahman* and *Saguna-Brahman*. *Nirguna-Brahman* is impersonal, without qualities, and certainly without interest in sentient beings like us.

Saguna-Brahman is personal, loving, and certainly interested in us. As we saw in the Bhagavad-Gita, Krishna (Vishnu) assures Arjuna that he loves and positively desires union with us. We also noted that some Hindus such as Sri Ramakrishna asserted God was both *Nirguna* and *Saguna*. This certainly violates linear logic, but, he argued, Divinity transcends logic. The kabbalistic answer is that God *as* God (*Ein Sof*—Infinite) indeed transcends time and is beyond being affected by creation in time. But once God manifested the Divine Self into the *sefirot* pattern, God could not be completely distinct from it. This is how Kabbalah works with the creative tension that daunts many philosophers.

The *sefirot* pattern is actually pervasive. The pattern is the face of God manifest. It is also the supernatural substructure of the universe. This is how we affect both God and the world by our deeds. Further, our souls, being in the image and likeness of God, are likewise spiritually structured in the *sefirot* pattern. Imagine our souls, the universe, and the Godhead-manifest as sharing the same underlying spiritual structure. We are extraordinarily spiritually potent in who we are and what we do.

Given this, we might also come to a great reverence in the joy and exuberance we see in the Hasidim. Life is joy, life is song, life is dance. The only caveat, and it is a big one, is that their kind of joy must be spiritually skillful. A *tish* is not an American New Year's Eve bash. A Hasidic wedding of drinking and dance is not like watching an exhilarating football game with beer and friends. Song intends to engage one's spirit and elevate one's consciousness, to take oneself underneath the music and discover the divine sparks. All this requires a mature soul and a very intentional life.

Notes

1. Lawrence Kushner, *Jewish Spirituality: A Brief Introduction for Christians* (Woodstock, VT: Jewish Lights, 2001), 38.

2. Ibid., 57.

3. Abraham Joshua Heschel, *I Asked for Wonder: A Spiritual Anthology*, ed. Samuel H. Dresner (New York: Crossroad, 1986), 89.

4. Ibid., 87.

5. John C. Merkle, *Genesis of Faith: The Depth Theology of Abraham Joshua Heschel* (New York: Macmillan, 1985), 208.

6. As cited in Jakob J. Petuchowski, *Our Masters Taught: Rabbinic Stories and Sayings* (New York: Crossroad, 1982), 52–53.

7. Merkle, *Genesis of Faith*, 130.

8. Adin Steinsaltz, *The Thirteen Petalled Rose: A Discourse on the Essence of Jewish Existence and Belief*, 2nd ed. (New York: Basic Books, 2006), 88–89.

9. This is my version of the story related in Kushner, *Jewish Spirituality*, 63–66.

10. Some of this material I have published in another form. See "Interrelatedness and Spiritual Masters: Why Martin Buber Still Matters," *The Way* 51, no. 3 (2014): 63–75.

11. Joseph Telushkin, *Jewish Literacy* (New York: Image Books, 1982), 216.

12. Elie Wiesel, *Four Hasidic Masters and Their Struggle against Melancholy* (Notre Dame, IN: University of Notre Dame Press, 1978), 14.

13. Much of my broad knowledge of Hasidism comes from the recently published and magisterial *Hasidism: A New History*, ed. David Biale et al. (Princeton, NJ: Princeton University Press, 2020). The volume's contributors are modern, world-class Jewish scholars.

14. Martin Buber, *Hasidism and Modern Man*, ed. and trans. Maurice Friedman (New York: Horizon Press, 1958), 51.

15. Wiesel, *Four Hasidic Masters*, 84.

16. Ibid., 61.

17. Ibid., 99–101.

18. Ibid., 61–62.

19. Biale, *Hasidism: A New History*, 175.

20. Ibid., 204.

21. Ibid., 194.

22. Ibid., 195.

23. Ibid., 210–11.

24. Ibid., 215.

25. Ibid., 217.

26. Ibid., 219.

27. Buber, *Hasidism and Modern Man*, 58.

28. Raymond P. Scheindlin, *Wine, Women, and Death: Medieval Hebrew Poems on the Good Life* (New York: Oxford University Press, 1986), 35.

29. Ibid., 37.

30. Ibid.

31. Ibid., 72.

5

How Might I Reimagine the Universe?

In Luke's gospel, Jesus is asked, "Teacher, what must I do to inherit eternal life?" Jesus then asked the man how he understood the law. His response was, "You shall love the Lord your God with all your heart, and with all your soul, and with all your strength, and with all your mind; and your neighbor as yourself." Jesus responded to him, "You have given the right answer; do this, and you will live." But then the man asked him, "And who is my neighbor?" Jesus uses this opportunity to tell the parable of the Good Samaritan:

> "A man was going down from Jerusalem to Jericho, and fell into the hands of robbers, who stripped him, beat him, and went away, leaving him half dead. Now by chance a priest was going down that road; and when he saw him, he passed by on the other side. So likewise a Levite, when he came to the place and saw him, passed by on the other side. But a Samaritan while traveling came near him; and when he saw him, he was moved with pity. He went to him and bandaged his wounds, having poured oil and wine on them. Then he put him on his own animal, brought him to an inn, and took care of him. The next day he took out two

denarii, gave them to the innkeeper, and said, 'Take care of him; and when I come back, I will repay you whatever more you spend.' Which of these three, do you think, was the neighbor to the man who fell into the hands of robbers?" He said, "The one who showed him mercy." Jesus said to him, "Go and do likewise." (Lk 10:30–37)

This is a famous story, but it needs to be unpacked. We clearly see that the Samaritan is the hero of the story and that the priest and Levite have failed morally. But Jesus chose two functionaries of the Temple, and for them, touching a corpse would have made them ritually impure. They would have had to risk violating purity laws to see if he was still living, and we might assume he looked dead to them. And of course, what would they do with a dead corpse of a stranger anyway? Further, were they neighbors? They were out of their neighborhood. What are the rules, the obligations, outside the neighborhood? We might blithely say that we would be like the Samaritan, and perhaps so. But perhaps we would not. Living outside the neighborhood is not easy.

A friend of mine had a grandmother who emigrated from Italy in the early twentieth century. The family settled in an Italian neighborhood in New York, and much of the family remained there for two generations. He told me that his grandmother never learned English. She didn't have to, since everyone spoke Italian and she rarely left the neighborhood. She understood the rules, the culture, and how to negotiate life there. She was comfortable. But she also had quite a narrow experience of US citizenship. Stretching ourselves to imagine other ways of thinking or being is both an adventure and an experience of disorientation.

More dramatically, consider leaving our world in a spacecraft and landing on a distant planet inhabited by aliens. Perhaps time is understood quite differently there. Morality has new rules and corresponds to a different kind of flourishing for very different beings. Obligations, cultural expectations, communication, and worldviews would all be different. What we would have to do first, I imagine, is to seek to understand how reality works there, and from this strive to understand how one might live in that new reality, how it might all make sense.

This chapter invites us to consider two ways of thinking about the universe that are very different from typical Western assumptions. These different worldviews are much more challenging to imagine than thinking of merely leaving the neighborhood. But they are not so extravagant that we see ourselves on another planet. In both cases, we find visions of a world that is highly interconnected and highly fluid. Reality is understood very differently in each, and both are very different from the way we usually assume reality works. We are taken far outside our neighborhood, and it can be disorienting. The payoff is that we are offered new ways of thinking about how the universe works and how we might flourish through new visions of our world.

Daoist Wisdom: Life Is Art—The Wu-Forms

Chinese religiosity is, in many ways, very different from a Western framework. Recent surveys on China have reported wildly different results on the question of religious self-identification. Of course, some Chinese might report that they are Confucian, or Daoist, or Buddhist, and so on. But, in fact, most moderately adhere to parts of several traditions. Twelfth-century Emperor Xiaozong once proclaimed, "Use Buddhism to rule the mind, Daoism to rule the body, and Confucianism to rule the world."[1] This demonstrates why many Chinese might hesitate to locate themselves in any particular religion. If specific and exclusive membership is required, then the Chinese populace would not look very religious at all. Yet the Chinese people broadly see themselves as religious. In the Chinese culture, life is more of an aesthetic exercise. Living richly, meaningfully, and artfully in ways that correspond to broad beliefs about how the universe works is, for them, a highly religious way of being.

They also see themselves and the universe quite differently. Two examples can illustrate this. The first is the very language of Chinese. Unlike English, Chinese has no articles (*the, a, an*), and Chinese also contrasts with English in that English nouns, verbs, adjectives, and adverbs make communication very specific. The Chinese language is less concrete. For the Chinese, reality is more fluid, more about relationships than individuation. In classical Chinese, the subject is even frequently omitted, thus strengthening the *event*-related focus of a sentence—a person is not a separate individual, an agent standing apart, but one in relationship, one involved in events.

My second example has to do with metaphysics, the nature of transcendent reality. From the Greek philosophical tradition we have words and concepts such as God (*theos*), who acts as the ultimate indemonstrable principle (*arche*), who created the universe with the divine organizing structure (*logos*), and did so in ways that are moral and just (*nomos*). We tend to see the universe as an ordered, divinely intended reality, governed by natural and divine laws that are intelligible to the human mind. The Daoist perspective, however, sees the world as virtually *acosmic*, with no absolute divinity or set of clear natural or divine laws. The closest Chinese word for cosmos is *yuzchou*, a term that expresses interdependence between time and space. There is no Absolute Reality, certainly nothing like the Hindu Brahman or Western God. There is just the ceaseless flow of life.[2]

All this is not to say that Daoism has no spiritual or transcendent principles that guide understanding; it surely does. It is just that the universe is not static, nor does it have an absolute Law Giver with immutable laws. Daoism relies on three particular dynamics. The first is the interflow of yin and yang as complementary energies or principles. Yin represents receptivity, darkness, earth, silence, stability, and femininity. Yang represents dynamism, light, heaven, sound, creativity, and masculinity. Yin and yang flow into each other and even carry the other within it, as the Daoist symbol suggests.[3]

The second dynamic is *dao*. *Dao* is a combination of two characters: *shu* (foot—meaning "to pass over," "go," or "lead through") and *shou* (head—meaning "foremost" or "leading"). What the term *dao* expresses is a skillful way or guidance in forging forward. *Dao* is the natural dynamic that undergirds all reality. It is spontaneous, nameless, and indescribable. It is the foundation of all things and the way in which all things follow their natural course. The ideal life and the ideal society exist insofar as they are solicitous to *dao* and aligned with *dao*. The first classic of Daoism, the *Daodejing*, begins thus:

> *The Dao that can be told is not the eternal Dao.*
> *The name that can be named is not the eternal name.*
> *The nameless is the beginning of heaven and earth.*
> *The named is the mother of ten thousand things.*
> *Ever desireless, one can see the mystery.*
> *Ever desiring, one can see the manifestations.*
> *These two spring from the same source but differ in name;*
> *this appears as darkness.*
> *Darkness within darkness.*
> *The gate to all eternity.*[4]

Here is another translation:

> *Way-making that can be put into words is not really way-making.*
> *And naming that can assign fixed reference to things is not really naming.*
> *The nameless is the fetal beginning of everything that is happening,*
> *While that which is named is their mother.*
> *Thus, to be really objectless in one's desires is how one observes the mystery of all things,*
> *While really having desires is how one observes their boundaries.*
> *These two—the nameless and what is named—emerge from the same source yet are referred to differently.*
> *Together they are called obscure.*
> *The obscurest of the obscure,*
> *They are the swinging gateway of the manifold mysteries.*[5]

I have consulted a number of translations of the *Daodejing*, and while they certainly show commonalities, what is striking is how different they are. The second translation has *dao* as "way-making," that is, *dao* is really about how to carry oneself in the world. The *dao* or the way or way-making all refer to the very nature of reality, which is mysterious but can be apprehended and engaged in how one lives. To be "desireless" is to stop trying to manipulate reality and allow it to unfold. Yet to have some kind of intentionality ("ever desiring") in what one does is valuable too. The challenge is to learn how to balance knowing and unknowing, or conceptualizing and recognizing the limits this brings. Learning how to embrace both at the same time is the art of living in and through the *dao*.

The third dynamic is *qi*, which refers to one's essence and vital force. *Qi* can be dissipated by one's passions. As we saw in chapter 3, being attached to a scenario or an outcome is a big problem. Being frustrated with one's experience or trying to manipulate one's circumstances goes against *dao* and weakens or drains one's *qi*. *Qi* is preserved by a skillful engagement with the world and a kind of equanimity in what one experiences. *Qi* can also be gained. In the ancient period some Daoist practitioners engaged in alchemy and the consumption of metals and herbs thought to extend life and even provide an immortal life in heaven. Daoism also developed what is known as *internal alchemy* (*neidan*) through meditative practices. Here the body is understood as the alchemist's cauldron and the practitioner seeks to transform body and soul into an *original state*. Daoist scholar Livia Kohn notes, "By preserving *qi* you can attain Dao, and through attaining Dao you can live long. Spirit is essence. By preserving essence you can reach spirit brightness."[6]

In Daoism, the universe we live in is not a large set of discrete individuals operating in the world, but an interpenetrating, always active, and changing series of relations. There is always continuity and novelty before us, and our mission is to most skillfully negotiate this dynamic. We are not passive participants in our experience, but we must be utterly sensitive to the fields of emerging energy and learn how to husband that energy. We are, with all others, co-creators of the moment. This kind of responsive participation requires the cultivation of *wu-forms*.

Wu is a prefix that, in and of itself, acts as a negation. *Wu-wei* literally means "no action." In Daoism, it refers to the value of being non-imposing in one's activity. One doesn't force something to happen, but learns to work with the energy at hand. The *dao* itself is noncoercive, and if we want to align ourselves to *dao*, we must be noncoercive as well. This allows one to be truest to the moment. One of the most important concepts in Daoism is *ziran* ("spontaneity" or "naturalness"), and life requires spontaneity. This is not randomness or impetuosity, but artful activity. Laozi writes:

> With the most excellent rulers, their subjects only know
> that they are there. The next best are the rulers they love
> and praise. Next are rulers they hold in awe. And the

worst are the rulers they disparage. Where there is a lack
of credibility, there is a lack of trust. Vigilant, they are
careful in what they say. With all things accomplished
and the work complete, the common people say, "We
are spontaneously like this."[7]

One sees here that excellent rulers are active agents. They are "vigilant," that is, they are attentive, mindful, and prudent. They are not lax, but their activity is *wu-wei*. Thus, their creative, moral presence is not even noticed. They are so aligned with the energy around them that the people's flourishing seems utterly natural to them.

Wu-wei is the most important *wu-form*, but there are others that one must necessarily cultivate. *Wu-zhi* (no knowing) refers to letting go of the kinds of artificial constructs that would hinder one from seeing the uniqueness of each new moment. *Wu-yu* (no desire) recognizes that reality is constantly morphing, constantly in flux. To "desire" in a way that is clutching dissipates *qi*, our vital force, and keeps us from being present to the changing moment. *Wu-ming* (no name) tells us not to assign an absolute fixed reference to anyone or anything, but rather to allow their mystery and complexity to reveal themselves. Even naming can have a quality of control. *Wu-qing* (no heart-and-mind) refers to unmediated feeling. Laozi announces, "The Sage has no fixed mind."[8] And finally, *wu-shi* (no business) refers to not interfering with others' business while going about one's own.

Not imposing, not contending, not possessing, not expecting reward, not lingering when work is done, not lording over, not manipulating, not meddling, casting off, knowing when to stop, knowing contentment, being tranquil within—this is the life of the Daoist sage.[9] It is not a guarantee that in being so, one would be free from suffering or difficulties. Rather, one ceases to try to control or manipulate the moment. For the most part, we are authors of our own pain by bringing our narrow minds to the moment. Second to Laozi in the influence of Daoism is Zhuangzi, who lived in the third century BCE. Zhuangzi writes:

Let your mind wander in simplicity, blend your spirit in the vastness, follow along with things the way they are, and make no room for personal views—then the world will be governed. I take inaction [*wu-wei*] to be true happiness, but ordinary people think it is a bitter thing. . . . The inaction of Heaven is its purity, the inaction of earth is its peace. So the two inactions combine and all things are transformed and brought to birth. . . . I say, Heaven and earth do nothing [*wu-wei*] and there is nothing that is not done. Among men, who can get hold of this inaction?[10]

What Can We Learn?

Western religious talk can be very dogmatic. You must believe X, you may not believe Y. There is right and there is wrong. When push comes to shove, however, we see that things are far more complicated. In the past several decades, there has been a growing awareness that what we see and how we see it are intrinsically dependent on the lens we use to interpret reality. This is the postmodern perspective. Many dogmas in Christianity, for instance, take for granted a Platonic metaphysics and rely on its first principles. Likewise, morality is often framed in terms of absolutes. There are natural and divine laws that cannot be violated for any reason. The Catholic Church, for example, has declared slavery to be intrinsically evil. This seems sound enough, but the Church supported the legitimacy of slavery up until the nineteenth century. Why wasn't this eternal divine law obvious before that? The same can be said of torture. What has changed is not better intellects weighing in, but a different perspective on human dignity. The same concerns can apply to areas of sexuality and reproduction. What appear to be absolute and universal proscriptions are often based on culturally specific ways of seeing things and the assumption that morality is static.

Daoism, in contrast, seems more aligned to a postmodern perspective, one where cultural assumptions are shown to create the lenses we use to interpret reality. Our insights are not as *objective* as we think. Daoist thinking is not relativistic by any means, and committed Daoists strive to be highly moral. The difference is that Daoism challenges us to consider the world as fluid, a world where what is moral or immoral is relationally complex. What is true or good involves what is emerging in this moment. Of course, there will be extraordinary continuity in what is considered moral behavior, as culture relies on that. Yet it is also a continuity that is sensitive and open to novelty. Morality is learning the art and practicing the habit of appropriately responding to every unique situation. This both frees us and commits us to far greater sensitivity to the ever-changing energies and interrelationships present. In this sense, Daoist moral action is very challenging. Daoists might see a "law-and-order" morality as lazy and insensitive, one where injustice is bound to occur.

I would like to share two stories, one I observed and one in which I took center stage. The first story describes a time when I was a seminarian helping at a church. I went to the hospital to be with a grieving family who had lost a loved one. I did not know the family and mostly kept out of the way. Two chaplains of the hospital spent time with the family that night. Both surely wanted to be a presence of healing for the distraught family. One seemed nervous. He spoke a lot, even though he got little response from the family, who answered his questions in monosyllables. He tried to help them reflect on life and death, and on faith and hope for the deceased's eternal life. He really seemed to get nowhere, and eventually he left for other calls. The other chaplain came a bit later. She said almost nothing. She just sat with the family. I noticed that twice she held the widow's hand quite naturally. She stayed about a half an hour until she also had to leave. The widow got up with her and hugged her. The difference between those two chaplains I imagine was not their interest in the family. Rather, the first was *pushing*. Ministers do things, and so he did them. Ministers share the good news, so he did. But this is not where the grievers were at. He misread the group and what they needed at the time; in this case, just a silent, loving presence and little more. The second chaplain came in softly, sensed the energy in the room, and attempted no agenda other than being present with them as a compassionate witness to the tragedy. Essentially, she did not do anything, and nothing was left undone.

My second story is about a time when I was a priest assisting a parish that had many weddings. I averaged a wedding a week. The pastor had asked one of our parishioners who was an acting coach to monitor my public presence and give me feedback. We had coffee a couple of times, and I learned a great deal, particularly about how I presided over weddings. She turned out to be quite a critic of me. One of the most difficult things about a wedding is that often those attending, even those of the same church, become incredibly passive. Given that this is a communal liturgy, one premised on active participation, I wanted them to sing, to pray, and to respond to the rite as they knew how to. These are good values, for sure. And I was frustrated that they were so passive. Thus I tried as much as I could to ramp up the often-flagging energy level and to model real engagement.

This was her criticism: "In trying to infuse energy into them, what you're really doing is fighting their energy. Even the enthusiasm you have when you pray works like a critique of their praying. You can't do their work for them. Instead, pay attention to the community. Work with what they're bringing and not with what you think they ought to be bringing." I took her advice. I still encouraged active prayer, but I was no longer fighting with what they brought. My energy was attentive to their energy. I noticed two things. First, I was less exhausted after the marriage rite than I had been. And second, comments after the wedding were different. They went from "Hey, I really like your enthusiasm, Father," to "That was a really prayerful wedding."

Daoism challenges us to be sensitive to the people, the energy, and the context we are in. This is, especially initially, very challenging. We like to take shortcuts. It is easier to put people into boxes than to allow the space for their best selves to emerge. Daoism challenges us to be ever responsive and never reactive. It requires a spacious heart and mind and demands we cultivate such a posture. The more we cultivate that kind of openness, the easier it gets for that to be our natural being-in-the-world. And we end up less frustrated that things did not go the way they *ought* to and more appreciative of the miracles and mystery around us. We have fewer walls and more open windows where fresh air is allowed to circulate. We find we have more energy, we are calmer, and we can reverence others far more easily. In a word, Daoism tells us: Life is really an art form. Engage yourself and your world this way and you will live creatively and robustly. You will be more human and more humane.

Buddhist Wisdom: The Way of the Bodhisattva

In chapter 2 we looked at Buddhism's understanding of *no self* and Buddha's expression of Nirvana. We have no essential self, Buddha taught, because we are made up of five "aggregates" of things, from materiality to consciousness, and all of them are impersonal. We exist as actual sentient beings, of course, but what makes us up has no underlying *selfhood*. Not realizing this, we cling, we create karma, and we end up with a new existence after death, only to go through the same pointless ordeal again and again. There is a technical term in Theravada Buddhism, "dependent origination," which describes our existence. It goes like this:

> *Ignorance conditions volitional [desire] formations,*
> *Which conditions consciousness,*
> *Which conditions mental-materiality,*
> *Which conditions the six-fold base [of physicality],*
> *Which conditions contact with the world,*
> *Which conditions feeling,*
> *Which conditions craving,*

Which conditions clinging,
Which conditions becoming,
Which conditions birth,
Which conditions aging and death,
Which conditions sorrow and grief.[11]

One ought not to consider dependent origination as a step-by-step set of causes. Think instead that all of these mutually interpenetrate and simultaneously contribute to what causes rebirth. Mahayana Buddhism also teaches dependent origination, but in a very different way. Rather than analyzing the specific conditions that bring about the rebirth of a sentient being, this term now typically refers to the arising of all reality together. The universe is an interdependent, wholly interconnected web of life. All beings are, in some sense, part of one another, with no absolutely hard boundaries. By seeing through the delusion that radically distinguishes self and other, one also sees that the sufferings of another are, in some sense, one's own. And the eradication of another's suffering is, in some sense, the eradication of one's own. Surely, one has a center of consciousness that is unique, and some attain Nirvana before others. But we are really never separated.

We also saw in chapter 2 that the Buddha was cagey regarding absolute truth and even the nature of Nirvana. Toward the end of the Buddha's life, one of his disciples, named Vaccha, asked him about what Nirvana would mean for him after death (*parinirvana*). The Buddha responded with a kind of simile. He asked Vaccha if there were a fire before him, would he know it? And if so, what did that fire depend on? Vaccha explains that it depended on grass and sticks. And if extinguished, where did the fire go? Vaccha tells him that this is not a good question. The fire did not go anywhere, rather it simply used up its fuel.

So too, Vaccha, the Buddha has abandoned that material form by which one describing the Buddha might describe him; he has cut it off at the root, made

it like a palm stump, done away with it so that it is no
longer subject to future arising [rebirth]. The Buddha
is liberated from reckoning in terms of material form,
Vaccha, he is profound, immeasurable, unfathomable
like the ocean. The term "reappears" does not apply,
the term "does not reappear" does not apply, the term
"both reappears and does not reappear" does not apply,
the term "neither reappears nor does not reappear" does
not apply. (*Majjhima Nikaya* 72.19–20)

So it seems that Nirvana and Final-Nirvana are both indescribable
and enigmatic. But one thing is certain, once the Buddha died, he
was no longer accessible. He had a long career as a teacher, some
forty-five years, and now he is gone. This is the Theravada telling.

Mahayana Buddhism provides a very different understanding
of the ministry of the Buddha and even of his purported enlightenment experience under the fig tree. According to the famous
Mahayana text, the Lotus Sutra, all this was show, since he had
actually attained Nirvana incalculable lifetimes ago. Here the Buddha is supreme and essentially always has been. He represents
a cosmic figure, now only experienced on the human plane of
existence.

In all the worlds the heavenly and human beings and
asuras [titans] all believe that the present Shakyamuni
Buddha, after leaving the palace of the Shakyas, seated
himself in the place of practice not far from the city of
Gaya and there attained *anuttara-samyak-sambodhi*
[perfect-supreme-enlightenment]. But good men, it has
been immeasurable, boundless hundreds, thousands, ten
thousands, millions of *nayutas* of *kalpas* [world cycles]
since I in fact attained Buddhahood. . . . Suppose all these
worlds, whether they received a particle of dust or not,
are once more reduced to dust. Let one particle represent
one *kalpa*. The time that has passed since I attained

Buddhahood surpasses this by a hundred, a thousand,
ten thousand, a million *nayuta asambkhya kalpas*. . . .
Constantly I have preached the law, teaching, converting
countless millions of living beings, causing them to enter
the Buddha way, all this for immeasurable *kalpas*.[12]

In Mahayana, this world is the historical Buddha's sphere of ministry, his Buddha-field (*Buddha-kshetra*). There are innumerable
worlds or universes, and each is its own Buddha-field. Buddhas
are embodiments of Buddha-nature (*tathagatagarbha*). According to Mahayana, all beings have within them an enlightenment-
awareness. The point of attaining enlightenment is to remove the
defilements of our minds and see the eternally and inherently pure
Buddha-nature shine forth.

There is one more contrast I would like to make between
Theravada and Mahayana Buddhism, and that is the role of the
bodhisattva. In Theravada, a spiritually developed being could
take a bodhisattva vow in which he commits himself to practicing
the ten perfections of Buddhism (generosity, morality, renunciation, wisdom, exertion, patience, determination, truthfulness, loving-kindness, and equanimity) to the superlative degree in order
to become a Buddha. This commitment far exceeds what is necessary to become enlightened and attain Nirvana. In the Theravada
canon, we find little interest in the bodhisattva vow. An *arhat*
refers to someone who is enlightened, and the Buddha seemed
to be singularly invested in helping persons become arhats. What
then is the motive for holding off Nirvana until one becomes a
Buddha? Texts speculate that it might be a better or higher Nirvana, or simply a greater hero's journey.

According to Theravada tradition, this vow was to be made
in front of a Buddha, and the being who became Siddhartha Gautama actually made this vow to a number of past Buddhas over
thousands of past eons. In the Mahayana tradition, the bodhisattva vow is likewise linked to the desire to become a Buddha, but
the reason for this is solely to serve all sentient beings. Through-

out Mahayana literature we find claims ranging from the belief that the arhat's Nirvana is limited, to the belief that the motive of the arhat is self-concerned and thus tainted, to the belief that an arhat's enlightenment is not real enlightenment at all. Regardless, full Buddhahood represents inexhaustible wisdom and inexhaustible compassion, and for this the aspirant must develop *bodhicitta* (awakened mind), which is focused on compassionate service.

Kamalashila, the great eighth-century Indian Buddhist, describes how *bodhicitta* can emerge on this arduous path. It is called the *Six Causes and One Effect*. A person begins by considering a friend, a neutral person, and an enemy. Since we have all lived an infinite number of lifetimes, we realize that at one time any of our friends were enemies and any of our current enemies (or difficult persons) were at one time our friends. Thus, no one is intrinsically friend or enemy. This is the start. The six causes are then: (1) realizing every sentient being was once my mother; (2) realizing that, as mothers, they suffered for my sake and were immensely kind to me; (3) realizing that right here and now, my past mothers are suffering and I have an obligation to them; (4) realizing that if I fail to attend to them, I am guilty of an immoral life; (5) generating great love and compassion for my mothers (all sentient beings); and (6) deciding to take upon myself the responsibility for alleviating their suffering, and to do this I must become a Buddha. These are the six causes. The one effect is *bodhicitta*, the overwhelming aspiration to become a Buddha in service to all sentient beings.

The premier text regarding training for one who has undertaken the bodhisattva vow comes from the eighth-century monk Shantideva and his classic *Bodhicaryavatara* (Undertaking the Way to Awakening). It is popularly known in the West as *The Way of the Bodhisattva*.[13] *Bodhicitta* dominates Shantideva's agenda. Shantideva distinguishes between *bodhicitta* in intent and active *bodhicitta*. It is commendable, he assures us, to aspire to enlightenment, and to do so out of compassion for others. Still, this is not yet an active effort. "*Bodhicitta* in intention bears rich fruit for those still wandering in *samsara*. And yet a ceaseless stream of merit does not follow from it; for this will arise alone from active *bodhicitta*" (1.17). The stakes are high. Human life is rare, and Shantideva asks rhetorically, "If the advantage is neglected now, how will this meeting come again?" (1.4). And the task is overwhelming: "Except for perfect *bodhicitta*, there is nothing able to withstand the great and overwhelming strength of evil. . . . Only this will save" (1.6–7).

The great Zen scholar D. T. Suzuki notes that when *bodhicitta* becomes an intense, spontaneous state of mind, one's whole consciousness changes. It "brings about a cataclysm in one's mental organization."[14] It is also karmically powerful. Shantideva writes, "For when, with irreversible intent, the mind embraces *bodhicitta*, willing to set free the endless multitudes of beings, at that instant, from that moment on, a great and unremitting stream, a strength of wholesome merit [karma], even during sleep and inattention, rises equal to the vastness of the sky" (1.18–19). In his third chapter, Shantideva describes how *bodhicitta* in action feels: "With joy I celebrate the virtue that relieves all beings from the sorrows of the states of loss, and places those who languish in the realms of bliss. . . . The intention, ocean of great good, that seeks to place all beings in the state of bliss, and every action for the benefit of all: such is my delight and all my joy" (3.1–4).

The issues I have chosen that distinguish Theravada from Mahayana Buddhism help us understand how a bodhisattva's compassionate service actually works. We see that serving others is intrinsically part of being a Buddha; that's what Buddhas do. They are forever in service. And becoming a Buddha means that one's service would be of the highest order. Likewise, reframing dependent origination—from individual causes of rebirth to a cosmology of interbeing—means that there are no hard disconnects between all sentiency. This is what allows bodhisattvas to share the good karma they have gained with those in need and take on the bad karma of those in states of suffering. Bodhisattvas cannot delete negative karma, but they can take it onto themselves and burn it off through their own store of good karma. Burning it off, however, means that they would take on the fruit of that karma, even personally suffering the temporal hell states others deserve. For Shantideva, the bodhisattva vows to become:

> doctor, nurse, the medicine itself. . . . For all sentient beings, poor and destitute, may I become a treasure ever plentiful. . . . And all my merits gained and to be gained, I give them all away withholding nothing. . . . Nirvana is attained by giving all, Nirvana the objective of my striving. Everything therefore must be abandoned, and it is best to give it to all others. . . . May I be a guard for those who are without protection, a guide for those who journey on the road. For those who wish to go across the water, may I be a boat, a raft, a bridge. May I be an Isle for those who yearn for landfall, and a lamp for those who long for light; for those who need a resting place, a bed; for those who need a servant, may I be their slave. (3.8–12, 18)

A virtual or perhaps literal eternity of living for others, of sharing the wealth of one's good karma and absorbing others' bad karma—and the pain that comes with that—is so daunting that one's head spins. And yet Shantideva assures us that this is exactly what Nirvana is about.

Paradoxically, when we live for others we ourselves are filled with joy. That too is what Nirvana is about. Toward the end of the *Way of the Bodhisattva* Shantideva assures us:

> All the joy the world contains has come through wishing happiness for others. All the misery the world contains has come through wanting pleasure for oneself. Is there need for lengthy explanation? Childish beings look out for themselves, while Buddhas labor for the good of others. See the difference that divides them? If I do not

give away my happiness for others' pain, Enlightenment
will never be attained, and even in *samsara*, joy will
fly from me. . . . If this "I" is not relinquished wholly,
sorrow likewise cannot be avoided. . . . To free myself
from harm and others from their sufferings, let me
give myself away, and cherish others as I love myself.
(8.129–36)

What Can We Learn?

All of this is a lot to take in. Like Daoism, we are invited to imagine a universe that is extraordinarily interconnected. In Mahayana, this is taken to the utmost level. We tend to think of ourselves
as rather separate individuals, but are we? Think about being at a
dinner party where the person you are sitting next to is seething
with rage. It may be held just under the surface, but one cannot
help but experience it. Our emotional life is affected. Our glands
start secreting stress hormones like cortisol and adrenaline. We
may end up leaving the party exhausted and with a headache just
by being next to this person. I may think that my thoughts are
independently happening inside my brain. And although this is
partially true, it is also the case that what I think and what I feel
are conditioned by this person. We could make a contrast. Say the
person beside me is holy and radiating love. Here too, I would
have decidedly different physical and emotional activity than I
would have otherwise. What I am, what I think, how I feel, and
what I do is conditioned by what is around me. I am not separate
from my environment; it interpenetrates. Now consider this on a
universal level. I may not be conscious of what is happening outside of my immediate vicinity, but this does not mean I am unaf-
fected. What if who and what we are has universal, albeit subtle,
effects on everything else? This leads me to consider a whole new
level of moral and spiritual responsibility.

Buddhist wisdom asks us to think about all persons as though
they were our mother. You may not be persuaded that we have lived

countless eons of lifetimes so that this is literally true. Still, what if we thought of them that way? Or how would we act if we considered every child of the world to be our own child? Most everyone would be horrified to know that one's own child is suffering disease, malnutrition, a polluted environment. Buddhism invites us to think that way and to live our lives such that we are motivated to do something extraordinary. Most Christians would say that all persons are children of God, made in God's image and likeness. And they would claim that Jesus is both our Lord and brother. Spiritually speaking, this does indeed make every person a member of our family.

The way of the bodhisattva is heroic. Imagine devoting an eternal existence to living for all others as their servant. Who would really want to do this? I was once on a Buddhist retreat and feeling very down because a friend of mine was addicted to drugs and couldn't seem to break free. He had just had another relapse, and the addiction was ruining him. I said to my Buddhist teacher that I would give my left arm for him to be truly free from his addiction. She looked at me suspiciously and said, "Really?" I assured her, "An arm compared to a life of someone I loved? Surely!" She replied, "I don't think you really would if it came to that." I've thought about this for years. She was right, I wouldn't.

The bodhisattva path takes some real courage, particularly as one starts. And it takes a great deal of maturity of spirit. I recall being present for a ritual by Tibetan monks who opened themselves to receive the bad karma in the world so that they could free others whose next rebirth could be hellish. They took that karma to themselves, now responsible for burning off the same bad karma through their lives of service and love. I asked another observer, a renowned teacher in Theravada meditation, whether he thought one really could take on another's karma. He replied, "I'm not sure. But I do know that you shouldn't attempt it without being deep in the path."

Just days before this writing, I attended a Zen center where a friend of mine was offering the *dharma-talk*. They ended the session as they always do, with a form of Bodhisattva vow:

Sentient beings cannot be counted, I vow to save them all.
Suffering is inexhaustible, I vow to end it.
Teachings are limitless, I vow to learn them all.
The Way of the Buddha is unsurpassable, I vow to
follow it.

One of the most important things to realize in Mahayana spirituality is that my deepest self is Buddha-nature, and Buddha-nature is compassion. Shantideva clearly recognizes how daunting his task is, and he repeatedly reminds the reader how easy it could be to lose one's nerve or aspiration. He also reminds us that this is actually a life of joy. If my deepest nature is compassion, then being devoted to the world compassionately is exactly my own flourishing. One cannot miss the dominant theme of joy in *The Way of the Bodhisattva*. And who does not want to be happy?

Notes

1. Timothy Brook, "Rethinking Syncretism: The Unity of the Three Teachings and Their Joint Worship in Late-Imperial China," *Journal of Chinese Religions* 21 (Fall 1993): 17.

2. Roger T. Ames and David L. Hall, *Daodejing: Making This Life Significant—A Philosophical Translation* (New York: Ballantine, 2003), 14.

3. Yin-Yang (in the public domain), https://publicdomainvectors.org/en/free-clipart/Yin-Yang/47093.html.

4. Lao Tsu [Laozi], *Tao Te Ching* [Daodejing], trans. Gia-Fu Feng and Jane English (New York: Vintage: 1972).

5. Ames and Hall, *Daodejing*, 77. I address much of this in the same way in *Encounters in Faith: Christianity in Interreligious Dialogue* (Winona, MN: Anselm Academic, 2011), 196–218.

6. Livia Kohn, *Readings in Daoist Mysticism* (Magdalena, NM: Three Pines Press, 2009), 9.

7. Ames and Hall, *Daodejing*, 102.

8. Feng and English, *Tao Te Ching*, no. 49.

9. Puqun Li, *A Guide to Asian Philosophy Classics* (Peterborough, ON: Broadview Press, 2012), 189.

10. Chuang Tzu [Zhuangzi], *Chuang Tzu: Basic Writings*, trans. Burton Watson (New York: Columbia University Press, 1964), 91, 112–13.

11. Bhadantacariya Buddhaghosa, *The Path of Purification* [*Visuddhimagga*], 5th ed., trans. Bhikkhu Nanamoli (Kandy, Sri Lanka: Buddhist Publication Society, 1991), XVII.2.

12. Burton Watson, trans., *The Lotus Sutra* (New York: Columbia University Press, 1993), 225.

13. I am normally using *The Bodhicaryavatara*, trans. Kate Crosby and Andrew Skilton (Oxford: Oxford University Press, 1995), but augment this translation with Shantideva, *The Way of the Bodhisattva*, trans. Padmakara Translation Group (Boston: Shambhala, 2003).

14. D. T. Suzuki, *Essays in Zen Buddhism* (London: Rider, 1950), 173.

6

How Might I Find Balance?

In the last chapter, we looked at the bodhisattva vow. Imagine a life or even billions of lifetimes devoted to nothing other than serving suffering humanity. Imagine a life committed to taking on the consequences of others' bad karma and burning through it by one's own merits, or perhaps suffering a lifetime of a hell state to save another who would otherwise end up there, and who actually deserves it. When I compare this to a Christian understanding of Jesus taking on the sins of the world by his sacrificial atonement on the cross, I not only see real, direct parallels, I also see something that looks even more heroic in the bodhisattva vow. It is an extraordinary hero's journey.

I also see serious potential problems with any given hero's journey. The first problem is that although extraordinary, intense spiritual practice can make one very holy, it tends to do so myopically. In a previous book, I addressed the nature of Zen enlightenment in Japan during the time of Japanese imperial expansion in the 1930s and '40s.[1] Zen masters, whose enlightenment experiences were tested and affirmed by other masters in venerable lineages, were recruited to train officers for the war effort. It is not the case that they were unaware of or merely tolerated the government's aggression; they actively participated in it by training men to serve. Philosopher and Buddhist teacher Brian Victoria has asked how it could be conceivable that highly regarded Zen masters could witness, without challenge, "what were clearly war atrocities committed against Chinese civilians, young and old, without having confronted the moral implications of . . . this mindless brutality."[2] Some Buddhists responded that these were clearly not authentically enlightened masters. To this, Victoria responds that such an excuse ignores the "sheer numbers of authenticated Zen Masters whose actions in the war fit this pattern."[3]

I noted, "Zen spirituality, like all spiritualities, exists in a culture, a paradigm . . . . In the monastic context, Zen enlightenment would depend on prior education, certain forms of socialization, customs, and specific training valued by that monastic community." I further noted, "[T]he mind is very complex. I have known many religious persons who have excelled in impressive ways along their respective spiritual paths, but who have significant blind spots as well as significantly underdeveloped parts of their psyche."[4]

What is omitted in many stories about spiritual virtuosos is a lack of balance or integration. Of course, this may not be true of all of them, but it is certainly true of many of them. Some Christian saints practiced asceticism so severe, it led to their early deaths. Others, in their spiritual confidence, promoted the Crusades, certain that battle against Islam was God's will. As one of my graduate students reported after having read St. Ignatius of Loyola's autobiography, "I learned that you can be a saint and crazy at the same time." And this is Ignatius, one of the Christian giants who was known as rather balanced (comparatively). God forbid they discover a biography of St. Catherine of Siena!

A second problem in looking to these heroes and spiritual virtuosos as exemplars is that their language and witness simply do not correlate with life as most people live it, even when we are at our most sincere and devout. Jesus tells his disciples, "If any want to become my followers, let them deny themselves and take up their cross daily and follow me. For those who want to save their life will lose it, and those who lose their life for my sake will save it" (Lk 9:23–24). The self-denial of Jesus and the way of his cross becomes the model then for all Christians. And yet, who lives this way?

I currently hold an endowed chair at the University of Toledo. This is how it happened. I was a full professor at the University of St. Thomas, a school I respected in a department of fine peers. I had published a couple of books, had another two coming out, and was finishing a manuscript for the fifth. I decided to give my CV (academic resume) a spin. I was offered this job that increased my salary by a full third and my research funds fivefold. I was also offered the support of a graduate research assistant. Great deal! So I took it, and was congratulated by all. I did think about the missions of the two departments and compared what I imagined my contributions in Toledo could be compared to what they were at St. Thomas, including how I might inspire students religiously. It all seemed pretty solid. I *did not* dwell on which appointment better fostered my self-denial, my dying to myself. On the contrary, I took it because it was a better job, a better deal. Who wouldn't? This is what life really looks like.

In this chapter, we look at two ways to consider living a balanced life. These ought not to be considered "selling out" or "the way of mediocrity," but being spiritual in a messy, complex world. The first is the kind of balance one finds in Jewish spirituality. As we saw earlier in chapter 4, even the holiest sing, dance, and drink wine. Judaism is not a highly ascetical religion, and it is proud that it is not. It imagines the world and human destiny in that world with another kind of agenda. The second comes from the Buddhist tradition. How ought one train oneself to engage the world most beautifully? How can one find balance? For Buddhism, it comes in holding together in a creative tension the four *divine abidings*.

Jewish Wisdom: Balance and the Two Impulses

The Greek philosopher Aristotle is known for many things, including his understanding of what constitutes ethical behavior, and how one can cultivate it. Among many of his principles and teachings is his understanding of the *golden mean*. Here virtues represent a balance between excesses. This is not a balance between virtue and vice, but rather finding a way to act with prudence, a way without deficiency and without excess. Thus, courage is found somewhere between cowardice and recklessness. Aristotle was not a moral relativist, but he understood that it is all too easy to get lost in an abstract ideal. Judaism is well known for its own version of the golden mean.

The rabbis of the Talmud did not idealize the ascetic who shuns the world and its pleasures. On the contrary, the wise person is the one who knows how to take pleasure in the richness of creation. Rabbi Hezekiah Kohen said, "A person is destined to give an accounting [before the heavenly tribunal] for everything he saw but did not enjoy."[5] These rabbis, obsessed with loving God with all their heart, mind, and strength (Deut 6:5), also commended the person who had "a beautiful home, a beautiful wife, fine furnishings," leading to "a happy frame of mind."[6] They objected to their ascetical peers taking on voluntary fasts. Rabbi Samuel even declared that someone who *indulges* in fasting "is called a sinner." And another unnamed rabbi of the Talmud declared, "If a person who withholds himself from wine is called a sinner, how much more is one a sinner who withdraws from all of life's enjoyments."[7]

This robust vision of engaging the world and purposefully enjoying it seems quite reasonable to most of us, but it is something of an outlier in typical religious framings. One of the great inspirations for Christian monasticism is Antony of Egypt, who fasted for twenty years in an enclosure. It is not as though he ate nothing, but his asceticism was severe. When he emerged from his enclosure, his biographer St. Athanasius declared, "Antony came forth as though from some shrine, having been led into divine mysteries and inspired by God."[8] Or consider St. Basil the Great, the principal guide for Orthodox monasticism. He described the perfect renunciant as "not having affection for this life."[9] The good monk, he declared, "repudiates all worldly affections."[10]

Both Buddhist and Hindu traditions also recommend meditating on the body in various ways to understand its "foulness."[11] In the classic *Maitri Upanishad* we find the following: "O Revered One, in this foul-smelling, unsubstantial body, a conglomerate of bone, skin, muscle, marrow, flesh, semen, blood, mucus, tears, rheum, feces, urine, wind, bile, and phlegm, what is the good of the enjoyment of desires?" (I.2).

Contrast these attitudes with a Jewish insistence on the blessings of having a body. Indeed, honoring the body is considered a religious obligation. There is a story in the Talmud about the famous Rabbi Hillel who had finished a teaching session with his pupils and was leaving the yeshiva with them:

> He accompanied them part of the way. They said to him, "Master, where are you going?" "To perform a religious duty," he replied. "Which religious duty?" they asked. "To bathe in the bath-house." "Is that a religious duty?" they wondered. He answered them: "One who is designated to scrape clean the statues of the king which are set up in theaters and circuses is paid for the work and he associates it with nobility. Surely must I, who am created in the divine image and likeness, take care of my body!"[12]

As we have seen earlier, Jewish spirituality is deeply grounded in engaging the world, not in escaping it to some ethereal sphere where the soul meets the Divine. Here is one more story, this in the context of the Roman persecution of Jews after the *Bar Kokhba* revolt:

> Simeon and his son hid themselves in the House of Study. His wife daily brought them a loaf of bread and jug of water. But when the persecution increased, they became afraid, and they hid themselves in a cave. There a miracle happened to them. A carob tree grew for

them, and a spring of water welled up for them. Daily they studied the Torah the whole day long. Only for the times of prayer did they get dressed, and after having prayed, they removed their clothes again, in order to not wear them out. In this manner, they remained in the cave for twelve years. Then the Prophet Elijah came, stood at the entrance of the cave and called out: "Who will make known to the son of Yohai that the Emperor has died, and that his decree is nullified?" Hearing this, they left the cave. When, passing an open field, they saw farmers ploughing and sowing, they became angry and said: "Those people are neglecting eternal life [i.e., the study of Torah] and are busying themselves with mundane matters!" And everything upon which they gazed was immediately consumed by fire. Then a Heavenly Voice was heard, saying: "Have you emerged from your cave in order to destroy My world? Go back to your cave!"[13]

There is a great deal here to unpack. In some sense Simeon and his son are heroes. They endure much hardship and God protects and supports them miraculously in their hiding from their persecutors. They are utterly pious, studying all day, every day, the Torah. They are so respectful that they save their clothes from rotting, only wearing them for prayer. Elijah himself announces their liberation. Now comes the oddest part. They curse the farmers and their land, that is, fellow Jews living productively, and the curse works! All before them gets consumed by fire. Thus, they really have developed some kind of supranormal powers due to their deep, obsessive spiritual focus. But they misuse these powers, and God rebukes them; his world is holy, clearly a holiness they did not appreciate.

How does the Jewish tradition understand that it is more than acceptable to be interested not only in being deeply grounded in a spiritual life of this concrete world, but also a spiritual life that has a decided interest in celebrating physical pleasures? Their answer is that we are created with two impulses, a good impulse (*yezer tov*) and an evil impulse (*yezer ra'*). Consider these as a selfless impulse and a self-interested impulse. We find in the Talmud, "Thus it is written: 'And you shall love the Lord your God with all your heart, and all your soul, and all your might.' With all your heart refers to both impulses, the good and the evil ones."[14]

The rabbis argued that, when taken beyond its limits, the evil impulse, one's self-interest, is destructive. And yet in its essential character it is not different from anything else God created. The Talmudists pronounced their judgment on the two impulses in commenting on creation:

> And God saw everything which He had made and behold it was very good. "Very good," say the rabbis, applies to those two impulses. "But," it is asked, "is the evil impulse very good?" The answer is that it is: Were it not for that impulse, a man would not build a house, marry a wife, beget children, or conduct business affairs.[15]

There is obviously a certain respect and honor given to the obvious, that we have and ought to have legitimate self-interest. To use religious language, e.g., *dying to oneself*, as though this were not the case is not only deluded but potentially interiorly disordered. The rabbis recognized that the so-called evil impulse generally dominates most lives. Yet as people spiritually mature, the good impulse gains ascendency until one finds an authentic balance.[16] In this balance, the two impulses actually work together.

What Can We Learn?

I want to pose a mythic world of my own making. Imagine living in a medieval town somewhere in central Europe. This town has everything you might imagine it ought to have. It is overseen by a noble prince living in a castle, and there is a splendid cathedral in the center of town. The main street is paved with stone and boasts of merchants' houses as well as many shops and places of business. West of town and beyond the fields is a massive, dense forest. In it dwell predators and prey, healing and poisonous plants, as well as a coterie of goblins, fey (fairies), and even several ogres. Some of these inhabitants are malicious, some peaceable and kind, and some could be one or the other depending on the circumstance. Beyond the deep, dark forest is a mountain, and on the top of that mountain is a cave. Inside the cave are treasure chests, each heavy enough to be filled with extraordinary riches and yet manageable enough to return home with. The greatest danger in seeking this treasure is that it is guarded by a man-eating dragon.

Others have tried to make it to the cave, only to return beaten and sore by the elements and various creatures of the forest. Some have actually made it to the cave, only to have been eaten by the dragon. Others have returned from battling the dragon maimed and with no treasure. But a select few over generations past have made it to the cave, subdued the dragon, and returned with fantastic wealth. Of course, they shared that wealth. The last one to succeed built the impressive cathedral church. The one before had saved the whole populace when both plague and drought threatened them in the same year. These are heroes whose memories remain through the generations.

If you decide to go on this hero's journey, you would have to give up everything. You would certainly fail unless you trained rigorously with a sword fighter and then with an archer. You would have to learn about the flora of the forest, which foods to eat and to avoid, which healing herbs would sustain you in case of injury and which would poison you. You would have to learn the ways of the fantastical creatures, their language, rites, charms, and sorcery. If you do, there is real hope that you would make it to the other side to take on both mountain and dragon. You might be wounded, you might die, or you might succeed to the joy and relief of the whole town.

Or you could live another way. You could take up a trade and work hard, be successful and respected among the townsfolk. You could tithe to your church and support its mission. You could be a loyal citizen to your lord and carry on a fine life. You could marry and raise children, teaching them to be good, moral, respectable citizens. If you lived this kind of life with real intention, you would have learned to be just and kind, faithful and hard-working, joyous and humble. Weathering the trials and delights of everyday life through the decades, you would live out the twilight of your life with great gratitude and no small amount of wisdom.

But there are dangers in this decision. The spouse you chose might turn out to be ill-tempered and constantly combative. Some of your children could be troublemakers well beyond adolescence, something that would weigh on you regularly. Your trade-work might fail by no fault of your own. You could die a pauper and alone. There is another kind of danger. You could have a happy family and a successful trade. You could be used to titles of honor and used to your own feather bed at home. You could become attached to a comfortable life. If a beggar came to your door, you might shoo that person away as lazy and unlike you. You do contribute to the church, but desire recognition for it. Little by little, your earnest dreams to be a truly honorable woman or man fade, and you're likely to spend more time in the tavern drinking mead than doing anything deeply meaningful. You could reach the twilight of your life a little greedy, a little self-pitying, and a little empty.

Since this is a mythic world, and one whose rules I am in total control over, I can assure you that wealth here is spiritual wealth. The hero's journey is to radical holiness. Returning to town after one's arduous adventure makes one wealthy (spiritually profound) and able to enrich others by love, compassion, service, and the like. You would be a saint, a guru. But taking this journey does not guarantee success, and there are many broken or disillusioned souls who tried. The Jewish mystical tradition tells of successes, those who ascended to the highest heaven, and failures, those who died trying or had a stroke due to the intensity of the mystical experience. Even if you succeed, parts of you might be a bit broken, as if maimed by the dragon, but still successful in beating the dragon and returning with the treasure. You may recall Sri Ramakrishna, the heralded modern Hindu saint and mystic from chapter 1. We can admire the overwhelming experiences he had, but his life was also incredibly neurotic, and during much of his life his emotions soared and sank dramatically and often. His mystical life took a heavy mental and emotional toll. Still, still, you could succeed!

The second way, the way of the town, looks like a way that does not seek high holiness, but a comfortable sort of a spiritual life, one where profound conversion of heart and mind need not take place or even be addressed. But it *could* be a holy life. The two impulses (self-interest and selflessness) need not fight each other. Rather, the spiritual quest could be seen as a gentler way of being. It respects the obvious, that I want my own good, but also that life is about faithfulness and sacrifice. Through life, I can learn to deepen a more holistic understanding of my existence and God's providence guiding me. I can learn to be proud of my family without being overly attached to their successes. I can more easily give of myself because day-to-day life has gently (or not so gently) showed me how. As the years go by, perhaps my *yezer ra'*, my self-interested impulse, now seeks not vain gratifications but more subtler gratifications, such as the ones that come from a loving family, a successful mission trip with my faith community, the bonding of neighbors, and the joy of seeing others around me flourish. These are indeed gratifying, but also deeply spiritual.

The spiritual writer, psychologist, and Zen Roshi John Tarrant writes like a Jewish wisdom figure in frequently challenging the notion that holiness is some absolute thing out there that needs to be captured by our idealism. He says this:

Some of the worst tyrannies of our era can be recognized as idealistic perversions of the spirit. . . . This crime is a vice of the spirit because it attempts, terribly, to subdue life to the idea, to make union only with the perfect, the unshaped. . . . Fundamentalism leads to tyranny because it tries to avoid the uncertainties of inner development. . . . Character development, on the other hand, evolves slowly, from within, and brings with it a relief and an experience-seasoned amusement about human flaws; it provides a gate for the spirit's boundlessness to appear in the soul's realm.[17]

Buddhist Wisdom: Divine Abidings

In Buddhism, the path to enlightenment or Nirvana contains three kinds of cultivation: virtue, concentration, and insight. The great fifth-century Buddhist master Buddhaghosa begins his massive *Path of Purification* with the puzzle: *How does one untangle the tangle with which one is entangled?* He answers, "When a wise person, established well in virtue, develops consciousness [concentration] and understanding [insight], then as a monk ardent and sagacious, one succeeds in disentangling the tangle."[18] Buddhaghosa then divides his book into the three kinds of cultivation. Essential to the path to enlightenment is meditation, but the path first depends on training in virtue; this grounds meditation.

In theory all Buddhists commit themselves to the five main precepts of virtue: (1) refraining from killing or physical violence; (2) refraining from what is not offered; (3) refraining from sexual misconduct; (4) refraining from false speech; and (5) refraining from intoxicants. Typically, these precepts are understood quite broadly. So, for example, the second precept is often imagined to be refraining from stealing. But this is too narrow. In refraining from what is not offered, one now has to live without the presumption of taking or using something that is not explicitly given. It provides a mental culture of non-acquisitiveness. Refraining from false speech is not merely about not lying, it also includes refraining from harsh speech, idle speech, and gossip. It has to be timely, beneficial, and without anger. Buddhaghosa also imagines his readership to be monks and nuns who then have hundreds of additional rules of behavior. It seems apparent that the focus of Buddhist morality is to lower the temperature of unskillful mental states and activities. Buddhaghosa writes that they bring "fewness of wishes, contentment, effacement, and [the ability for] withdrawal."[19]

Nearly half of Buddhaghosa's *Path of Purification* is devoted to the third cultivation, that is insight or wisdom. This involves a series of meditative practices that deconstruct the self to discover there is no permanent self underneath it all. What I would like to focus on here is the second cultivation, that is, concentration, often referred to as *samadhi*. Concentration meditations have three ends. First, they suppress and, to a degree, eliminate that which keeps the mind from being self-possessed. Traditionally, the impediments to self-possession are the *five hindrances* of lust, ill will, torpor, agitation, and uncertainty. These hindrances are mental dispositions that interfere with both meditative concentration and insight. Second, these meditations are designed to support strengths in the psyche. For example, someone with a natural disposition toward faithfulness would do well to meditate on the Buddha's qualities. Such a practice would naturally draw on what is already an inherent predilection of this type of personality. Third and conversely, some are designed to reverse unskillful mental states. For example, he recommends that a greedy or sensuous personality type would do well meditating on the *foulness of the body*.[20]

Knowing one's personality predilections is important. Buddhaghosa writes, "When a person cultivates what is unsuitable, their progress is difficult and their direct knowledge is sluggish. When they cultivate what is suitable, their progress is easy and their direct-knowledge swift. This refers to both the severing of impediments and to the object choices in meditation."[21] Buddhaghosa lists six different personality types (sensuous, angry, dull, faithful, intelligent, and speculative). They can also be understood as only three, depending on one's interior development. So, sensuous aligns with faithful, angry with intelligent, and dull with speculative. Buddhaghosa also lists forty different meditations, each useful depending on one's personality.

This is how one would meditate: At a suitable time when one's energy is good and the mind is somewhat quieted, one takes up a meditation object, say, *the generosity of the Buddha*. Once settled, one experiences several mental characteristics: applied and sustained thought, that is, solid focus on the meditation subject; happiness; bliss; and one-pointedness. This is the first level of mental absorption. Fully immersed in the quality of the meditation subject, one lets go of it and focuses on the status of one's mind, thus experiencing happiness, bliss, and one-pointedness. This is the second level of absorption. Realizing that the mental quality of happiness is coarser than bliss and one-pointedness, one directs one's concentration to those latter qualities allowing happiness to subside. This is the third mental absorption. Finally, one realizes that bliss is less sublime than one-pointedness. One stays focused there, as bliss diminishes. Having succeeded in this, one enters into the fourth level of absorption.[22] There one stays for an hour, two hours, or even longer for those with enough mental strength.

Buddhaghosa lists a group of four meditation subjects that in Buddhism are universally understood as appropriate for everyone: the divine abidings. These are *loving-kindness, compassion, sympathetic joy*, and *equanimity*. Taken collectively, and truly integrated into one's psyche, Buddhist wisdom sees them as the kind of attitude or posture toward the world that corresponds to an enlightened person, that is, they are quasi-nirvanic. It is not as though practicing these would bring one to Nirvana; this can only be attained through insight meditations. Rather, it is how persons who have attained Nirvana look at the world of sentient beings.[23]

There are various ways of practicing these meditations, and my following description is but one, yet it is a typical framing. Regarding loving-kindness, one begins a kind of mantra with oneself and progressively extends the meditation universally.

> *May I be happy and safe.*
> *May I be free.*
> *May I be filled with joy.*
> *May my life end with ease.*

Once one experiences a deep level of concentration, one moves to a benefactor, toward whom it is easy to express the same desire. Placing an image of that benefactor in one's mind, one returns to the mantra: May you be happy; May you be free; May you be filled with joy; May your life end with ease. Again, when loving-kindness is strong here, one then moves to a neutral person, say a relative stranger you see periodically. Then one moves to a difficult person, someone toward whom one experiences aversion. One then applies loving-kindness to all sentient beings in each of the four cardinal directions (east, south, west, and north). And then finally, one applies loving-kindness to all beings universally.

The other divine abiding meditations begin with others rather than the self. For the cultivation of compassion, Buddhaghosa recommends beginning with an unhappy person, then an unlucky person, then a dear person, then oneself, and then universally. For sympathetic joy, one begins with a dear person, a neutral one, then universally. And finally, for equanimity one begins with a neutral person, then a dear person, then an aversive person, and then universally. The mantras correspond to those qualities. So, for compassion, one's mantra could be: May you be free of all pain; May you be free of all suffering; May you be free from all tribulation. For sympathetic joy: May your happiness and success never end; May your good grow greater; May you stay happy. For equanimity: Your joys and sorrows depend upon your actions and not my wishes; Your outcomes depend on your choices not my wishes; The eternal law is you reap what you sow.

One would only practice a given divine abiding meditation at one time, and perhaps it would be best to devote an hour or two a day for a week (or month) on a given category before moving to another. Collectively, one's posture to the world is a deep care for others' flourishing and freedom from suffering. The final divine abiding meditation, equanimity, ensures that one would not get lost or enmeshed in the lives of others. One cannot change the fact that others suffer and may or may not have success. The law of karma is a natural and universal law. Equanimity balances the others and allows them context in a complex world.

The effects of the divine abiding meditations are extraordinary. The Buddha once declared that there are eleven benefits from practicing loving-kindness:

> One sleeps well; gets up well; does not have nightmares; becomes affectionate to human beings; becomes affectionate to non-human beings; the deities protect one; neither fire nor poison nor a weapon affect one; one's mind becomes calm immediately; one's complexion brightens; one dies without confusion; beyond that, if one does not comprehend the highest, one goes to the world of the brahmas.[24]

Recently, studies on monks and nuns who have practiced these meditations deeply have shown that their brains are not like other brains.[25] Rather, these brains get rewired—they literally become loving, compassionate minds.

With the exception of equanimity, which can be taken to the fourth level of mental absorption, the other three can be taken to the third level (bliss and one-pointedness). What we have then is a mind utterly infused with universal love, universal compassion, and universal joy for others that is both other-centered and feels completely blissful to the mind.

The Buddhist tradition also describes *near and far enemies* of the divine abidings.[26] The far enemies might be obvious. Hatred or anger is the far enemy of loving-kindness. Cruelty is the far enemy of compassion. Jealousy is the far enemy of sympathetic joy. And attachment or reactivity is the far enemy of equanimity. The near enemies are more difficult to recognize because they resemble the kind of mental state one seeks, even as they undermine the true qualities being sought. Love in most human experience is highly preferential; it is self-interested; this is the first near enemy. True loving-kindness seeks flourishing without exception or expectation as to how this affects me. Pity seems like compassion, but it is not. Pity condescends. It is as though I am looking down on that "poor person" whose suffering unnerves me. Pity does not enter into another's suffering, but reacts against it. Sympathetic joy can be confused with unfounded merriment or frivolous excitement. It can also be tainted with some subtle thoughts about when "my turn" might come. Finally, equanimity can degrade into lack of concern. This is to say that having equanimity could simply mean that I've chosen not to know about or be invested in the lives of others. This is hardly a virtue.

What Can We Learn?

The divine abiding meditations work together. One hopes for, and thus seeks, the universal flourishing of all sentient beings. Those who follow this path cultivate a sense of balance. One cares about the joy and fulfillment of all. Compassion is concerned about the universal suffering that simply goes with existence. The Sanskrit term for compassion is *karuna*, which literally means the "fluttering of the heart." We become people who are moved from the center at the mass of suffering in this world. But this too is balanced by sympathetic joy, by rejoicing in the successes and happiness of others. So our hearts incline toward this reality too. And, as noted above, equanimity keeps us grounded so that we do not lose ourselves and become attached. We need equanimity if we are going to respond well to others and not out of a reactive state.

Allow me to reflect on each of these divine abidings. Many years ago, I was a faculty member at a seminary. Most of the priests, including me, lived together in community on site. It was a fine group of bright, thoughtful men, but there was an exception. Fr. Jerry was a rather toxic presence, and he was quite taxing on the rest of us. In fact, over the years, several faculty members moved out because of Jerry. I realized that I held a lot of negative judgment of Jerry as well as a good deal of resentment. Thus, I decided to change my morning meditational strategy and do loving-kindness meditation, with Jerry being my "difficult" candidate. There were times when after picturing myself, a benefactor, and a neutral person that I got to Jerry and lost concentrative momentum. I had to go back to my benefactor to reinvigorate loving-kindness. And yet, over the next two months of an hour a day of loving-kindness meditation I came to see Jerry differently. When I greeted him, I felt a warmth for him I had never previously had. And when seeing him in the evening and asking about his day, I found that I really cared. I found myself rooting for him without even trying. I never stopped feeling some aversion for his personality, even though this had been significantly reduced. But he wasn't an *enemy* anymore. He became to me more of a challenging brother whom I cared about.

If we only knew how much people suffered, we would be different. The divine abiding of compassion helps us to lean into that truth. One of the most important qualities of care is paying attention. Compassion pays particular attention, and in doing so sensitizes us to the ongoing struggle that life often brings. It also brings us greater sensitivity to our own suffering. Compassion makes the heart more malleable, gentler, softer. People are afraid of pain, and when we see it in others we tend to react. What others need from us is not pity or horror, but someone who is willing to walk with them and be attentive to them in their sorrow.

With regard to sympathetic joy, this kind of meditation is filled with light, and is often regarded as the easiest and most delightful of the four. The challenge is to integrate sympathetic joy into our daily lives. I ask my students to consider the following: Say you had a very hard math exam and you ended up getting a B as your grade. Say also that you discovered it was the highest grade in the class. Half the class failed, and the rest got Ds and Cs. Wouldn't you actually feel good? Now say that you got a B, but this was the lowest score in the class. Virtually the whole class was in the A range. Wouldn't you feel deflated? My students nod both times. So, our relationship to our experience has little to do with the experience itself. Rather, it has to do with how we are doing *compared* to everyone else. Sympathetic joy moves us to simply celebrate others' happiness with no need to be interested in our own. Ironically, if we can successfully integrate this divine abiding meditation, we find that we are really quite happy much of the time.

Equanimity is perhaps the most interesting of the four. In an interview with Bill Moyers, the great scholar of world mythology Joseph Campbell told a story of meeting a Hindu guru in India. Campbell asked the guru what he considered the most essential teaching. He responded, "Say *yes* to everything." Campbell's response was, "Yes to war? To poverty? To injustice?" The guru laughed and said, "When I was your age, I asked my master the same question. He gave me the answer I gave you and my response was exactly yours." And he laughed again. When I heard that story by Campbell, I shook my head. "So superficial," I thought. Years later, I realized what was going on. It is not as though war, poverty, injustice, or any other evil is somehow good or somehow not devastating to the lives of many. Rather, the difference is whether one is going to live reactively or responsively to what is before one. To say, "No! I do not accept this," now seems idiotic to me. It *is* the fact before me. *Yes* to life is yes to life *as it is*, not yes to some eternal Platonic form. This is what the reality of the moment is. Only by accepting that this is the real present, am I able to engage well. Now, what shall I do about it? Saying *yes* is not acquiescing to evil, but keeping one's mind and heart spacious and free enough to see how one ought to most skillfully respond. I might have to respond vigorously to work against an injustice. Equanimity tells me that there is suffering in the world. I cannot change the fact that the world is what it is. Equanimity does not inhibit or counteract the other divine abidings. Rather, it frees us to engage the world as it is.

Equanimity also frees one from getting caught and lost in the story lines of others. I once spent a summer as a chaplain intern in a substance abuse hospital. I learned that the co-dependent person is, in some ways, almost as sick as the substance abuser. He or she is on a roller coaster of loss, fear, cautious hope, possible relief, and then more loss, and then more fear. One of the first rules is, if an addict wants to use, the addict will use. You cannot change this. You cannot control an addict's use or recovery. You can, of course, support that recovery, but only with a mind balanced in equanimity. Not only is this crucial for one to keep one's own sanity, it actually best supports the abuser's recovery.

The divine abidings represent a truly balanced perspective in the world. Collectively, they create a mind and heart that is deeply loving and caring; profoundly sensitive to hearing the small and large cries in the hearts of those we encounter; happy and filled with wonder at the good fortunes of others; free and spacious enough not to get lost in it all. These meditations do not speak to everything about our lives. They intend to create a universal perspective, but humans are local; we are social animals. Our brains are wired to prefer our closest loves, and this is as it should be. If my wife asks me if I love her, I will not respond, "Of course I love you, just as I love all people, just as I love the neighbor's dog and the student who rarely shows up to class." I love her more because I'm bonded to her more, because we are together creating an intimate life and future. I love her more because I prefer her company to any other. I also know that I will love her best if I also love all beings in the universe. Then love is what my mind is infused with.

Notes

1. See Peter Feldmeier, *Experiments in Buddhist-Christian Encounter: From Buddha-Nature to the Divine Nature* (Maryknoll, NY: Orbis Books, 2019), 150–51.

2. Cited in Dale Wright, *What Is Buddhist Enlightenment?* (Oxford: Oxford University Press, 2016), 92–93. See Brian Victoria, *Zen War Stories* (London: Routledge/Curzon, 2003); and *Zen at War* (New York: Rowman & Littlefield, 2005).

3. Wright, *What Is Buddhist Enlightenment?*, 93.

4. Feldmeier, *Experiments in Buddhist-Christian Encounter*, 153–54.

5. *Talmud, Yesushalmi* 4:12 (66d). *The Talmud*, trans. and ed. Ben Zion Bokser and Baruch M. Bokser (New York: Paulist Press, 1989). All citations of the Talmud are taken from this text unless otherwise noted.

6. *Talmud, Barakot* 57b.

7. *Talmud, Taanit* 11a.

8. Athanasius of Alexandria, *The Life of Antony and the Letter to Marcellinus*, trans. Robert C. Gregg (New York: Paulist Press, 1980), 42.

9. Basil the Great, *St. Basil: Ascetical Works*, trans. Monica Wagner (New York: Fathers of the Church, 1950), 254.

10. Ibid., 253.

11. For example, the great synthesizer of Theravada Buddhism, Buddhaghosa, devotes an entire chapter on various ways to meditate on the foulness of the body. See Bhadantacariya Buddhaghosa, *The Path of Purification* [*Visuddhimagga*], 5th ed., trans. Bhikkhu Nanamoli (Kandy, Sri Lanka: Buddhist Publication Society, 1991), 173–90. And see the *Maitri Upanishad* I.2–4.

12. *Talmud, Leviticus Rabbah* 34:3.

13. *Talmud, Shabbath* 33b, as cited in Jakob J. Petuchowski, *Our Masters Taught: Rabbinic Stories and Sayings* (New York: Crossroad, 1982), 13.

14. *Talmud, Mishnah* 9:5.

15. *Talmud, Genesis Rabbah* 9:7.

16. Cited in Bokser and Bokser, *The Talmud*, 18.

17. John Tarrant, *The Light Inside the Dark: Zen, Soul, and the Spiritual Life* (New York: Harper Perennial, 1998), 149, 175–76.

18. Buddhaghosa, *The Path of Purification* [*Visuddhimagga*], 1.1.

19. Ibid., 2.78.

20. "In this body there are head hairs, body hairs, nails, teeth, skin, flesh, sinews, bones, bone marrow, kidney, heart, liver, midriff, spleen, lungs, bowels, entrails, dung, bile, phlegm, pus, blood, sweat, fat tears, grease, spittle, snot, oil of the joints, and urine" (*Path*, 8.44).

21. *Path*, 3.116.

22. Some meditation subjects even allow for four additional levels of mental absorption called *arupa-jhanas*. Further, the fourth level as one-pointedness also carries with it a high level of equanimity.

23. We find versions of these meditations in a number of sermons in the Buddhist canon. Perhaps the most famous is the *Brahmavihara Sutta* (*Anguttara Nikaya*, 10.208).

24. *Mettanisamsa Sutta* as cited in Mahathera Gunaratana, *Bhavana Vandana: Book of Devotion* (Taipei, Taiwan: Bhavana Society, 1990), 163.

25. See Eugene d'Aquili and Andrew B. Newberg, *The Mystical Mind: Probing the Biology of Religious Experience* (Minneapolis: Fortress Press: 1999); and Andrew Newberg, Eugene D'Aquili, and Vincent Rause, *Why God Won't Go Away: Brain Science and the Biology of Belief* (New York: Ballantine Books, 2002).

26. Buddhaghosa describes them in *Path* 9.98–101.

7

How Might I Live in the Natural World?

Religions have, within their histories and theologies, resources for both good and ill, much like everything else that is part of the human condition. Islam's great culture of learning and tolerance in the medieval period resulted from rapid military expansion, as Muslims conquered the Middle East, northern Africa, and Spain. Christianity brought Europe libraries, hospitals, art, and a deep appreciation for the common good. It also brought the Crusades, anti-Semitism, and colonialism that exploited Indigenous societies. Hinduism has provided systems of yoga that generate extraordinary possibilities of interior transformation as well as the theological justification for caste oppression and, currently, anti-Islamic policies in India. And one can find a rationale for each of these developments and actions within the sacred traditions themselves.

The same can be said about how one ought to imagine the created world. Is it holy? Is it neutral? Is it an evil that ought to be jettisoned? We saw in chapter 5 that Daoism is highly sensitive to the ways of nature and the need to live in its rhythms. But it is also true that the practice of alchemy and ingesting metals for spiritual immortality was tantamount to self-poisoning. Many of my Christian students are Evangelicals who believe that the Second Coming is imminent; thus, care for the environment is simply not on their spiritual radar. Many also think of the created world as made exclusively for human beings. On this view, animals and plants have no intrinsic value or dignity and thus cannot ever be exploited; they are not valuable enough to merit that term. Consider the Christian Bible. On the one hand we find:

> But the day of the Lord will come like a thief, and then the heavens will pass away with a loud noise, and the elements will be dissolved with fire, and the earth and everything that is done on it will be disclosed. . . . But, in accordance with his promise, we wait for new heavens and a new earth, where righteousness is at home. (2 Pet 3:10–13)

On the other hand, St. Paul writes:

> For the creation waits with eager longing for the revealing of the children of God; for the creation was subjected to futility, not of its own but by the will of the one who subjected it, in hope that the creation itself will be set free from its bondage to decay and will obtain the freedom of the glory of the children of God. (Rom 8:19–21)

Here Paul imagines that the created world itself will become transformed, that it too is part of God's redeeming plan. But the future cannot include both of these visions (the Petrine and the Pauline), can it?

In Hinduism, the created world is *maya*, and *maya* can be variously understood. The great eighth-century mystic and philosopher Shankara (700–750) understood creation itself as an illusion, whereas Ramanuja (1017–1137), an equally great mystic and philosopher, understood *maya* as Brahman's expression of its very self, of Brahman's creative power. Which is it?

What if creation *is* intrinsically valuable? What if the created world shared in the spiritual life of God, each sentient being in its own way? And if that is the case, then what if exploiting and abusing the created world is not just understood as bad form or bad for the future of humans, but as an assault on something holy, perhaps even an assault on God? In this chapter we look at two very different traditions: the Roman Catholic view as articulated by Pope Francis and the Native American view, with a particular interest in Black Elk and the Lakota people. As you read, imagine how differently you would live if you actually thought these perspectives were guides for ethical behavior.

Christian Wisdom:
St. Francis, Pope Francis, and *Laudato Si'*

In the modern era, several recent popes have come out strongly against humanity's exploitation of the natural world. In 1971, Pope Paul VI wrote in his apostolic letter *Octogesima Adveniens*, "Due to an ill-considered exploitation of nature, humanity runs the risk of destroying it and becoming in turn a victim of this degradation."[1] Pope John Paul II called for a global economic conversion that takes into "account the nature of each being and its mutual connection in an ordered system."[2] John Paul was followed by Pope Benedict XVI who challenged us to see that "the book of nature is one and indivisible," and that "the deterioration of nature is closely connected to the culture which shapes human existence."[3] Pope Francis's encyclical *Laudato Si'* (On Care for Our Common Home) aligns with what preceded him in calling for a complete rethinking of our relationship to the environment.[4] What makes *Laudato Si'* different is the spirit that runs through the encyclical; it is a spirit of St. Francis of Assisi, whose name Cardinal Jorge Bergoglio took when he became pope.

St. Francis (d. 1226) is popularly depicted as a charming monk with a bird on his shoulder, but he is much deeper than that. He praised poverty and simplicity; these are the qualities that he believed allow the human spirit to find God everywhere and to love God in everyone and everything. He loved humility, as he saw this as necessary for being a servant of God. And he loved contemplation, through which he experienced the physical and spiritual unity of the world and the glory of God that held it all into being and penetrated it all. Pope Francis called his encyclical *Laudato Si'*, meaning "Be Praised." It is a direct reference to St. Francis's most famous poem *Canticle of the Creatures*. Here is the Canticle in full:

> Most high, all-powerful, all good, Lord!
>> All praise is yours, all glory, all honor
>> And all blessing.
>
> To you, alone, Most High, do they belong.
>> No mortal lips are worthy
>> To pronounce your name.
>
> Be praised, my Lord, through all that you have made,
>> And first my lord Brother Sun,
>>> Who brings the day; and the light you give to us
>>> through him.
>
> How beautiful is he, how radiant in all his splendor!
>> Of you, Most High, he bears the likeness.
>
> Be praised, my Lord, through Sister Moon and Stars;
>> In the heavens you have made them, bright
>> And precious and fair.
>
> Be praised, my Lord, through Brothers Wind and Air,
>> And fair and stormy, all the weather's moods,
>> By which you cherish all that you have made.
>
> Be praised, my Lord, through Sister Water,
>> useful, lowly, precious and pure.
>
> Be praised, my Lord, through Brother Fire,
>> Through whom you brighten up the night.
>> How beautiful is he, how happy! Full of power
>> and strength.
>
> Be praised, my Lord, through Sister Earth, our mother,
>> Who feeds us in her sovereignty and produces
>> Various fruits with colored flowers and herbs.

> *Be praised, my Lord, through those who grant pardon*
>   *For love of you; through those who endure*
>   *Sickness and trial.*
> *Happy those who endure in peace,*
>   *By you, Most High, they will be crowned.*
> *Be praised, my Lord, through Sister Death,*
>   *From whose embrace no mortal can escape.*
> *Woe to those who die in mortal sin!*
>   *Happy those She finds doing your will!*
>   *The second death can do no harm to them.*
> *Praise and bless my Lord, and give him thanks,*
>   *And serve him with great humility.*[5]

This canticle reflects St. Francis's attitude toward the natural world. There is a mutual interplay of all creation, and this must be seen in the context of his fundamental theological belief in God as Creator, Redeemer, and Sanctifier, as revealed by Jesus Christ, Lord and as crucified Servant. The Canticle falls into four parts. In the first part St. Francis deals with God: one stanza is devoted to direct praise of God, while the second sets up the paradox in attempting to praise God, declaring that "No mortal lips are worthy to pronounce your name."

The second part is a cosmological section of seven stanzas devoted to praising the Creator as revealed "with" and "through" his creatures, with the sun (the central manifestation of divine light and goodness) being given the primary role. The first three stanzas deal with the heavenly realm of sun, moon, and stars, each of which is characterized by splendor and beauty. The next four stanzas describe the four elements of terrestrial cosmology (air, water, fire, earth). Air is how the world is cherished by God; Water is useful, precious, pure; Fire is beautiful, happy, powerful; and Earth produces and feeds. Francis wrote this in the Umbrian dialect that uses *laudato*, a passive imperative. God is praised by and through the created world, which manifests his glory.

In the third part, which is anthropological, two stanzas praise those who pardon others for love's sake and those who bear infirmity in peace, in what we might describe as the fundamental active and passive dimensions of St. Francis's understanding of following Christ.

Finally, the last part is eschatological, or about final things. Here God is praised through *Sister Death*. St. Francis expresses his hope to die in God's will. Bodily (not spiritual) death carries no fear for the person who has understood the true meaning of praise. Francis posits a solidarity between the human and cosmic order, portraying an experience of the world as a single harmonious theophany, a visible manifestation of God.

This is not only St. Francis of Assisi's vision; it is also the vision of the current pope who took his name. In *Laudato Si'*, Pope Francis says time and time again that we are all interconnected, that humans are part of the natural world along with non-human animals and plant life, and that that inter-human relations and human relations with God imply each other. We flourish together or we die together. He writes, "The violence present in our hearts, wounded by sin, is also reflected in the symptoms of sickness evident in the soil, in the water, in the air, in all forms of human life" (no. 2).

Much of the encyclical details the consensus among climate scientists on global warming, such as polluted water supplies, deforestation, and so on. Unless we change, Pope Francis warns, "this century may well witness extraordinary climate change and an unprecedented destruction of ecosystems with serious consequences for us all" (no. 24). And challenging both climate deniers and obstructionists, he writes, "Evasiveness serves as a license to carrying on with our present lifestyles. . . . [T]his is the way human beings contrive to feed their self-destructive vices: trying not to see them, trying not to acknowledge them, delaying the important decisions and pretending that nothing will happen" (no. 59).

Pope Francis reminds Christians that a repeated principle in the Bible is that the created world comes from God as a gift to embrace, but it ultimately belongs to God: "The Bible everywhere reminds us that the earth is the Lord's and all within it" (Ps 24:1; Deut 10:14), and that "God rejects every [human] claim to absolute ownership" (no. 69). "Dominion" over the earth in Genesis, he argues, was never meant by the Bible to mean exploitation, but rather husbanding and guardianship. Further, quoting the Catholic Catechism, he writes: "Each creature possesses its own particular goodness . . . [and] reflects in its own way a ray of God's infinite wisdom and goodness" (no. 69); "God wills the interdependence of creatures" (no. 88); "We are linked by unseen bonds and together form a kind of universal family, a sublime communion which fills us with the sacred, affectionate and humble respect . . . . We ought to feel the desertification of the soil almost as a physical ailment, and the extinction of species as a painful disfigurement" (no. 89).

Pope Francis ends the encyclical by inviting us to have what he calls a mystical life: "The universe unfolds in God, who fills it completely. Hence, there is a mystical meaning found in a leaf, in a mountain trail, in a dewdrop, in a poor person's face. . . . [T]he mystic experiences the intimate connection between God and all beings" (nos. 233–34).

What Can We Learn?

One of the most important things we can learn here is that there are many resources in the Christian tradition that support a truly holistic understanding of the world and our place in it. Pope Francis alludes to Genesis, where "dominion" ought to be understood as "husbanding" or "guardianship." We might do well to look at the text itself, as it has been used to actually justify exploitation of the natural world.

> So God created humankind in his image, in the image of God he created them, male and female he created them. God blessed them, and God said to them, "Be fruitful and multiple, and fill the earth and subdue it; and have

dominion over the fish of the sea and over the birds of
the air and over every living thing that moves upon the
earth" (Gen 1:27–28).

Pope Francis's interpretation of Genesis follows the consensus of
scholarship. In the *New Jerome Biblical Commentary* we find that
being created in the image and likeness of God makes one an icon
of God and a representative of God's authority. Being the pinnacle
of creation has with it the responsibility to act as God would act.[6]
The *Oxford Bible Commentary* notes:

> The ordinance that mankind is to rule over the animal
> kingdom, like the statement that the sun and moon
> are to rule over the day and night (1:16), determines
> mankind's function in the world. It does not imply
> exploitation, for food or for any other purpose; rather,
> it is a consequence of the gift to mankind of the image
> of God. Mankind is, as it were, a manager or supervisor
> of the world of living creatures.[7]

We saw in chapter 1 that St. Paul interprets Jesus much like
Wisdom in the Old Testament, the creative power of the Divine
through whom the universe was made. The Wisdom of Solomon,
a very late book, shares the same image of the world, where "the
spirit of the Lord has filled the world. . . . For he created all things
so that they might exist; the generative forces of the world are
wholesome" (Wis 1:7, 14). Many Christians imagine that the
world is ours to do with as we wish, that God created all things
only for humans—but Pope Francis reminds us that the world is
God's, not ours. Consider the following medley:

- [Moses speaking to Pharaoh]: "I will stretch out my
  hands to the Lord; the thunder will cease, and there will
  be no more hail, so that you may know that the earth is
  the Lord's" (Ex 9:29).

- "The heaven of heavens belongs to the Lord your God, the earth with all that is in it" (Deut 10:14).
- "For the world and all that is in it is mine" (Ps 50:12).
- "The heavens are yours, the earth also is yours; the world and all that is in it" (Ps 89:11).
- "The earth and its fullness are the Lord's" (1 Cor 10:26).

This sample of verses could be multiplied tenfold. The point is that the natural world is simply not ours to do with as we wish. It is God's to do with as God wishes.

What both St. Francis of Assisi and Pope Francis bring to this widely attested perspective is a deeper appreciation of the interconnectedness of all of nature. Thus, not only is the world not ours, but we can only understand ourselves well by seeing the human condition as a part of a spiritual whole that includes all sentient beings. Part of Pope Francis's call to conversion is an invitation to a richer life. He says it begins with gratitude, a recognition that the world is God's loving gift. It involves awareness of the interconnection of life. Francis reminds us that we are "joined in a splendid universal communion" (no. 22). Once freed from our obsession with consumption and compulsion to dominate, we are spiritually available to appreciate the beauty of creation. "This is not a lesser life or one lived with less intensity; on the contrary we enjoy more, live better, shedding unsatisfied needs, reducing our obsessiveness and weariness" (no. 223). "No one can cultivate a satisfying life," he says, "without being at peace with him or herself. Inner peace is related to care for ecology and for the common good because it is reflected in a balanced lifestyle, a capacity for wonder, an ability to listen and be present" (no. 225).

The real problem is not with advances in technology or consumption per se, but with a worldview that is "technocratic, consumerist, materialistic, and individualistic." Francis calls these perspectives dangerous "myths" in which human dignity and the dignity of the planet are ignored and humans and the earth are exploited (no. 112), and he calls us to repentance for these myths.

The early church fathers regularly referred to the soul's problem as *scotosis*, Greek for "blindness." They used the term to describe the soul's cultivated habit of not seeing the truth: if we practice long enough, we really do become blind and cannot see what is right before us. Pope Francis challenges the world to recognize its *scotosis*, to see the scientific data for what it is and its implications for what they are; to see the natural world as having intrinsic dignity and to see ourselves as part of it, not outside of it. He also challenges us to see others, particularly the poor, in a plight that the first world has inflicted upon them.

Pope Francis invites us to see new possibilities; a new vision where the earth is enjoyed, where wonder is still possible, where humans globally are recognized as brothers and sisters; where our compulsivity, our unquenchable habits, and our boredom are replaced by inner and outer peace, inner and outer harmony. *Praised be*, St. Francis proclaimed eight hundred years ago. This is our question: Will we live a life where we praise God through all that God has given us; where we cherish life, so full of wonder and the divine presence? Or will we live a life that is a curse to ourselves, to the poor, and to creation?

Native American Wisdom: God Indwells in Everything

Decades ago, when I was in college, we learned that Indigenous traditions were typically *animistic*, that is, they believed that all living things, from humans to animals to plants, had a spirit or soul. In some traditions, this spirit was believed to be divine and in others the spirit was specific to that type of being. Today, animism is something of an archaic term rarely used in academic circles. One reason is that it is too fuzzy a term. Those two framings, divine manifestation versus individual souls, are too radically different to be lumped together. Another reason is that many world religions that are not considered animistic believe the same kinds of things. Mahayana Buddhism widely believes that every sentient being has a Buddha-nature, a universal seed of enlightenment and the foundational essence of all that exists. And, as we saw in Hinduism, Brahman is the transcendental essence that pervades all sentiency. Would these then not be animistic too?

Still, maybe the term does help us here. While we will see that Native American spirituality shares many of the intuitions we found in Pope Francis's *Laudato Si'*, its vision extends far beyond what Francis had in mind. In the Christian tradition (Jewish and Islamic too), human souls are imagined to be uniquely or qualitatively different from whatever spiritual quality might exist in animals. Most Christians would simply deny that there are any other beings with souls, and there is nothing Pope Francis says that ought to lead us to think otherwise. What I would like to do in this section is to explore how three different Native American traditions understand the interconnectedness of beings, in terms of one's spirit or soul.

Thomas Banyacya (1909–1999) was a Hopi traditional leader in northeastern Arizona. He was one of four Hopis who were named by elders to speak to the general public after the atomic bombings of Hiroshima and Nagasaki. Banyacya and his brothers were peace activists during the war and after, sharing Hopi traditional teachings and even Hopi prophecies regarding the future of the world, in light of human violence and environmental degradation. Banyacya continued to be a public prophetic presence for the rest of his life, and in 1992, he addressed the United Nations General Assembly. Before he began, he sprinkled corn meal next to the podium in order to consecrate it for this sacred purpose. The following is an excerpt of what he said:

> My name is Banyacya . . . and I am a member of the Hopi sovereign nation. . . . The traditional Hopi follows the spiritual path that was given by *Massau'u*, the Great Spirit. We made a sacred covenant to follow his life plan at all times, which includes the responsibility of taking care of this land and life for his divine purpose. . . . Our goals are . . . to pray for

and to promote the welfare of all living beings and to preserve the world in a natural way. . . . In the Earth today, humans poison their own food, water, and air with pollution. Many of us, including children, are left to starve. Many wars are being fought. Greed and concern for material things is a common disease. . . . Nature, the First People and the spirit of our ancestors, is giving you loud warnings. Today, December 10, 1992, you see increasing floods, more damaging hurricanes, hailstorms, climate changes, and earthquakes as our prophecies said would come. Even animals and birds are warning us with strange changes in their behavior. . . . Why do animals act like they know about the earth's problems and most humans act like they know nothing? If we humans do not wake up to the warnings, the great purification will come to destroy this world. . . . If we return to spiritual harmony and live from our hearts, we can experience a paradise in this world. If we continue only on this upper path [of separation], we will come to destruction. This is now a time to weigh the choices for our future. We do have a choice. If you, the nations of this Earth create another great war, the Hopi believe we humans will burn ourselves to death with ashes. That's why the spiritual Elders stress strongly that the United Nations fully open the door for native spiritual leaders to speak as soon as possible. Nature itself does not speak with a voice that we can easily understand. Neither can the animals and birds we are threatening with extinction talk to us. Who in this world can speak for nature and the spiritual energy that creates and flows through all life?[8]

The night before Thomas Banyacya's speech and those of other native wisdom figures, there was a total eclipse of the moon over New York City, and the sky was exceptionally clear. The night after the speech, rain fell so hard that New York experienced its worst flood to date in modern memory. The subfloors of the United Nations Building were flooded. In the ground-floor meeting room, Thomas called all the participants gathered to form a great circle to pray. The storm quickly subsided. It could all have been a coincidence, but it is certainly uncanny.

In 1978, the Iroquois Nation of northeast America submitted a formal statement of beliefs to a United Nations conference. This is a portion of that statement:

> We remember the original instructions of the Creators of Life on this place we call *Ionkhi'nistenha onhwentsia*—Mother Earth. We are spiritual guardians of this place. . . . In the beginning we were told that the human beings who walk about the earth have been provided with all the things necessary for life. We were instructed to carry a love for one another, and to show a great respect for all the beings of this Earth. We are shown that our life exists with the tree life, that our well-being depends on the well-being of the vegetable life, that we are close relatives of the four-legged beings. . . . Ours is a Way of Life. We believe that all living things are spiritual beings. Spirits can be expressed as energy forms manifested in matter. . . . The spiritual universe, then, is manifest to man as the Creation, the Creation that supports life. We believe that man is real, a part of the Creation, and that his duty is to support life in conjunction with the other beings. . . . The original instructions direct that we who walk about on the earth are to express a great respect, an affection, and a gratitude toward all the spirits that create and support life. We give a greeting and thanksgiving to the many supporters of our own lives—the corn, beans, squash, the winds, the sun. When people cease to respect and express gratitude for these many things, then all life

will be destroyed and human life on this planet will come
to an end. . . . We are not a people who demand or ask
anything of the Creators of Life; instead we give greetings
and thanksgiving that all the forces of life are still at
work. . . . Many thousands of years ago, all the people
of the world believed in the same Way of Life, that of
harmony with the universe. All lived according to the
natural ways.[9]

One of the most fascinating biographies of Native American voices is that of Black Elk (1863–1950), an Oglala Lakota
Indian representing the Sioux nations. He was born on the Pow-
der River at the border of South Dakota and Wyoming. His
father and grandfather were medicine men, and his cousin was
the famous Crazy Horse. From the time Black Elk was a child,
he had visions and heard the voices of spirits and deceased relatives. He would eventually become a prophet and medicine man.
As a young man, he joined Buffalo Bill's Wild West show, which
took him to major cities in the United States and Europe. Returning, he settled down, got married, and became a store clerk and
medicine man (*yuwipi*) for the next fourteen years. Due to Jesuit
missionary activity, he became a Catholic during this time, and
was baptized on December 6, 1904. This was on the feast of St.
Nicholas, and he took Nicholas as his first name, usually going by
Nick. Black Elk also became a Catholic catechist and was instru-
mental in converting over 400 Native Americans to the Christian
faith. He ended up becoming a godfather to 113 fellow Lakota
Indians. Biographer Damian Costello argues persuasively that he
never denied his Lakota tradition but reinterpreted it in light of
Catholicism. "Black Elk makes an explicit theological connection
between Lakota and Catholic traditions. According to Black Elk,
the two traditions are not similar or parallel; rather, they are inter-
nally connected in a way that *precedes* separation."[10]

Black Elk died on August 19, 1950, at his home in Mander-
son, South Dakota. Both Lakota and Jesuits observed strange

lights in the sky on the night of his wake. William Siehr, a Jesuit brother at Holy Rosary Mission, remembers, "The sky was just one bright illumination. I never saw anything so magnificent. I've seen a number of flashes of the northern lights here in the early days, but I never saw anything quite so intense as it was that night. . . . It was a sort of celebration."[11] Actually, Black Elk predicted this to his daughter Lucy: "I have a feeling when I die, some sign will be seen. Maybe God will show something. He will be merciful to me and have something shown which will tell of his mercy."[12]

The following is a glimpse of Black Elk's cosmology:

> We are Earth People because we live close to our mother, the Earth. . . . We are part of the rock, or earth, and a part of the water and a part of the green, or living. That way we were able to communicate with all the living. . . . We have a biological father and mother, but our real Father is *Tunkashila* [Creator], and our real mother is the Earth. They give birth and life to all the living, so we know we're all interrelated. We all have the same Father and Mother. That is why you hear us always saying *mitakuye oyasin*. We say these words as we enter the sacred *stone-people-lodge* [sweat lodge] and also at the end of every prayer. It means "all my relations." It helps to remind us that we are related to everything that exists.[13]

For Black Elk, "We should know that He [the Great Spirit] is within all things: the trees, the grasses, the rivers, the mountains, and all the four-legged animals, and the winged peoples; and even more important, we should understand that He is also above all these things and peoples."[14] Black Elk's eschatology includes the second comings of both Jesus, who will judge the living and the dead, and the White Buffalo Woman who gave the Sioux the sacred pipe. She too will return at the end of this world, "a coming which we Indians know is now not very far off."[15] This is how she gave the Sioux the sacred pipe:

> With this sacred pipe you will walk upon the Earth; for the Earth is your Grandmother [ground] and Mother [creator of growth] and She is sacred. Every step that is taken upon Her should be as a prayer. The bowl of this pipe is of red stone; it is the Earth. Carved in the stone and facing the center is this buffalo calf who represents all the four-leggeds who live upon your Mother. The stem of the pipe is of wood, and this represents all that grows upon the Earth. And these twelve feathers which hang where the stem fits into the bowl are from *Wanbli Galeshka*, the Spotted Eagle, and they represent the eagle and all the wingeds of the air. All these peoples, and all the things of the universe, are joined to you who smoke the pipe—all send their voices to *Wakan-Tanka*, the Great Spirit. When you pray with this pipe, you pray for and with everything. The *waken* woman then touched the foot of the pipe to the round stone which lay upon the ground, and said: "With this pipe you will be bound to all your relatives: your Grandfather and Father, your Grandmother and Mother. This round rock, which is made of the same red stone as the bowl of the pipe, your Father *Wakan-Tanka* has also given you. It is the Earth, your Grandmother and Mother, and it is where you will live and increase.[16]

The tradition of the sacred pipe is revealing. It is given by a courier of God to the people. Each part of the pipe refers to different parts of the universe and all sentient and spiritual realities in that universe. It is a microcosm of all that is. Thus, the ritual smoking of the pipe draws the whole of the universe together. Smoking the pipe is a sacrament that instantiates and participates in universal life.

What Can We Learn?

The examples above are but snapshots, yet I think fair representatives of broad Native American belief. And they all reveal similar spiritual visions of the relationship living things have with each other and with God. If one were to compare their creation myths or their rites, one would find great diversity, and little could be culled that is universal among them. And yet, given that they are quite different from one another, it is particularly interesting that they share the same intuitions about nature and life. In each, for example, human beings are privileged above other animals. But they are so only in that they have the kind of consciousness to voice concern and to support universal life. Thomas Banyacya speaks on behalf of the created world, urging its protection and care. The Iroquois understand part of their mission as one of gratitude and explicit respect. Expressions of these become part of what keeps the world united under God. And, as we just noted, the sacred pipe ritual becomes a way to maintain and live out the unity of all sentiency. In this sense, the Native American and Christian and Jewish understanding of humans as guardians of the world converge.

On the other hand, in the Native American vision the difference between humans and other forms of life does not elevate them above other beings; rather, it charges humans with greater responsibility in the universal web of life. For it is obvious that, in terms of intrinsic value, humans share the same dignity—not more or less—as all living beings. All are relatives, and this is meant literally. Without anthropomorphizing the animal world and imagining a kind of human consciousness as applied to horses, turtles, muskrats, and so on, what if we were to imagine that they really were our relatives, truly part of our family? Recall from chapter 5 the bodhisattva pursuit of *bodhicitta* or awakened mind. Here one realizes that every person, throughout the many eons of rebirths, was once your mother who now needs you. Buddhists take this very literally. Every being *was in fact* my mother in a past rebirth.

This dramatically changes one's perspective. So too, what if we were to literally see all beings as relatives?

Many Native American creation myths include animals that the tribe needs for its own support as making covenants with humans. The myths surely are useful in allowing the tribe to hunt animals who are *relatives*. But the myth also instructs the tribe on having respect and gratitude for the life they know they have to take. The animal kingdom is one of predator and prey, for sure, and humans are not exempt. But the rites engaged in the hunt, the consuming of animal meat, and the full use of the animal for clothing, shelter, and so on, teach them to be respectful; to not hoard, to hunt only what is necessary, and to become highly sensitive to the circle of life. The contrast between this perspective and the one utilized to support, say, factory farming, is dramatic. Would you want your worst enemy to live the life of cattle encaged and knee deep in feces? Or the life of chickens bred with breasts so large they cannot walk, living in cages and enduring bird droppings from the cages above?

What if we really thought other life forms were intrinsically valuable, not just useful for our appetites alone? We would buy differently. We would eat differently. We would live differently. Most human societies have laws against animal cruelty. We know that other animals can flourish or suffer, and intentionally torturing or even neglecting these animals is a crime. This is good. But most societies also exempt animals used for food production from these protective laws. How can this not be duplicitous or immoral? Imagine the scenario from a Native American vision of life. Then it becomes blasphemous as well.

One of the most interesting themes that come up in all three Native American examples is the belief that we are on a historical precipice. Thomas Banyacya was a draft resister during World War II, and spent seven years in prison because of that. He became a public peace activist upon release and for the rest of his life. During the first Gulf War, Banyacya feared that humanity was on the brink of World War III, and that this would lead to the collapse of the current world before it is re-created anew by the Divine. His speech to the United Nations warns that this would be the case unless humanity dramatically changed course. In his message to the United Nations he articulates this concern: "If we humans do not wake up to the warnings, the great purification will come to destroy this world." The Iroquois also warned, "When people cease to respect and express gratitude for these many things, then all life will be destroyed and human life on this planet will come to an end." And Black Elk likewise imagined that the end of the world and the return of both Jesus Christ and the White Buffalo Woman would be soon.

One might dismiss these apocalyptic prophecies. Certainly, in the Christian tradition the consensus of the theological community is that imagining an imminent second coming is a fool's errand. But one ought not to dismiss these apocalyptic scenarios so lightly. Not only is climate change a settled truth in the scientific community, it is also clear that most countries lack the political will to seriously address it, thus imperiling the natural world in unprecedented ways. Currently, 194 countries have signed the Paris Agreement on climate change. According to the non-profit Climate Action Tracker, of them just seven (Morocco, Gambia, India, Costa Rica, Ethiopia, Bhutan, and the Philippines) have made significant progress. None of the other countries has come close to meeting the Paris Agreement's short-term aims. Some of the worst offenders include the United States, Russia, Turkey, Ukraine, and Saudi Arabia. China and Canada have done next to nothing.[17] What our future looks like is a global increase in temperatures of 3.5 degrees Fahrenheit, mass destruction of species, ocean levels rising several feet (potentially eight feet in the worst-case scenario), severe drought in some areas and severe flooding in others, a deadly acidification of the oceans, and for humans, massive deaths of the most vulnerable.[18] This is apocalyptic indeed.

To me, Native American Wisdom appears to be saying that what is needed is a whole new conception of our relationship with the natural world. And really it goes beyond this to a complete paradigm shift. If one were to ask many first-world citizens what the relationship is between humans and the natural world, one would get a variety of answers. But if one were to ask a Native American, the response might be more like a shake of the head. "Everything is sacred. We do not have a *relationship* with the natural world. We, and everything around us, *is* the natural world." Imagine thinking like this.

Notes

1. Pope Paul VI, encyclical letter *Octogesima Adveniens*, 21 AAS 63 (1971), 416–17. This and other papal texts are cited in Pope Francis's *Laudato Si'* (On Care for Our Common Home) (Vatican City: Libraria Editrice Vaticana, 2015).

2. Pope John Paul II, encyclical letter *Redemptor Hominis*, 15 ASS 71 (1979), 287.

3. Pope Benedict XVI, encyclical letter *Caritas in Veritate*, 51 ASS 101 (2009), 687.

4. Pope Francis I, *Laudate Si'* (2015), www.vatican.va.

5. St. Francis of Assisi, *St. Francis of Assisi: Writings and Early Biographies*, 4th ed., ed. Marion Habig (Chicago: Franciscan Herald Press, 1983), 130–31.

6. Richard Clifford and Roland Murphy, "Genesis," in *The New Jerome Biblical Commentary*, ed. Raymond Brown et al. (Englewood Cliffs, NJ: Prentice Hall, 1990), 11.

7. John Barton and John Muddiman, eds., *The Oxford Bible Commentary* (Oxford: Oxford University Press, 2001), 41.

8. "HOPI Message to the United Nations, 12/10/1992," http://www.nativeamericanchurch.com/Signs/HOPI-UNMsg.html.

9. Akwesasne Notes, ed., *Basic Call to Consciousness* (Summertown, TN: Native Voices, 1978), 85–86, as cited in Louis Vaughn, ed., *Anthology of World Religions: Sacred Texts and Contemporary Perspectives* (New York: Oxford University Press, 2017), 45–56.

10. Damian Costello, *Black Elk: Colonialism and Lakota Catholicism* (Maryknoll, NY: Orbis Books, 2005), 85.

11. Ibid., 13.

12. Ibid.

13. Vaughn, *Anthology of World Religions*, 57.

14. Black Elk, *The Sacred Pipe: Black Elk's Account of the Seven Rites of the Oglala Sioux*, ed. Joseph Epes Brown (Norman: University of Oklahoma Press, 1953), xx.

15. Ibid., xix–xx.

16. Ibid., 5–7.

17. Carmen Singer et al., "The 7 Countries Actually Living Up to the Paris Climate Agreement," *Global Citizen*, October 12, 2018, https://www.globalcitizen.org/en/content/7-countries-paris-climate-agreeement/.

18. "The Effects of Climate Change," NASA, https://climate.nasa.gov/effects/.

8

How Might I See God?

In the famous Hindu *Chandogya Upanishad* we find a Brahmin priest, Uddalaka Aruni, who welcomes his son Shvetaketu home after twelve years of study to become a priest like his father. But Uddalaka is not impressed by his son. Shvetaketu knows the Vedas, all the right chants, and the specifics of all the proper rituals. Given this, he thinks quite well of himself. But Uddalaka is disappointed. Does his son have even an inkling of what underlies them all? His father says to him, "Shvetaketu, since you are now so greatly conceited, think yourself well-read and arrogant, did you ask for the instruction by which the unhearable becomes heard, the unperceivable becomes perceived, the unknowable becomes known?" To which the son responds, "How, Venerable Sir, can there be such a teaching?" (VI.1.4). The conversation goes on and Shvetaketu learns about Brahman, that ultimate reality underlying all phenomenal reality.

But how indeed can one hear the unhearable, perceive the unperceivable, know the unknowable? By definition you can't. Religions widely attest that God is beyond knowing *as* God. Our intellects are designed to know about objects in the created world, and our minds can only conceptualize "things." God is not a *thing*, not another object among objects in the universe. The great Christian theologian and mystic Gregory of Nyssa likened seeing

God to what happened to Moses on Mount Sinai, where "Moses drew near to the thick darkness where God was" (Ex 20:21). Only when Moses is surrounded by a dark cloud of unknowing does he encounter God *as* God, at least insofar as one can in this life. What then sees or knows when the very faculty of the intellect is shut down? St. Gregory argues that we have *spiritual senses*, including a kind of knowing faculty that is within the soul. This part of us can *know*, but it cannot translate that knowledge to objectifiable data perceivable to the intellect.[1]

Thomas Aquinas understood God in two ways. The first is Absolute Mystery. We can speak of God only analogically by using terms that make sense to us, such as God is goodness and God is truth. These claims, he believed, were certainly true. But it is not simply that God is infinite goodness and truth while we only know their relative levels. More fully, God is good *as God*, while we only understand what goodness can mean in the created world. God is truth *as God*, but we can only know conceptual truths related to our own existence. Jane is good *as a human*. God is good *as God*. These do not parallel each other, but they are analogous. Thomas's second depiction of God is that God is pure Subject. We can point directly to objects, anything in the created world, but we cannot point to God; God cannot be objectified—God is only Subject, never object. Surely, when we use language we have to refer to God as though God were an object of our discussion, but again, such a maneuver is as concealing as it is revealing about God. This is why the mystical traditions in both West and East use metaphors and paradoxical language to address the mystery of knowing what cannot be known and speaking about what is ineffable.

This particular chapter is not exactly about those ways of unknowing, but this does not completely free us from that intractable problem of saying what cannot be legitimately said and seeing what cannot be seen. This chapter is devoted to "seeing" God. Just as I drew on only one religion in chapter 4 (Judaism), I will also restrict myself to one religion here, in this case Christianity.

I do so because it is Christianity that claims Jesus as divine in ways that have no other historical parallel—for Christians, Jesus is what God looks like.

Christian Wisdom:
Seeing Humanity, Mediating God

We read in First John, "No one has ever seen God; if we love one another, God lives in us, and his love is perfected in us. . . . God is love, and those who abide in love abide in God, and God abides in them" (4:12–16). This is Christianity's first and biggest clue in understanding and *seeing* God. Although we cannot literally see God, we can perceive human love, or rather we can perceive divine love working through humans. Humans in Christianity (and in most religions) are considered uniquely created. In the second creation story in Genesis we find that Adam is created with two ingredients: dust and God's breath or *ruah* (2:7). Hebrew biblical scholar Mark Smith notes, "This *ruah* is in some sense integrally related to divinity. . . . [It] is somehow divine not only in its origins but also in its ultimate destiny."[2] And in the first creation story, God made humans in God's own image and likeness (1:26). This *imago Dei* is the foundation for why Christians and Jews believe that human life is intrinsically valuable. In Christianity, after Adam and Eve's fall, we are said to have lost much of our likeness to God and even marred the image. The Greek Fathers regularly described the task of humanity as removing the stains of sin so that both our image and likeness shine forth. St. Diadochus of Phontiki, one of the great monastic fathers, saw baptism as the beginning of the way to restore the full image of God; and then the spiritual work begins:

> With all his will to desire the beauty of the likeness [he] stands naked and undaunted in this work, then grace causes virtue upon virtue to blossom in us and it raises the form of the soul from glory to glory and bestows on the soul the form of likeness.[3]

Other Greek Fathers understood image to refer to humanity's potential for holiness and union with God, while the likeness represents realizing divine holiness.[4]

There is something mystical and hidden about the image and likeness of God because God is unknowable. We can experience this reality in ourselves and in others, but it is elusive. The great Orthodox theologian Vladimir Lossky notes that "the image of God in humanity, in so far as it is perfect, is necessarily unknowable . . . for as it reflects the fullness of its archetype, it must also possess the unknowable character of the divine Being. . . . We can only conceive it through the idea of participation in the infinite goodness of God."[5]

In Catholic and Orthodox thought, sacraments are symbols that participate in the very reality they symbolize. They *realize* the reality or instantiate the reality exactly through their symbolic representation. And it can only be this way. God and God's grace are of the eternal and spiritual world, not the temporal and physical world. Yet the only way to engage them in this life is through the created world. This is analogous to humans' own spiritual life. Consider love: it is not a physical thing, but the only way to express it is through the physical. For example, say I love someone and show that love by an embrace. The physical dimension is just a body performing a physical act. But that physical act not only points to the love I have, it actually participates in it. The embrace incarnates the love.

The Christian tradition sees Jesus Christ as the incarnation of God, *the* symbol of God, *the* sacrament of God, one in whom the image and likeness of the Divine is perfected and present before us. The gospels of Matthew and Luke strive to make sense of this in their infancy narratives where Jesus is described as conceived by the Holy Spirit. Luke's version is a bit more dramatic. He said that the angel Gabriel was sent to Mary,

> And he came to her and said, "Greetings favored one!
> The Lord is with you." But she was much perplexed
> by his words and pondered what sort of greeting this

might be. The angel said to her, "Do not be afraid, Mary, for you have found favor with God and now, you will conceive in your womb and bear a son, and you will name him Jesus [God saves]. He will be great and called the Son of the Most High, and the Lord God will give him the throne of his ancestor David. He will reign over the house of Jacob forever, and of his kingdom there will be no end." Mary said to the angel, "How can this be, since I am a virgin?" The angel said to her, "The Holy Spirit will come upon you, and the power of the Most High will overshadow you; therefore the child to be born will be holy; he will be called Son of God." (Jn 1:28–35)

Mark's gospel has no narrative, but simply begins, "The beginning of the good news of Jesus Christ, Son of God" (1:1). John's gospel is more poetic and philosophically loaded:

In the beginning was the Word, and the Word was with God and the Word was God. All things came into being through him and without him not one thing came into being. What has come into being in him was life, and the life was the light of all people. The light shines in the darkness, and the darkness did not overcome it. . . . And the Word became flesh and lived among us, and we have seen his glory, the glory as of a Father's only son, full of grace and truth. . . . No one has ever seen God. It is God the only Son, who is close to the Father's heart, who has made him known. (Jn 1:1–18)

Here we find that Jesus is both referred to *as* God and as being *with* God. Jesus had a God whom he regularly called Father (*Abba*) and to whom he prayed. But he is no mere human who has fully expressed the image and likeness of God—he is the divine presence of God in the world. It took centuries for the Church to hammer out dogmatic issues related to the Trinity and the person of Jesus Christ, particularly the human and divine natures of Christ and how they are related (or not). These need not concern us here, as we addressed some of this in chapter 1. For Christians, Jesus is the instantiation of the divine—the divine before us. This is what God looks like. Jesus himself, not his words, not his acts, is *the* revelation of the Divine.

At Vatican II, the Catholic Church makes this clear in a statement that is surely shared by Protestant, Catholic, Orthodox, and Evangelical Christians:

> It pleased God, in his goodness and wisdom, to reveal himself and to make known the mystery of his will. His will was that humans should have access to the Father, through Christ, the Word made flesh, in the Holy Spirit, and thus become sharers in the divine nature. . . . The most intimate truth which this revelation gives us about God and the salvation of humanity shines forth in Christ, who is himself both the mediator and the sum total of Revelation. (*Dei Verbum*, no. 2)

Here lies the problem. Jesus, as sacrament of God, is experienced in time, in history, in the particularities of culture, and with a human body. When we ask, "What does God look like?" the answer is certainly not a Semitic man who ate, slept, and preached throughout various Middle Eastern provinces of the Roman Empire. Perhaps the paradox might be framed instead as: God does not look like a human person, but this particular human person looks like God. And yet, how?

Israel experienced God as One who saves and blesses. God's universal love and compassion express themselves particularly in responding to the cry of the oppressed and those in need. Where there is life there is God's blessing, and where there is oppression and death God reacts. The prophetic worldview was one in which true fasting was acting justly (Is 58:1–9), reversing oppression was the only way to make the Temple holy (Jer 7:3–11), and where sacrifices were only acceptable (and not blasphemous) when care for those in need came first and foremost (Am 5:21–24). God can also be angry and threatening, but God's judgment and punishment correlate with God's love and compassion for those mistreated. "God reacts against the injury of the weak *because* God loves and has compassion. And God's judging is precisely a continuation of God's saving activity."[6]

And then came Jesus. Jesus preached the kingdom of God; this was his dominant message, his *master symbol*. Theologian Dermot Lane observed, "Everything that Jesus says and does is inspired from the beginning to the end by his personal commitment to the Reign of God in the world. The controlling horizon of his mission and ministry is the Kingdom of God."[7] The biblical symbol of the reign of God, the *malkuth Yahweh*, reaches back to the time of the Judges where God was Israel's king, and then to the monarchy where the human king was God's regent. Progressively, Israel looked to a kind of paradisal future where captives will be freed and those who mourn will be comforted (Is 61:1–3). Jesus announces that these words are being "fulfilled in your hearing" (Lk 4:21).

The kingdom of God was not, for Jesus, a definitive social, political, or religious agenda. Rather, it represented salvation, a life of flourishing, justice, peace, and communion with the Divine. As a sure sign of the kingdom's advent, Jesus performed exorcisms, healings, and "mighty deeds." The kingdom of God was both a future realization and an event created by Jesus himself; "[I]f it is by the finger of God that I cast out demons, the kingdom of God has come to you" (Lk 11:20). Jesus was a holy man who spoke with the authority of the Divine. And those who followed him experienced the inbreaking of the kingdom before them. Jesus's kingdom was also empowering. Midway through his ministry he sent out his disciples to villages to prepare for his arrival and he spiritually empowered them: "So they went out and proclaimed that all should repent. They cast out many demons, and anointed with oil many who were sick and cured them" (Mk 6:12–13).[8]

But Jesus also had enemies, including Pharisees, chief priests, scribes, Sadducees, and Herodians. Collectively, they held many types of power: economic, political, religious, and military. Those among these groups who were his enemies represent the *anti-kingdom*, a division most clear in John's gospel where one must decide to be a child of God who lives in the light and has life, or a child of Satan who lives in the darkness and represents death. Jesus's condemnation of the latter also looks like the God of Israel. In this world, the powers of the anti-kingdom often prevail. This was certainly the case with Jesus. He was condemned by the Jewish court of the Sanhedrin for blasphemy and crucified by the Romans for sedition. "We found this man perverting our nation, forbidding us to pay taxes to the emperor, and saying that he himself is the Messiah, a king" (Lk 23:2). And so, he needed to be killed, sacrificed for an imagined greater good: "[I]t is better for you to have one man die for the people than to have the whole nation destroyed" (Jn 11:50). So, Jesus was sacrificed.

In the Temple, many different kinds of sacrifices were made. A sacrifice could be a peace offering that included ratifying covenants.[9] There were also thanksgiving offerings in which an animal is offered to God and then slaughtered and cooked. Those offering this sacrifice present a banquet to God, who accepts it and invites the worshippers to dine with him (Deut 12:7–18). Imagine this kind of sacrifice as follows: Jews present to God what is vital and dear to them, and in this way recognize God's sovereignty. In order to offer sacrifice to God, they separate the offering from the profane world and introduce it into the sacred world; they make it sacred. The Latin etymology of "sacrifice" is worth noting. It is *sacrum facere*, "to make holy." God then receives this holy offering and takes it to himself, making it take on divine holiness. It is then eaten by those offering the sacrifice. In doing so they consume and ingest something of the very holiness of God. One can see here how these sacrifices align with Jesus. His new covenant is ratified in his own blood on the cross, and this sacrifice provides for communion with the Divine. This is, in part, how the Roman

Catholic and Eastern Orthodox Churches understand the Eucharist they celebrate.

Finally, there were also sacrifices for the atonement of sins.[10] The most important sacrifice in the Temple was the Sin Offering, which is especially holy.[11] Once a year, on the Day of Atonement, two goats are brought to God in the Temple and then lots are thrown. The goat that *wins* is the one that will be sacrificed. The high priest takes the goat that loses the lots and confesses Israel's sins over it so that the goat ritually takes on those sins. Then the goat is sent out into the desert to die. This is the *scape-goat*.[12] It is this kind of sacrifice that Christians focus on: Jesus took on the sins of the world and died for those sins. Paul will even declare something shocking: "For our sake he [God] made him to be sin who knew no sin, so that in him we might become the righteousness of God" (2 Cor 5:21). The New Testament sees Jesus as the person Isaiah prophesied about in his Servant Songs.[13] Isaiah writes, "Surely he has borne our infirmities and carried our diseases; yet we accounted him stricken, struck down by God, and afflicted. But he was wounded for our transgressions, crushed by our iniquities; upon him was the punishment that made us whole, and by his bruises we are healed" (Is 53:4–5).

How can this possibly be? One thing to understand is that it is *not* an angry God who needs to be appeased with blood. Pagan sacrifices were meant to influence divine forces or neutralize evil. Sacrifice in the biblical sense is different. As Gerhard Lohfink observes, "Sacrifice in the biblical sense . . . signifies self-surrender, listening with one's whole existence to what God wills. Then it is no longer about one's own cause but about God's."[14] As most realize, modern culture in the West is strikingly individualistic. Imagining someone as a representative of anything but oneself, much less a whole people or even the world, simply does not resonate well. But the biblical world is very different—representative substitution and atonement are normative ways of thinking.[15] Lohfink writes,

The questions might be asked: how can another do for me what I must do for myself? How can I be redeemed by another? But we are all dependent on other people. We rely on an endless number of surrogates, representatives. In all this, representation or substitution never means dispensing the other from her or his own action, faith, and repentance. Rather, substitution is intended to make one's own action possible.[16]

Elsewhere, he notes,

"Atonement" is a new enabling of life given by God. "Atonement" is the gift of being able to live in the presence of the holy God, in the space where God is near, despite one's own unholiness and constant new incurring of guilt. Effecting "atonement" means *not* appeasing God or making God amenable to reconciliation, but allowing ourselves to be rescued by God's own self from the death we deserve.[17]

This new freedom, given the graciousness of God, has divine possibilities for us. In declaring Jesus "sin" that we might be God's righteousness, Paul declares, "So if anyone is in Christ, there is a new creation. . . . All this is from God, who reconciled us to himself through Christ, and has given us the ministry of reconciliation; that is, in Christ God was reconciling the world to himself" (2 Cor 5:17–19).

There is more. In the synoptic gospels of Matthew, Mark, and Luke, Jesus is taunted by his enemies with versions of "He saved others, but he cannot save himself."[18] These words were meant by the evangelists to be something of an unintended truth. While Jesus did save others, he was not able to save himself, but *unable* only in the sense that he was *unwilling* to disregard his Father's will. "For the Son of Man came to seek out and to save the lost" (Lk 19:10). As Francis Watson notes, "Others are saved, but he is lost; they are saved, but at his expense. In that sense, he dies as the *substitute*. . . . The substitution draws attention to the contrast between the Son of God's unreserved participation in the depths of human misery and the well-being he achieves for others."[19] In Jesus, the incarnation of God, the Divine enters into a realm God seemingly would not have been able to legitimately enter—alienation from God. And if God is exactly life, in the death of Jesus the God-man enters death in order to bring life. He dies that they might live.

There is still more. We saw above a portion of one of Isaiah's *servant songs*. There are four total: Isaiah 42:1–9; 49:1–6; 50:4–11; and 52:13–53:12. Here is something of a shortened medley of them:

- Here is my servant, whom I uphold. . . . I have put my spirit upon him; he will bring forth justice to the nations. He will not cry or lift up his voice or make it heard in the street; a bruised reed he will not break, and a dimly burning wick he will not quench. . . . I have given you as a covenant to the people, a light to the nations, to open the eyes of the blind, to bring out the prisoners from the dungeon. . . . See, the former things have come to pass, and new things I now declare.

- The Lord called me before I was born, while I was in my mother's womb he named me. . . . And he said to me, "You are my servant, Israel, in whom I will be glorified. . . . And now the Lord says, who formed me in the womb to be his servant, to bring Jacob back to him, and that Israel might be gathered to him. . . . It is too light a thing that you should be my servant to raise up the tribes of Jacob and to restore the survivors of Israel; I will give you as a light to the nations, that my salvation may reach to the ends of the earth.

- The Lord God has opened my ear and I was not rebellious, I did not turn backward. I gave my back to those who struck me, and my cheeks to those who pulled out the beard: I did not hide my face from insult and spitting.

- Just as there were many who were astonished at him—so marred was his appearance, beyond human semblance, and his form beyond that of mortals. . . . He had no form or majesty that we should look at him, nothing in his appearance that we should desire him. He was despised and rejected by others; a man of suffering and acquainted with infirmity; and as one from whom others hide their faces he was despised, and we held him of no account. Surely he has borne our infirmities and carried our diseases; yet we accounted him stricken, struck down by God, and afflicted. But he was wounded for our transgressions, crushed for our iniquities; upon him was the punishment that made us whole, and by his bruises we are healed. . . . The righteous one, my servant, shall make many righteous.

As we saw, Jesus became a representative or symbol of Israel and indeed the human race. He is an icon of the human condition, and this allowed for his substitutionary atonement. Isaiah depicts the servant of God as a humble declarer of the truth, and because of this he was rejected. Yet still he persists in his saving work, even to his suffering and demise. These themes appear throughout Isaiah's servant songs. And in the New Testament, Jesus was arrested at night; he endured priestly reviling, spitting and slaps on his face, direct strikes to his body, and the condemnation of the Sanhedrin. Given over to Pilate, the Roman governor of Judea, he was flogged, crowned with thorns, and mocked. Then he was brutally made to carry his cross to the site of his crucifixion. Looking at Jesus now is to look at the ravages that sin inflicts on the human condition. Isaiah reflects that the servant of God was "marred beyond human semblance" such that they could not look at him but had to "hide their faces" as he "carried our diseases."

In the baptismal ritual of the Catholic Church, the one baptized renounces sin "and the glamor of evil." Evil does have some

kind of glamor or it would not attract us. There has to be some
kind of perceived good about it. The only way to escape tempta-
tion is to unveil it, to see its true ugliness. But we do not want
that. How often we have a public figure lie, get caught, and reply,
"I realize I wasn't as transparent as I could have been," or "We
could have been more forthcoming." We? How many times we
have seen someone selfishly cause great harm and reply, "Mistakes
were made, and for that I am sorry." Hardly a confession of sin
here. How many times have we ourselves expressed a version of
these? Humans are the masters of pretensions and euphemisms.
After Jesus's flogging and humiliation, Pilate brings him before the
people and demands, "Look at the man!" (Jn 19:5).[20] Look at the
ugliness. Look at the human condition that does not show itself to
be the image and likeness of God, but humanity disfigured. Jesus
is ugly because our sins are ugly. We now see another layer of St.
Paul's profound claim, "He became sin."

We can also see in Jesus the prophetic call to confront sin,
human disfigurement, and the death it causes. St. Óscar Romero,
the martyred Archbishop of San Salvador, framed it thus:

> Now we realize what sin is. We realize that offenses
> against God bring death to human beings. We realize
> that sin is truly death-dealing; not only does it bring
> the interior death of the one who commits it; it also
> produces real, objective death. We are thus reminded
> of a basic truth of our Christian faith. Sin caused the
> death of the Son of God; sin still continues to cause the
> death of the children of God.[21]

There is more, for Jesus is not only an icon of humanity, but
also of God. The Gospel of John begins with the great prologue
announcing Jesus, Word made flesh. The rest of the Gospel
works like a progressive unveiling of this truth. While we find
miraculous deeds in this gospel, none of them are called miracles. Rather, they are *signs*. At the wedding in Cana, Jesus trans-

forms water into wine and John notes, "Jesus did this, the first of his signs, in Cana of Galilee, and revealed his glory, and his disciples believed in him" (Jn 2:11). What was the sign about? Consider this representing the revelation and wisdom he brings from God, fulfilling the Old Testament promises of abundance of wine and blood in the messianic days.[22] In John, there are seven total signs, the last being Jesus raising Lazarus from the dead while proclaiming to Lazarus's sister Martha, "I am the resurrection and the life. Those who believe in me, even though they die, will live, and everyone who lives and believes in me will never die" (Jn 11:25–26).

This claim to be the resurrection and the life is just one of many seemingly superlative self-designations Jesus makes. "I am the light of the world," he insists. "Whoever follows me will never walk in darkness but will have the light of life" (Jn 8:12). Jesus also compares himself to the manna God offered to the Israelites as they escaped through the desert from slavery in Egypt. Jesus reminds his listeners,

> Very truly, I tell you, it was not Moses who gave you the bread from heaven, but it is my Father who gives you the true bread from heaven. For the bread of God is that which comes down from heaven and gives life to the world . . . . I am the bread of life. Whoever comes to me will never be hungry, and whoever believes in me will never be thirsty. (Jn 6:32–35)

If to see Jesus is to see God and to commune with Jesus is to commune with God, then with Eucharistic overtones, Jesus proclaims:

> I am the living bread that came down from heaven. Whoever eats of this bread will live forever; and the bread that I will give for the life of the world is my flesh. . . . Very truly, I tell you, unless you eat the flesh of the Son of

Man and drink his blood, you have no life in you. Those
who eat my flesh and drink my blood have eternal life,
and I will raise them up on the last day. (Jn 6:51–54)

Jesus is not only the bread from heaven but life-giving water:
"Let anyone who is thirsty come to me, and let the one who
believes in me drink. As the scripture has said, 'Out of the
believer's heart shall flow rivers of living water'" (Jn 7:37–38).
Perhaps the crescendo of Jesus's self-revelation comes by his
identifying with God's very name. In comparing himself to
Abraham who lived and died almost two millennia earlier, he
announces, "'Before Abraham was I Am.' So they picked up
stones to throw at him" (Jn 8:58–59). "I Am" is God's name.
When God called Moses to lead the Israelites from slavery,
Moses asked God,

> If I come to the Israelites and say to them, "the God
> of our ancestors has sent me to you," and they ask me,
> "What is his name?" what shall I say to them? God said
> to Moses, "I AM WHO I AM." He said further, "Thus
> you shall say to the Israelites, I AM has sent me to you."
> (Ex 3:13–14)

By proclaiming himself the I AM, Jesus was seen to be blasphem-
ing, and he probably would have been if it were not true.[23]

To encounter the grace of Jesus is to find in him the new wine
of the kingdom, bread from heaven, life-giving waters, light, and
life. These are metaphors, so we cannot take them literally. Still,
they are meant to be taken truly, deeply. Metaphors are not analogies. An analogy is a comparison between two things. One knows
the properties of one of the things but not the other. For someone
to say to me, "Mary runs like a deer" is to suggest the following: I don't know anything about Mary's running abilities, but I
do know that a deer is fast and agile. So I now understand that
Mary runs very fast and with deft agility. Metaphors are not these.

Analogies are about information. Metaphors are images that are access points for the imagination. They invite us to engage the subject of the metaphor through the lens of the metaphor itself. Consider St. Ignatius's prayer, the *Anima Christi*:

> *Soul of Christ, sanctify me.*
> *Body of Christ, save me.*
> *Blood of Christ, inebriate me.*
> *Water from the side of Christ, wash me.*
> *Passion of Christ, strengthen me.*
> *O good Jesus hear me.*
> *Within your wounds conceal me.*
> *Do not permit me to be parted from you.*
> *From the evil foe protect me.*
> *At the hour of my death call me.*
> *And bid me to come to you,*
> *To praise you with all your saints*
> *forever and ever.*[24]

For Ignatius, we are saved by Christ's body, inebriated by his blood, cleansed by the waters flowing from his crucified side, and safely hidden in his wounds—all metaphors, and all very real.

There is more. We saw in the synoptic gospels that Jesus was the suffering servant. In his suffering he entered fully into human alienation from God, thus destroying all alienation. In the cross's cruelty and abuse Jesus is an icon of the human condition ravaged by sin. In John's gospel, we have something else. It is precisely on the cross where Jesus reveals God, where he looks like God. Here, the cross is not the imagined and short-lived victory of evil, but Jesus's glory. "The hour has come for the Son of Man to be glorified" (Jn 12:23). In the synoptic gospels we find Jesus in the Garden of Gethsemane anticipating his passion and praying to God: "'Father, if you are willing, remove this cup from me; yet not my will but yours be done.' . . . In his anguish he prayed more earnestly, and his sweat became like great drops of blood falling down on the ground" (Lk 22:42–44).[25]

John's gospel understands it differently. Just before going to the garden to pray and to be arrested, Jesus "looked up to heaven and said, 'Father, the hour has come; glorify your Son so that the Son may glorify you'" (Jn 17:1). In the garden there is no angst, no tears, no beseeching the Father to take away the cup. Rather, when he is confronted by the soldiers who come to arrest him he asks them, "'Whom are you looking for?' They answered, 'Jesus of Nazareth.' Jesus replied, 'I am he.' . . . When Jesus said to them, 'I am he,' they stepped back and fell to the ground" (Jn 18:4–6). He does not fall; his enemies fall. Jesus's response, "I am he," is the same term he used to identify with God, (*egō eimi*), "I Am." Earlier, he declared, "When you have lifted up the Son of Man, then you will realize that I Am" (Jn 8:28). This term, *egō eimi*, can mean "I am he," but the association John makes with the cross and Jesus's glory suggests otherwise. It is in his passion that Jesus shows the Divine to those who have eyes to see. The cross itself is magnetic: "And I, when I am lifted up from the earth, I will draw all people to myself" (Jn 12:32). Being "lifted up" is not the resurrection or the ascension; it is the crucifixion. There one sees God.

What does it mean to see God in the dying of Jesus of Nazareth? It surely means that divine love is self-offering, self-emptying, a complete giving, and holding nothing back. In John, it is on the cross where Jesus gives God's gifts of life. To the beloved disciple, a character who symbolically represents the church and ideal discipleship, Jesus entrusts his mother (Jn 19:26–27).[26] Jesus gives the church Mary as its mother. It is also on the cross where Jesus "gives up his spirit" (19:30), with the double meaning of both literally dying and gifting the Holy Spirit.[27] And finally, postmortem, Jesus's side is pierced. "But when they came to Jesus and saw that he was already dead, they did not break his legs. Instead, one of the soldiers pierced his side with a spear, and at once blood and water came out" (Jn 19:34). Raymond Brown notes, "The scene of the piercing of the dead Jesus' side is particularly Johannine, fulfilling both 7:37–39 that from within Jesus would flow living water symbolic of the Spirit, and since the bones of the paschal lamb were not to be broken (1:29) that he was the Lamb of God."[28]

What Can We Learn?

One of the most important lessons we can learn from Christian wisdom is that God is a God of paradoxes, a God whose face no one can see but who is paradoxically revealed by the human face of Jesus. Discipleship too has to take on this kind of paradox. Authentic discipleship is no small order:

> The hour has come for the Son of Man to be glorified. Very truly, I tell you, unless a grain of wheat falls into the earth and dies, it remains just a single grain; but if it dies, it bears much fruit. Those who love their life lose it, and those who hate their life in this world will keep it for eternal life. Whoever serves me must follow me, and where I am, there will my servant be also. (Jn 12:23–26)

In *Soul Searching*, sociologist Christian Smith's book on American adolescent religiosity, he concluded that most Americans—young and old—know little about their religion and embrace a broad generic worldview he has labeled *moralistic-therapeutic-deism*. On this view, there is a God who wants people to be good and fair, and the goal of life is to be happy and adjusted. God is not much involved in our lives except perhaps when needed to solve a problem. And, finally, nice, good-hearted people go to heaven when they die. Here God is not very demanding of us nor very relevant to the human condition. I recall several years ago I was waiting for my step-daughter to finish dance class, so I could drive her home. Her best friend's mom was waiting too, and we got to talking. She knew I was Catholic and that I had been a priest some years back. She told me that she had a conflict with her pastor over a policy in her church's parochial school, where her daughter was attending. Thus, they quit the school *and* the church. I really did not need to know any of this. But she also assured me, "We're still Christians, we still believe." My response, after some hesitation, was that Christianity was more than just signing off on faith claims, but a real engagement with that faith, particularly in community. "Maybe," I offered, "you could look for another church." She certainly did not want to do that. But she was thrown enough to repeat the encounter with her daughter, who told my step-daughter, who told me. I believe I upset her moralistic-therapeutic-deism.

Erich Fromm, most known for his famous book, *The Art of Loving*, also wrote *The Pathology of Normalcy*. Here he describes the typical role of therapy as helping clients to be adjusted to the culture. His critique is that culture is itself pathological, and simply fitting in or being "adjusted," while better than being mentally ill, is hardly a real accomplishment for human flourishing. Christian wisdom challenges "normalcy" with the paradoxical language of death, of self-emptying. This kind of death-to-self is a death to the *false self*, by which we might discover, as St. Paul did, that "it is no longer I who live, but it is Christ who lives in me" (Gal 2:20).

This life of Christ within the disciple, one where the image and likeness of God shine, looks like Jesus's life, a man of sorrows and glory. This is the one who enters the depths of the human condition, in order to commune with those who suffer, and the one who reveals the face of God as self-giving love. St. Macarius, one of the most authoritative desert monastics, describes how life is experienced when one is *christified*:

> Those who have been deemed worthy to become children of God and to be reborn by the Holy Spirit from above, who have within themselves Christ,

illuminating and bringing them rest, are guided in many and various ways by the Spirit. . . . Sometimes they find themselves immersed in weeping and lamenting over the human race and in pouring out prayers on behalf of the whole human race of Adam. . . . At another times, they are so enflamed by the Spirit with such joy and love that, if it were possible, they would gather every human being into their very hearts, without distinguishing the bad and good. . . . Sometimes they are lifted up in "joy unspeakable."[29]

The great C. S. Lewis, in distinguishing the *pathology of normalcy* with *christifying discipleship*, describes the latter as a life of actual freedom where our most authentic self emerges as a real image and likeness of God. Again, it is a framing that seems paradoxical.

The more we get what we now call "ourselves" out of the way and let Him take us over, the more truly ourselves we become. . . . It is no good trying to *be myself* without Him. The more I resist Him and try to live on my own, the more I become dominated by my own heredity and upbringing and surroundings and natural desires. In fact what I so proudly call "Myself" becomes merely a meeting place for trains of events which I never started and cannot stop. What I call *my wishes* become merely the desires thrown up by my physical organism or pumped into me by other men's thoughts or even suggested to me by devils. . . . It is only when I turn to Christ, when I give myself up to His Personality, that I first begin to have a real personality myself. . . . Until you have given your self to Him you will not have a real self.[30]

Notes

1. Perhaps the best treatment of the issue is Paul Gavrilyuk and Sarah Coakley, eds., *The Spiritual Senses: Perceiving God in Western Christianity* (Cambridge: Cambridge University Press, 2012).

2. Mark Smith, *How Human Is God?* (Collegeville, MN: Liturgical Press, 2014), 88.

3. As cited in Andrew Louth, *The Origins of the Christian Mystical Tradition: From Plato to Denys*, 2nd ed. (Oxford: Oxford University Press, 2007), 126.

4. Kallistos Ware, *The Orthodox Way*, rev. ed. (Crestwood: NY: St. Vladimir's Seminary Press, 1979), 51.

5. Vladimir Lossky, *The Mystical Theology of the Eastern Church* (Crestwood, NY: St. Vladimir's Seminary Press, 1976), 118.

6. Roger Haight, *Jesus, Symbol of God* (Maryknoll, NY: Orbis Books, 1999), 92.

7. Dermot Lane, *Christ at the Centre: Selected Issues in Christology* (New York: Paulist Press, 1991), 11.

8. See also Mt 11:1 and Lk 9:1–6.

9. See Gen 15:7–20; Ex 24:1–8; and connections with Jesus: Lk 22:19–2; 1 Cor 11:23–26.

10. There is a list of faults for which atonement sacrifices may be offered in Lev 4:1–6:7 and Num 15:22–31.

11. See for these, Lev 6:17–23; 7:15.

12. See Lev 16.

13. See, for example, Acts 8:30–37.

14. Gerhard Lohfink, *No Irrelevant Jesus: On Jesus and the Church Today*, trans. Linda Maloney (Collegeville, MN: Liturgical Press, 2014), 101–2.

15. Gerhard Lohfink, *Jesus of Nazareth: What He Wanted, Who He Was*, trans. Linda Maloney (Collegeville, MN: Liturgical Press, 2012), 262.

16. Lohfink, *No Irrelevant Jesus*, 99.

17. Lohfink, *Jesus of Nazareth*, 265.

18. Mt 27:42–43; Mk 15:31–32; Lk 23:35.

19. Francis Watson, *The Fourfold Gospel: A Theological Reading of the New Testament Portraits of Jesus* (Grand Rapids, MI: Baker Academic, 2016), 153–54.

20. Some translations, such as the *NRSV*, have "Here is the man." But in the Greek text, Pilate is not merely bringing Jesus forward. The text reads: *idou ho anthrōpos*, with *idou* being the imperative: Look!

21. As cited in Gustavo Gutiérrez, *We Drink from Our Own Wells: The Spiritual Journey of a People*, trans. Matthew O'Connell (Maryknoll, NY: Orbis Books, 1972), 99.

22. Prov 9:4–5; Sir 24:20; Amos 9:13–14; Gen 49:10–11. See Raymond Brown, *An Introduction to the New Testament* (New York: Doubleday, 1997), 340.

23. Raymond Brown et al., eds., *The New Jerome Biblical Commentary* (Englewood Cliffs, NJ: Prentice Hall, 1990), 967.

24. "Anima Christi," United States Conference of Catholic Bishops, https://www.usccb.org/prayer-and-worship/prayers-and-devotions/prayers/anima-christi.

25. Matthew renders the moment like this: "Then he said to them, 'I am deeply grieved, even to death; remain here, and stay awake with me.' And going a little farther, he threw himself on the ground and prayed, 'My Father, if it is possible, let this cup pass from me; yet not what I want but what you want'" (26:38–39). Mark writes, "He took with him Peter and James and John, and began to be distressed and agitated. And he said to them, 'I am deeply grieved, even to death; remain here, and keep awake.' And going a little farther, he threw himself on the ground and prayed that, if it were possible, the hour might pass from him. He said, 'Abba, Father, for you all things are possible; remove this cup from me; yet, not what I want, but what you want'" (14:33–36).

26. Brown, *Introduction to the New Testament*, 369.

27. Ibid., 358; see also John Barton and John Muddiman, eds., *The Oxford Bible Commentary* (Oxford: Oxford University Press, 2001), 995.

28. Brown, *Introduction to the New Testament*, 358.

29. As cited in Vincent Pizzuto, *Contemplating Christ: The Gospels and the Interior Life* (Collegeville, MN: Liturgical Press, 2018), 132–33.

30. C. S. Lewis, *Mere Christianity* (New York: Harper and Collins, 1952; 2001), 223–25.

9

How Might I Consider Death and Beyond?

In the great Hindu epic, the Mahabharata, Yudhistira asks Krishna what the greatest mystery is. He replies with something that is both witty and insightful. He instructs Yudhistira that we all know that every person is going to die, but each person lives as though this would not happen to them personally. Of course, we all know that we are mortals, and as we age the trajectory of death becomes increasingly clear, at least conceptually. And yet we still cling to useless self-images, to egos we both defend and advance. We still seek so much of what is perishable. To counter this rather universal mental and spiritual habit, Western monastics for centuries repeated the following phrase throughout the day: *memento mori* ("remember that you die").

What exactly happens to us after we die? Christians might be surprised that the New Testament does not provide a clear answer. In First Thessalonians, St. Paul addresses a question from the community. They had expected the second coming to be imminent but wondered about those believers who had already died. What was their fate regarding the second coming? Paul answers,

> But we do not want you to be uninformed, brothers
> and sisters, about those who have died, so that you
> may not grieve as others do who have no hope. . . . For

> this we declare to you by the word of the Lord, that
> we who are alive, who are left until the coming of the
> Lord, will by no means precede those who have died.
> For the Lord himself, with a cry of command, with the
> archangel's call and with the sound of God's trumpet,
> will descend from heaven, and the dead in Christ will
> rise first. Then we who are alive, who are left, will be
> caught up in the clouds together with them to meet the
> Lord in the air; and so we will be with the Lord forever.
> (1 Thess 4:13–17)

Here Paul imagines that he will still be among the living when the
second coming arrives. But those dead and asleep in the ground
will awaken and rise, joining the living in being lifted into heaven.[1]
This contrasts with Paul's letter to the Philippians. In this letter,
Paul is deathly ill and in prison, and he anticipates that he may
not survive. No matter, he says, he would then be with Christ.
"My desire is to depart and be with Christ, for that is far better; but to remain in the flesh is more necessary for you" (Phil
1:23–24). This seems to correspond to the promise Jesus makes
to the "good thief" who repents on the cross next to his: "Then he
said, 'Jesus, remember me when you come into your kingdom.' He
replied, 'Truly I tell you, today you will be with me in Paradise'"
(Lk 23:42–43).

Which is it? Do we "rest in peace" (RIP) until the second
coming? Or do we immediately go to heaven? The Catholic
funeral rite plays it both ways. The funeral Mass ends by chanting a prayer for the angels to take the loved one to paradise, while
at the grave site the prayers suggest waiting in the grave until the
second coming. Odd indeed.

The question before us in this chapter is less about death itself
and more about the lives we lead and the spiritual practices we
pursue during life as they relate to our death and beyond our
death. Virtually every religion sees death as a crisis and a portal
to a different existence. Is there a waiting period and, if so, how

long and what happens during it? We will also consider what the final outcome looks like. This chapter looks at two very different perspectives on these themes. One is the Tibetan Buddhist understanding of the *bardo* or in-between period after death and before rebirth. The other represents something of a pan-religious understanding of union with God.

Buddhist Wisdom: *The Tibetan Book of the Dead*

Buddhism did not take hold in Tibet until the eighth century. Indigenous Tibetan religion was focused on the world of shamans, those spiritual adepts who could enter trance states and engage the worlds of the spirits, gods, and demons. Some of these shamans even went to India to learn esoteric practices from Hindu and Buddhist spiritual masters. The Buddhist practices included creating *mandalas*, which are visual symbols of a kind of perfect environment of Buddha-lands. Such mandalas could be physical two- or three-dimensional visuals or could be created in the meditative imagination of the practitioner. Shamans also learned various forms of *tantras*. A tantra is a spiritual technology, provided personally by a guru/lama, which quite literally creates versions of the realm of enlightenment. *Vajrayana* means "diamond way" or "way of the thunderbolt," and is so-named to highlight the power and brilliance that can be experienced by the use of tantras. For this reason, sometimes Vajrayana Buddhism is called "Tantric Buddhism."

The single most important development of Buddhism in Tibet was that of the work of Atisha (982–1054). He was trained at a university at Vikramashila, near Nalanda, which was the center of Buddhist scholarship in India. Atisha founded the first of the great Tibetan monastic orders and strove to integrate various forms of Buddhism he found in Tibet. He also provided a philosophical framework for melding tantric practices into standardized monastic practice. In his famous *Lamp on the Path to Awakening*, Atisha clearly argues for the superiority of Mahayana Buddhism over Theravada Buddhism, and this is important for the development of Vajrayana Buddhism. Recall that the historical Buddha did not seem to place much interest in anything but attaining Nirvana, and that after an enlightened person had died, she or he was essentially inaccessible. In contrast, Mahayana emphasized the interdependence of all things and that Buddhas and bodhisattvas were present and available to minister to all. One of the most important innovations in Mahayana is that everyone has within them a Buddha-nature, a core reality that permeates the universe and whose essence is infinite wisdom and infinite compassion.

Of course, the core Buddhist teachings were shared by all branches; the first and foremost teachings are the Four Noble Truths on suffering and liberation and the belief that our past karma dictates our future rebirths. Karma reflects not only our deeds and their effects, but also the kind of mental state that these deeds create in us. Maybe our rebirth or some event in our next life has to do with a long-ago deed whose *karma has ripened*, but for the most part our next life reflects the kind of person and the activities we pursued in our current life. In this sense, our next life is just part of the continuum we've been living in all along. This continuity is crucial to understanding what Tibetan Buddhists think happens during the transition from life to life.

Buddhists of all stripes broadly agree that there are six categories of possible realms of existence with thirty-one variants as well as the kinds of beings that inhabit them. The first and lowest would be hell-states. These are produced by actions driven primarily by hate. Next would be the realms of the *pretans*, who are sometimes called *hungry ghosts*. They are not really ghosts at all, but beings who are hungry and thirsty. Beings come to these realms due to a past karmic life of greed. In this existence they are understood as having giant stomachs and narrow throats—some miles long—with pinhole mouths. So they are forever hungry and can never satisfy their hunger. They simply cannot get enough food. For those particularly greedy in their past lives, pretans experience swallowing as painful burning and the food they find is virtually unpalatable. A third kind of rebirth is the animal realm. One is reborn as an animal if one lived with particular ignorance, folly, or stupidity. Human rebirth is the fourth realm. It is particularly valuable as humans have the consciousness to be aware and to act freely. And human life is a mixture of pleasure and pain, of happiness and despair. It is considered a rare and valuable birth as one is most likely to further one's spiritual practice on the long journey to enlightenment. An interesting fifth kind of rebirth is that of the *asuras* or titans. These beings exist in realms that are quite pleasant, but they are contentious beings and are constantly fighting each other. Typically, their own next rebirth will be a hell state. The sixth and highest rebirth is that of the heavenly states. These are *devas*, sometimes rendered gods as they live in a quasi-divine realm. The most complicated list of rebirths is that describing these possible divine states. This list proceeds from those who experience extraordinary pleasure and bliss analogous to a physical existence to those who experience deep meditative states of the bliss of, say, love, to those who experience a kind of formless state of deep meditative absorption. These devas live a long life—potentially eons—but they rarely spiritually develop. So taken by the very bliss of their existence, they do not seem to have the motivation for ongoing spiritual practice. None of these states is permanent, and once one has burned through good and/or bad karma from the past and concluded their life, they return to another life to start it all over again. One can also see that each rebirth, save human rebirth, is an exaggerated or heightened experience of their karmic past. To be greedy in a human life is to live a misdirected and empty life. To be a pretan is to suffer extraordinarily from this quality.

Most Tibetans are unnerved by death and what may come to them in the future. This actually comes from the earliest Buddhist traditions, where one has to go to Yama, the god of the underworld, to be judged by one's deeds. The Buddha declares, "You are now like a yellowed leaf. Even Yama's men have come for you. You stand at the mouth of death, with no provisions for the journey."[2] Many Buddhists see Yama as terrifying and something of a personified wild creature with fangs and claws.

The indigenous Tibetan religion, called *Bon*, focused on four primary activities. One was divination, that is, seeking the future through ritual and portents. Another was exorcism of evil spirits from persons or places. A third was coercing beings in the spirit world to either free them from harm or produce a boon for a person or community. And finally, the *Bon* tradition ushered the newly deceased into the afterlife, principally to make sure that this newly deceased person would not haunt those still living. This latter activity is the foundation for the famous *Tibetan Book of the Dead*, which Tibetans call *Bardo T'odrol*, though more formally it is *Bardo thos grol chen mo*, *The Great Book of Natural Liberation through Understanding in the Between*.

For Tibetans there are several *bardos* or "between" states, such as life itself (between birth and death) or sleep and waking. This particular "between" state is that of death and rebirth. By tradition, *The Tibetan Book of the Dead* was written by Padma Sambhava in the eighth or ninth century, but only came to prominence in the fourteenth century. It is thoroughly Buddhist, but it also relies on the pre-Buddhist belief that there is a forty-nine-day transition in dying and moving on. This between state is spiritually potent and brings with it possibilities of ensuring better rebirths or even attaining enlightenment itself. For most people, the death transition is so dominated by one's own karmic energy that one is just carried along through the process. For those who have diligently and skillfully practiced, however, parts of the process can even be slowed down and the dynamics of the process can be analyzed and engaged by the dead/dying person's subtle consciousness. Thus, both practice for death and the practices during the forty-nine day process can be extremely fruitful.

Before exploring the stages of death and the spiritual practices associated with them, it is worth our while to explore the Vajrayana understanding of the makeup of the human person.[3] With regard to the most material qualities, a person has a *gross body* and a *gross mind*. A gross body is made up of physical things that correspond to the elements of earth, water, fire, and air. The gross mind is associated with our ability to sense these elements as well as the mind's use of concepts and volitions, all of which are associated with the gross body.

There is then also a *subtle body*, which refers to our neural energies and pathways. This is not so much the hard matter of the pathways as it is the pattern structuring them into vessels of experience. They are strung together on a three-channel central axis that predominantly corresponds to a Hindu understanding of chakras, which are spiritual and physical energy centers from the genitals to the head (genitals, abdomen, heart, throat, brain, and top of the head). Without deep spiritual practice, we are unaware of these energies. Within this network of pathways are "drops" of awareness-transmitting substances, directed by subtle energies called winds. The *subtle mind* corresponds to these energies and consists of three interior states: luminance (subtle), radiance (more subtle), and immanence (the most subtle).

The *extremely subtle body* is a tiny energy pattern existing in the center of the heart chakra, and the *extremely subtle mind* can know this energy pattern. The extremely subtle mind corresponds to it as the intuition of clear light (transparency)—consider this Buddha-nature. Here the mind-body distinction is abandoned. To achieve conscious identification with this nonduality is tantamount to attaining Buddhahood. It is realizing one's true self.

There is far more complexity to all of this—one learns by training and experience multiple channels, the scheme of different subtle winds, their various main lines and subsidiary branches, and even their specific bases, ranges, colors, functions, and characters. Rather than getting bogged down in the details, however, what we ought to take from this at least is that becoming aware of each quality of the body and mind is how Vajrayana techniques help one gain control over life and death functions.

There are eight stages of death or the dissolution process, and these correspond to the gross, subtle, and extremely subtle bodies and minds discussed above:

- Stage 1: Our materiality starts to break down and becomes indistinct: earth dissolves into water;
- Stage 2: Sensations disappear, the ear sense begins to fail: water dissolves into fire;
- Stage 3: The energy of desire fades and notions dim: fire dissolves into air;
- Stage 4: Breathing stops and the body sense utterly fades: wind dissolves into consciousness [from a Western point of view, now one is clinically dead];
- Stage 5: Here the gross consciousness with its instinct patterns dissolves and one's awareness descends from the central channel of the chakras to the heart chakra. One inwardly perceives within the mind-space a vast sky of white moonlight: the gross consciousness dissolves into luminance;
- Stage 6: The awareness "drop" rises from the genital chakra toward the heart chakra and one perceives a sky full of orange sunlight: luminance dissolves to radiance;
- Stage 7: The awareness "drops" of luminance and radiance meet at the heart chakra and one perceives the sky full of bright *dark-light*: radiance dissolves into immanence;
- Stage 8: One gains an unaccustomed kind of non-dual consciousness, the heart chakra unravels, and our extremely subtle consciousness flies out of its location: immanence dissolves into translucency. This, in Vajrayana Buddhism, is the real moment of death, presumed to have taken forty-nine days to accomplish.

How then is rebirth attained? One's extremely subtle body and mind will then start the process over again, but this time in reverse, literally creating a new being that emerges from extremely subtle body and mind, then regathering the energies and dynamics of the subtle body and mind, and finally reestablishing oneself into the gross body and mind. Voilà, a new rebirth somewhere in the thirty-one possible rebirth scenarios within the six realms. Robert Thurman, perhaps the West's foremost scholar in Vajrayana, notes,

> The whole science and art of navigating the between-state bears down on this moment, assisting a person to use the transition between habitual lives to enter this extremely subtle awareness that is naturally at one with blissful freedom, total intelligence, boundless sensitivity—that is, perfect enlightenment. . . . Most people traverse these dissolutions without recognizing what is happening to them, not being able to rest in the clear light, not realizing their essential freedom, happiness, and natural and joyous boundless participation in the lives of all beings. They will mentally shoot through the void's clear light and rise back up into gross embodiment. . . . They will faint again at immanence, then rise through dark-light, radiance, sunlight, and luminance moonlight into instinctually dominated consciousness, then reassociate themselves with wind, fire, water, and earth.[4]

What is going on is that on some level of consciousness, we who are unprepared for what we experience in this process are alarmed by it or simply do not recognize that this mysterious reality emerging from the heart chakra is actually our deepest identity, Buddha-nature itself. We want our bodies back—we think we need them, we think we *are* them. We want our personalities back for the same reason. Instead of this being an experience of liberation, it is an experience of terror, and we cling to the only reality we understand. *The Tibetan Book of the Dead* is a manual of instruction that a lama or friend gives to one who is dead/dying, and explains what is going on and how one ought to proceed at each stage. But for the dead/dying person who is not well trained, these instructions would be very hard to appreciate. As Thurman observes, "[O]ne's egocentric instinctual drives and the fear and terror during this high crisis makes liberation difficult."[5] Here is an example of what a lama would announce to a dead/dying person on the seventh day, although it would actually be much, much longer than what I provide here:

> Hey, noble one! Listen without wavering! On the seventh day a five-colored, rainbow-striped light will dawn to purify your instincts by immersion in reality. At that time . . . Padmanarteshvara [Amitabha Buddha] will arise, his body lustrous with the five colors, his consort the Red Angel wound round his body, performing the dance of chopper and blood-filled skull bowl, striking the gazing posture toward the sky. . . . Hey, noble one! Spontaneously purifying instincts in reality, the five-colored wisdom light striped like colored threads wound together dazzles . . . it blinds your eyes and penetrates into your heart center. At the same time the soft green light of the animal realm dawns together with the wisdom light. . . . Therefore, don't be afraid of that energetic, piercing, five-colored light! Don't be terrified! Recognize it as wisdom! . . . The sound is fierce, reverberating, rumbling, stirring, like fierce mantras of intense sound. Don't fear it! Don't flee it! Don't be terrified of it! Recognize it as the exercise of your own awareness, your own perception.[6]

Tibetan Buddhists have practices that assist one in exactly preparing for this momentous experience. There are ordinary preparations and extraordinary preparations. Some of the ordinary preparations are associated with being a good Buddhist monk, such as learning the sutras, living ethically, particularly in

terms of generosity and compassion, and learning the philosophical details of Buddhist thought: for example, emptiness, dependent
origination, and Buddha-nature. They also include the Buddhist
meditations of mindfulness and concentration that we saw in
chapter 3. In most copies of *The Tibetan Book of the Dead* there
is also a collection of "Root Verses of the Six Betweens." One
verse, intended to encourage serious spiritual practice throughout
one's life, begins this way:

> *Hey! Now when the life between dawns upon me,*
> *I will abandon laziness, as life has no more time,*
> *Unwavering, enter the path of learning, thinking,*
> *   and meditating,*
> *And taking perceptions and mind as path,*
> *I will realize the Three Bodies of enlightenment!*
> *This once that I have obtained the human body*
> *Is not the time to stay on the path of distractions.*[7]

The extraordinary preparations are almost completely related
to one's relationship with her or his lama and various meditations.
For example, the trainee could visualize an enormous mandala
of assembled Buddhas, bodhisattvas, and lamas of one's lineage.
Once fully realized in the trainee's mind, the trainee prostrates
to them 100,000 times. Or one could receive from one's lama
a patron deity or bodhisattva and recite the deity's 100-syllable
mantra 100,000 times. The purpose of the former is to integrate
into one's consciousness that the world of Buddhahood is really
one's own truth; the purpose of the latter is to self-identify with
the patron deity and in a sense embody that deity, becoming the
truth of awakening. There are actually four stages of training:
(1) Preliminary Stage of Teaching; (2) Lama Yoga Stage, which
includes complete devotion to one's lama as an instantiation of
Buddhahood and receiving advanced practices suited for the specific trainee; (3) Creation Stage, which involves learning to create mandalas of Buddha-worlds; and (4) Perfection Stage, which
includes yoga tantras that empower the trainee to channel the

various subtle and extremely subtle parts of one's body and mind. And each of these stages has substages and multiple permutations.

The point of these training stages is to gain mastery over every part of one's body and mind to the subtlest level. This itself could condition enlightenment or Nirvana here in one's life. Short of that, it gives the aspirant the tools to understand what is happening at death and to negotiate what one experiences so as to be fully liberated in the very natural process of dying.

What Can We Learn?

One of the most important insights we can take away from Buddhist wisdom is that the universe may be far more complex than we think. When the Buddhist aspirant creates a mandala of a Buddha-land, this is believed to correspond to what actually exists in the cosmos. Or when one practices tantric meditation in order to instantiate the presence and power of a deity such as a bodhisattva, this presence and power is actually experienced within one. So these practices are not merely intense uses of the imagination. Rather, they correspond to the actual state of affairs in the cosmos. What's out there? It would be easy to dismiss these ideas if they do not correspond to our current understandings; it just seems a bit bizarre. But how do we know our own assumptions are either accurate or complete? Jewish Kabbalah has a cosmos that includes God, sefirot, supernal beings, seraphim, angels, and humans. Islam has God, angels, Jinn, and humans. American Sioux religion has God, cosmic powers, cosmic presentations (of living things), spirits of the dead, humans, animals, and plants. Hindus have God (Brahman), brahmas, high gods, devas, dangerous beings, humans, animals, and beings in hell states.

I ask my students to reflect on these multiple versions. The majority of my students are Christian, and they widely believe that the spiritual universe only contains God, angels (good and bad), and humans (dead and alive). These are the only beings referenced in the Bible, as far as they know. I ask them, "How do you know it is not more complicated?" In fact, the Western tradition of Christianity has included more beings: seraphim, cherubim, thrones, dominions, principalities, powers, virtues, archangels, and angels. These categories were taken from Colossians 1:16; 2:8–10 and Ephesians 1:21; 3:10; 6:12. These are not versions or ranks of angels, but different specific types of beings. They became ranks of angels only later in the medieval period. Has our imagination become too small?

Another insight we can take away is that the process of dying and the transition from one's life to what is beyond could be far more complex than we think. We only register life when there is breath and activity in the brain, but according to Vajrayana Buddhism, this is only the most exterior part of the human (the gross body and mind). Could there be more? And, if so, how ought that *more* be understood? I also ask my students if they believe in ghosts, and the majority of them say they do, despite the fact that there is no theological room for them in traditional Jewish, Christian, or Islamic traditions. Could it be that these beings are humans who did not transition well?

Perhaps the most important insight in Tibetan wisdom is the power of our habits. The bardo offers an opportunity for great spiritual advancement between lives and even the possibility for enlightenment. But, as we saw, most do not—because they cannot—take advantage of this opportunity. The power of our habits and the weight of our clinging to the gross self makes us not understand the process as it is happening. The very lights that represent subtle energies are experienced as overwhelming and even horrifying. And so for the most part our next rebirth corresponds to who we are in this life. What you get is who you are. What you get is what you've become. This makes deep spiritual practice in this life urgent, as our next existence will correspond to the one we have. Are we practicing love, generosity, and compassion? Are we *becoming* loving, generous, and compassionate deep down? Are we tightening our grip on the delusions of an ego, or are we stripping ourselves of that false self?

Finally, we might find comfort in the possibilities of the bardo. For the most part, our karmic lives determine our next rebirth, and we get what we deserve. But the universe is structured for more; for freedom, for liberation. What we see in the bardo, the between state, is that our deepest, truest self reveals its full spiritual nature. One does not have to believe that at the core we are Buddha-nature to see that the cosmos—God if you will—desires our liberation and desires our discovery that we are indeed utterly precious at the center. If only we lived that truth day to day.

The Endgame: A Pan-Religious Consideration

In chapter 2 we wrestled with the question "Who am I?" and addressed both Islamic and Theravada Buddhist understandings of this very question. It is a huge question, for sure, and it relates to two others quite directly. The first is, who or what is the Divine? Knowing who we are and what the Divine is gives us some direction on how to relate to the Divine and what we can expect of the Divine. The second question is, given answers to the first two questions, what is the divinely intended fulfillment of human life? What is the *telos* or completion? What is the endgame?

We should not be surprised that different religions come up with different answers to all three questions. We have already seen that Hinduism has versions of identification between the self (atman) and the Divine (Brahman). In this chapter, we have also seen that the core reality of ourselves is Buddha-nature. And realizing this is exactly enlightenment, the experience of Nirvana. Hinduism and Buddhism on this score are really quite different, and both differ from the emphasis on our being creatures, as we see in Judaism, Christianity, and Islam. All these three Western traditions believe that humans have intrinsic value and profound spiritual potentiality, but that humans are not God. The Sioux religion sees human existence as potentially very *wakan* (holy), but we are not *Wakan Tanka* (God). Still, I ask you to consider the following medley of witnesses from mystical traditions in several religions. These are taken either from canonical texts or the writing of exemplars, those spiritual proficients who have taken their tradition to the limit.

- **Plotinus** (204–270, Greek philosopher): "Many times it has happened: lifted out of the body into myself; becoming external to all other things and self-encentered; beholding a marvelous beauty . . . acquiring identity with the divine."[8]
- **Abraham Abulafia** (1240–1292, Jewish): "[The soul] will be united with it [God] after many hard, strong and mighty exercises, until the particular and personal prophetic [faculty] will become universal, permanent and everlasting, similar to the essence of its cause, and he and He will become one unity."[9]
- **Adin Steinsaltz** (1937–2020, Jewish): "At the highest level of holiness are those persons who have achieved a state in which their whole personalities and all of their actions are joined to the divine holiness. Of these persons it is said that they have become a 'chariot' for the *Shekhinah* [Divine Manifestation] . . . and they will constitute a part of the throne of glory itself."[10]
- **Bernard of Clairvaux** (1090–1153, Christian): "In the kiss of his mouth we receive a full infusion of joys, a revelation of secrets, a wonderful and inseparable mingling of the light from above and the mind on which it is shed, which, when it is jointed with God is one spirit with him."[11]
- **John of the Cross** (1542–1591, Christian): "Having been made one with God, the soul is somehow God through participation. . . . For the will of the two is one will, and thus, God's operation and the soul's are one. . . . A reciprocal love is thus actually formed between God and the soul, like the marriage union and surrender, in which

the goods of both (the divine essence that each possesses freely by reason of the voluntary surrender between them) are possessed by both together."[12]

- **Abu Yazid al-Bistami** (804–874; Islamic): "I looked at my Lord with the eye of eternity, after that he turned me away from all that was not he, and had illumined me with his light; and he showed me marvels from his secret being, and he showed me his *He-ness*. And through his *He-ness* I looked on my *I-ness*, and it vanished away. . . . And he transmuted me from my *I-ness* into his *He-ness*, and caused me to cease from my self-hood in his *He-ness*."[13]

- **Jalal ad-Din Rumi** (1207–1273, Islamic): "The prayer of the holy one is different from other prayers. He has so completely dissolved his ego—*nothinged* himself—that what he says is like God talking to God. . . . His spirit grows wings, and lifts. His ego falls like a battered wall. He unites with God, alive, but emptied of identity."[14]

- **Prasna Upanishad** (Hindu): "He who knows, O my beloved, that Eternal Spirit wherein consciousness and the senses, the powers of life and the elements find final peace, knows the All and has gone into the All."[15]

- **Svetasvarata Upanishad** (Hindu): "When a man knows God, he is free: his sorrows have an end, and birth and death are no more. When in inner union he is beyond the world of the body, then the third world, the world of the Spirit, is found, where the power of the All is, and man has all: for he is one with the ONE."[16]

- **Master Bukko Kokushi** (1226–1286, Buddhist): [Bukko describes the fruition of meditating on the Zen Koan *Mu* for six years.]: "'Mu' became so inseparably attached to me that I could not get away from it even while asleep. This whole universe seemed to be nothing but 'Mu' itself. . . . All of a sudden the sound of striking the board in front of the head monk's room reached my ear, which at once revealed to me the *original man* in full. . . . I laughed loudly, 'Oh, how great is the Dharmakaya! [Ultimate Truth]. . . . My eyes, my mind, are they not Dharmakaya itself? . . . Today even in every pore of my skin there lie all the Buddha-lands in the ten quarters.'"[17]

- **Tathagatagarbha Sutra** (third century, Buddhist): "All living beings . . . have the Buddha's wisdom, Buddha's eye, Buddha's body sitting firmly in the form of meditation. . . . They are possessed of the Matrix of the Tathagata [Buddha], endowed with virtues, always pure. . . . Having thus observed, the Buddha preached the doctrine in order to remove the defilements and manifest the Buddha-nature within all living beings."[18]

- **Yan Hui** (521–481 BCE, Confucian/Daoist): "I leave behind my body, perception and knowledge. Detached from both material form and mind, I become one with that which penetrates all things."[19]

- **Zhang Zai** (1020–1077, Confucian/Daoist): "Now I am grasping its [life's] beginning and can go beyond the maker's wheel. Through solitary vastness I ascend to the Great Silence, meeting only the clear and the perfected. Pure and shining I encompass primordial harmony, joined with pure energy in mutual relation."[20]

As we have seen throughout this book, the first principles, philosophical commitments, anthropologies, and so on, from these religions are often very different from one another, and in some cases contradicting. Further, we can already see that these witnesses are not exactly the same. Some seem to claim an identity with Absolute Reality, while others are much more relational. And we already saw in chapter 5 that Daoism does not seem to have a Divine to reference. Indeed, whenever such comparative texts are lined up as I have just done above, I can hear critics balking: "You must respect the uniqueness of each religion," or "You are cherry-picking texts to make a strained point."

Anticipating such objections, I would like to say, "Well, yes and no." Religions are certainly very different from one another, and it is a problem to collapse them together under the heading *mysticism*. It is also the case that John of the Cross did not think he was practicing mysticism but Christianity. And all his energies were spent engaging the sixteenth-century monastic path of the Christian faith. So too, Bistami, who was not practicing mysticism but Islam of the Sufi variety. The unity they appear to claim is not exactly the Advaita Vedanta seemingly claimed in the *Chandogya Upanishad*, and Buddha-nature ought not to be exactly equated with God. I also admit that I am choosing citations that show a kind of alignment. But this is no foul. The citations that I have chosen represent both their authors and the traditions in which they are revered. Further, it is true that some of these see God as personal, while others as impersonal. It is also true that some describe communing with or coming near to Absolute Reality, while others seem to fuse or identify with Absolute Reality. *What is remarkable is that, given their respective differences in theology, philosophy, culture, and time, they are so strikingly similar.* In each, the spiritually adept so unites with the Divine that distinctions begin to blur. Their previous self-identification gets lost. They may retain a "conventional" self, one that negotiates society, has friendships, and so on. But they no longer identify their deepest, truest, core self with that personality or its roles. Rather, their identity seems to be lost in divine communion. God becomes their deepest identity.

What Can We Learn?

The human *telos* or end, the goal to achieve in this life or the next is not simply some kind of paradise that is extremely blissful. It is God. We attain God. The Divine Reality, in some clear but mysterious sense, is who we are or who we will become by participation. One of my favorite authors is the twentieth-century monk and spiritual writer Thomas Merton. While living a strict Trappist life in a monastery in Louisville, Kentucky, he corresponded with philosophers, writers, poets, and religious leaders throughout the world. He also had a great interest in the writings of other religious traditions. Merton wrote some sixty books, many of them short. The following selections come from two of his more famous books written later in his life, *New Seeds of Contemplation* and *Conjectures of a Guilty Bystander*. I want to end this chapter with parts of them, for they represent his vision of the reality we are discussing here.

Merton on the Soul's Identity

The secret of my full identity is hidden in him. . . . To say that I am made in the image of God is to say that love is the reason for my existence, for God is love. Love is my true identity. Selflessness is my true self. Love is my true character, Love is my name. . . . [One] lives in emptiness and freedom, as if he had no longer a limited and exclusive *self* that distinguished him from God and other persons. . . . What happens is that the separate identity that is *you* apparently disappears and nothing seems to be left but a pure freedom indistinguishable from the infinite Freedom, love identified with Love. . . . He is the *I* who acts there. He is the one Who loves and knows and rejoices.[21]

Merton on the Center of the Soul

At the center of our being is a point of nothingness which is untouched by sin and by illusion. This is a point of pure truth, a point or spark which belongs entirely to God, which is never at our disposal, from which God disposes of our lives. It is inaccessible to the fantasies of our mind or the brutalities of our will.

This little point of nothingness and of absolute poverty is the pure glory of God in us. It is, so to speak, His name written in us. As our poverty, as our indigence, as our dependence, as our son-ship, it is like a pure diamond blazing with the invisible light of heaven. It is in everybody. And if we could see it we would see these billions of points of light coming together in the face and blaze of a sun that would make all the darkness and cruelty of life vanish completely. I have no program for this seeing; it is only given. But the Gate of Heaven is everywhere.[22]

Notes

1. In 1 Cor 15:8, Paul refers to the faithful dead as "asleep in Christ."

2. Dhammapada, #235.

3. I am relying on Robert Thurman's description here. See Robert Thurman, *The Tibetan Book of the Dead: Liberation through Understanding in the Between* (New York: Bantam, 1994), 35–41.

4. Ibid., 44–45.

5. Ibid., 44.

6. Ibid., 145–46.

7. Ibid., 115.

8. Plotinus, *The Enneads* [IV.8.1], trans. Stephen MacKenna (New York: Penguin, 1991).

9. Cited in Moshe Idel and Bernard McGinn, *Mystical Union in Judaism, Christianity, and Islam: An Ecumenical Dialogue* (New York: Contiuum, 1996), 30.

10. Adin Steinsaltz, *The Thirteen Petalled Rose: A Discourse on the Essence of Jewish Existence and Belief*, rev. ed., trans. Yehuda Hanegbi (New York: Basic Books, 2006), 62.

11. Bernard of Clairvaux, Sermon 2, in *Bernard of Clairvaux: Selected Works*, trans. G. S. Evans (Mahwah, NJ: Paulist Press, 1987).

12. John of the Cross, *Dark Night*, II.13.11, in *The Collected Works of John of the Cross*, rev. ed., trans. Kieran Kavanaugh and Otilio Rodriguez (Washington, DC: ICS Publications, 1991).

13. Cited in R. C. Zaehner, *Hindu and Muslim Mysticism* (Oxford: Oneworld, 1960), 198–99.

14. Jalal al-Din Rumi, *The Essential Rumi*, trans. Coleman Banks (New York: HarperSanFrancisco, 1995), 163.

15. Prashna Upanishad IV.11.

16. Svetasvatara Upanishad I.11.

17. Cited in D. T. Suzuki, *Essays in Zen Buddhism* (London: Rider, 1973), 254–55.

18. Tathagatagarbha Sutra, cited in Peter Feldmeier, *Experiments in Buddhist-Christian Encounter* (Maryknoll, NY: Orbis Books, 2019), 95.

19. Zhuangzi, *The Zhuangzi*, trans. and intro. Hyum Hochsmann and Yang Guorong (New York: Pearson Longman, 2007), 123.

20. Zhang Zai, *Ximing*, trans. Wing-tsit Chan, *A Source Book in Chinese Philosophy* (Princeton, NJ: Princeton University Press, 1963), 497–98.

21. Thomas Merton, *New Seeds of Contemplation* (New York: New Directions, 1961), 33, 60, 210, 283, 286–87.

22. Thomas Merton, *Conjectures of a Guilty Bystander* (New York: Image Books, 1968), 158.

10

Considering Everything

Considering Religions

Throughout this book, I've tended to speak about God as the Divine. Implicitly, I have been writing as though all of the religions we have seen are addressing the same referent, although often differently imagined. Is this legitimate? In some sense no, since we have seen, for example, that Daoism does not exactly have a functional equivalent to God, and that to equate Mahayana Buddhist beliefs with theistic beliefs is very complicated. Some have imagined that the Buddhist equivalent to the Divine is Buddha-nature, this central core reality at the heart of all sentient beings that is absolute compassion and absolute wisdom. But others have suggested it is *dharmakaya*, the "truth-body," that is really the comparative notion.[1] Both are good candidates, and neither is an excellent candidate. You have to swallow a lot of philosophical differences to consider either of them as equivalent to God. Theravada Buddhism is even more problematic. And we have not even begun to look at, say, Japanese Shinto, which has a divine creator couple (*Izanami* and *Izanagi*), but they do not have the supremacy of God proper.

And yet I think my reference to "God" has been legitimate overall. *If* God does exist, and it should be obvious that this is a first principle of this book, and *if* God represents Absolute Reality (another guiding assumption), *then* religions in the main are referring to the same thing. In this sense, whether we call God Brahman, Wakan-Tanka, Trinity, Yahweh, and so on, we are all talking about the same referent, Ultimate Reality. Surely, all these religions think about God both differently and similarly, and they cannot all be correct in that some of their respective claims contradict those of others. On the other hand, why would we imagine that this matters so much that it trumps all other considerations? In fact, it would be strikingly odd if all religions thought about the Divine in the same way. Religions look like the specific cultures, histories, and spiritual practices that have developed uniquely. Ancient India is not ancient Greece, and these are not like ancient South America, and none of them cleanly represent their modern correlates. It would be an impossible expectation that their language, experience, and philosophical commitments should align.

There is a well-known Hindu parable that speaks to the problem of many religions. It goes like this: Suppose there are six blind men who have never heard of an elephant, and they are led to one and allowed to feel the animal. Feeling the trunk, one concludes it is like a large snake. Feeling the tail, another concludes it is like a large feather duster. Feeling the side, another concludes it is like a curved wall. Feeling a leg, yet another concludes it is like a tree trunk. Feeling an ear, another experiences it like a basket. And the final blind man feels the tusk and concludes it is like a plow. In coming to these conclusions, we would say that with modest accuracy, they all spoke the truth about their experience; what they said was right. The problem, as the parable has us consider, is when they extrapolate their limited experience to the whole of the elephant.

Obviously, in this parable the elephant is God, and the six blind men represent different religious traditions. Each religion experiences God quite directly and profoundly. Each then provides access to God according to its experience. Where they may go awry is when they overshoot their experience as though they can speak about all of God. Added to this problem is the widely held claim that God transcends human concepts. So any of their claims can only approach something of the Divine by analogy anyway.

I share this parable with my world religion students on the first day of class. For many, it makes all the sense in the world. It explains religious plurality. It explains why there are similarities in various religions as well as why there would be real differences. It also explains why religions speak with such authority, as they really are in intimate contact with the Divine. We could go further in affirming the parable. Different spiritual practices are going to yield different religious experiences, that is, they would access the Divine differently. This explains why very different spiritual practices exist between religions as well as within a given religion. In Christianity, for example, charismatic prayer (speaking in tongues) would allow one to experience God very differently than monastic contemplative prayer would. This was probably the original purpose of the Hindu parable: to show how different spiritual paths in Hinduism might access the same God, but in different ways.

Some of my most alert students, however, see a looming problem. If everyone is "right," then everyone is "wrong." They are right in that their religion really does correspond to something of the Divine. But they are wrong in saying that what they believe is universally true or that their truth claims speak for the entirety of the Divine. Interestingly, in the Buddhist canon, the Buddha himself referred to this parable.[2] In doing so, he was criticizing his fellow religionists. They were, for him, blind guides for the blind. Nirvana, he taught, is the absolute goal, and the Eightfold Path is the *only* way to attain it. Supporters of the parable would have to say that the Christian belief in the Trinity is just one among other ways to talk about God who, *as God*, is ineffable anyway. In this view, a Christian who affirms the parable would not exactly say that Jesus is the universal Lord, but rather that the Lordship of Jesus is one of many skillful means of talking about salvation. Did Jesus die for the sins of the world? Here, one would have to hedge; that is *one* way of talking about the nature of salvation among so many others.

There is yet another problem in the parable. Although an elephant has "parts" that can be experienced variously, the Divine is rather universally believed to be purely singular and without parts. Presuming this is true, there can be no good parallel to a blind man touching a tusk and another a leg. All the differences would be caused by the different kinds of "touching" that singular and pure Divine essence. Recognizing this, sharing religious insights from one religion to another, as we have done in this book, would not be some version of "this is what the divine tusk is like, now inform me what the divine leg is like." Rather, it would have to be some version of "when we practice our faith and consider the Divine to be like X, we experience Y, now inform me what you experience when you consider the Divine to be like A and experience B."

Several times in this book I have mentioned something about postmodern thought. The principal point in postmodern thinking is that to understand anything one has to approach it with a given lens of interpretation. There is no blank slate upon which one can receive information "objectively." Rather, our understanding and experience are viewed through our particular lens. There are data we ignore or are not even aware of, because these data are not interesting to the lens. And there are data we pay attention to. Further, we only pay attention to that data according to the lens we see with. This makes universal claims very difficult to sustain, since it would be tantamount to imagining that one has been able to rise above every specific way of thinking and take on some kind of meta-perspective. No one can do this; language and conceptuality itself forbid it. Words and concepts are only meaningful in their own *field* of meaning.

What ought we do with such a challenge? The first thing we might consider is whether we ought to have confidence that what we think is ever universally true, particularly religiously true. How do you know (or have confidence) that your own religion is "right"? We ought not to throw up our hands and claim something like, "That's why they call it *faith*; you just have to believe." Some religious claims are simply not trustworthy. In the 1990s, Marshall Applewhite and Bonnie Nettles started a religious community called Heaven's Gate. They taught that souls were imprisoned in human bodies and that these souls had an opportunity to be released and transformed. When the Hale-Bopp comet approached the Earth, Applewhite assured believers that Nettles, who had died earlier, was on an alien spacecraft trailing behind the comet's tail. If they all committed suicide on March 26, 1997, when the comet was closest, they would be beamed up to the spaceship and carried to TELAH, a form of existence higher than the human one. All thirty-nine members happily took their lives believing such a claim. They clearly had "faith" and proved it dramatically. But I trust the reader would not think these beliefs are even remotely true. Warranted confidence in one's religious life can come from many places. A religion can have a philosophically convincing perspective, making it right by reason. One might also have dramatic religious experiences in a given religion or find real interior transformation. A religious tradition might also carry a long lineage of respectable adherents who attest to its authenticity. These represent solid ground for confidence. We have not exactly solved our problem though. Many persons have experienced all three of these qualities in different religions.

I have solved the problem for myself in the following way. I am a Christian, and I believe that Jesus Christ is both divine and human. In some sense, God has entered the created world personally. As creatures (and not the Creator), we can only live in time, in history. So, for God to actualize salvation in an absolute way *for us* it seems quite reasonable for there to be a salvation event that conditions its possibility of absolute salvation in time, in history. It is unreasonable to me for this to happen outside of time and outside of the human condition. We saw in the last chapter that many venerable religious traditions witness to an extraordinary possibility of union with the Divine. Jesus Christ instantiates that universal truth in his very being. So I am a Christian. I have also had enough dramatic religious experiences in the Christian tradition to add justification to my confidence. Of course, if I were a Muslim I might say, "Christianity is a philosophical nightmare, and it's impossible to imagine it to be true."

I have not completely solved the problem, however. I also believe that the insights of postmodernity are fundamentally right. We have no access to some pure form of knowledge that is free from the interpretive lens we bring to our experience. This keeps me humble and willing to learn from other ways of thinking, worshipping, and being. At the very least, what I can learn is how to stretch my small mind and broaden my imagination that I might be a more interesting Christian. One fellow Christian, Father Robert Kennedy, spent years devoted to Zen practice along with his Christian practices. Insightfully, he writes:

> I never have thought of myself as anything but a Catholic and I certainly never have thought of myself as a Buddhist. . . . What I looked for in Zen was not a new faith, but a new way of being Catholic. . . . Yamada Roshi [his Zen teacher] told me several times that he did not want to make me a Buddhist but rather he wanted to empty me in imitation of "Christ your Lord" who emptied himself, poured himself out, and clung to nothing. Whenever Yamada Roshi instructed me in this way, I thought that this Buddhist might make a Christian of me yet![3]

There is another way for us to ensure we do not fall into the metaphysical mush of relativism: religious ways can also be evaluated. Dale Cannon, in his *Six Ways of Being Religious*, describes how one might responsibly assess religious authenticity.[4] Cannon's six ways are: Right Action; Reasoned Inquiry; Sacred Rite; Devotion; Shamanic Mediation; and Mystic Quest. To each of these categories he suggests three different criteria for assessment. They are: competency, balance, and selflessness. So, for example, right action is competent when it lives out its ideals in decisive and courageous ways and is realistic with obstacles. It is incompetent when it is frenetic, shows little inward reflection, is ignorant of what is right, or is unaware of the shortcomings of the status quo. It is balanced when it is passionately committed without being utopian and when it is open to reassessment. It loses balance with utopian idealism, when it cannot distinguish between its own agenda and the divine ideal, or when it is legalistically obsessed with the letter rather than the spirit of obligation. It is selfless when the welfare of all is considered and when it is not defensive but open to criticism. It is egoistic when it is morally hypocritical or pretentious, when it nurses resentments, or when the welfare it seeks is at the expense of others. Applying these three criteria to Cannon's six categories can help one see the strengths and shortcomings of a given religious tradition as well as one's own religious community, and even the state of one's own soul. Cannon also shows that while all religions have each of the six ways of being religious (even versions of shamanism), religions tend to emphasize some of the ways over others. And this would be true for a local community and ourselves personally. This ought not to be a fatal problem, but it ought to lead to critical assessment as to whether some of these ways are highly developed while other ways are ignored or suffer spiritual atrophy.

Considering Spiritual Maturity

Holiness is an astoundingly problematic term. Who gets to decide what exactly constitutes holiness and by what criteria? Further, as I observed about Zen enlightenment in chapter 6, high holiness exists in a culture and with a particular vision. Specific training in that culture seeks a specific outcome, not a universal one. I also noted that because the human mind is complex, one can have parts of one's personality or soul highly transformed, while other parts stay immature. With all this in mind, I think it wise to consider what spiritual maturity looks like. After thirty years of deeply studying the spiritualities of many religions, I have come up with thirteen qualities that seem to me rather universal for spiritual maturity. These do not necessarily imply profound holiness, but collectively they do reflect a wise, seasoned soul.

Generosity

At the end of Georges Bernanos's 1936 novel *Diary of a Country Priest*, Fr. Laydu, the protagonist of the book, lays suffering and dying of cancer, but he is at peace. His final words are, "It's all grace." When we realize that we have been graced, that everything comes from God and everything will return to God, then we also realize that there is nothing we need to cling to. Recall the example in chapter 2 that one can catch a monkey as it clings to a treat in a trap. The trapped monkey need only release its grip on the treat and slip its "hand" out. It is trapped by its own greed and failure to imagine a free life. Spiritually mature persons are those whose hands, metaphorically and otherwise, are open to receive gifts and to give gifts. There is no hoarding of time, treasure, or talent. No one is holy who is a miser.

Kindness

Just as spiritual maturity is marked by generosity, it is also marked by kindness. This need not be the kindness of a "bleeding-heart" who seems lost in the moment and gushes everywhere with emotive warmth. Rather, it seems to me that kindness here is a simple kind of posture to the world around us. One's personality is simply kind, and is so when one is taking a solitary walk, talking to a friend, or accosted by a beggar. Kindness is who one becomes. In Jesus's image of the final judgment, he describes those who will enter paradise and those who will be sent to eternal punishment (Mt 25:31–46). Those who enter paradise gave food to the hungry, clothed the naked, cared for the sick, and visited prisoners.

This is not meant to be a specific or exhaustive list; the point is that there is great need and suffering in the world, and that the spiritually mature walk in kindness, especially with the poor and suffering.

Patience

Patience has to it a kind of constancy of spirit and acceptance of what is before one. Above all, one has to be patient with oneself. The road to holiness is long, often involving one step backward before one can take two steps forward. A developed soul knows how to wait for things to emerge in their own time. There comes, in the process of interior maturity, an intuition that considers when and how to anticipate resolutions. Sometimes you have to wait. This does not mean one ought not to act with urgency when the moment demands. Rather, one learns to be comfortable with time and even comfortable with feelings of discomfort.

Compassion

Jesus's parable about the last judgment could be used here as well. There is great suffering in the world, and a holy person has the honed skill to lean into it. As we saw in the divine abiding meditations in chapter 6, compassion is not pity. It is not a reactive place of fear in response to the suffering of another. Nor is it a place of superiority, in which one is saddened by the pain someone else has and is just glad it isn't our own. So important is compassion that we saw it as one of two intrinsic qualities of Buddha-nature, and we saw that it is the cornerstone of an authentic Jewish piety. I remember being an idealistic and rather judgmental young man. My mentor, Fr. Bill Kenny, told me that he didn't think I had much compassion, and he thought this was because I hadn't suffered enough personally. I dismissed this until I went through a dark night of the soul some years later. I was never more compassionate as at that time. I learned what it means to *lean in*.

Humility

Traditionally in Christianity, the fall of Adam and Eve was due to the sin of pride. They wanted to be gods, but they were made of dirt. "Pride goeth before the fall," as the saying goes. To be puffed up about oneself is not to know much about oneself. We are prideful when we forget our contingency. Everything that we are has to do with the many supports around us. There is no "self-made" man (or woman). Above all, we are contingent on God. Spiritually mature persons experience their contingency deep down, and they are aware of their own shortcomings. There is a Buddhist saying that goes, "Self-awareness is no good news." But humility is not the opposite of confidence. There are many saints in various traditions who were very confident, presumably because of their closeness to God. And because of that intimacy, they were strikingly humble.

Selflessness and Self-possession

There is a kind of paradox in the spiritual life. The more self-less we are, the more self-possession we have. As we saw in chapter 2, the Buddha taught that we have no self, but rather are a collection of impersonal aggregates. The way to discover this is through deep self-awareness. When one becomes selfless, one becomes free; free of the tyranny of the ego. With nothing to protect and nothing to advance we have the spaciousness to live authentically. That is the very spaciousness we also need to know ourselves, be at home with our selves, and carry ourselves in freedom. Mature souls are not reactive souls, and they have spent enough time in spiritual practice that they know who they are. Once, while I was getting my PhD in Berkeley, California, my friends and I were praising one of our professors who did not seem to have an ego that needed to lord over anything or anyone. One noted thoughtfully, "It is obvious that Beth has done her inner work."

Questioning

I was once on a retreat in the midst of a spiritual crisis, and my retreat director told me, "Do not be afraid of looking deeply. Where the truth is, there is God." God is Truth—not my religion, not my sacred texts. If I really believed that, then I would be free to question any and everything. God could hardly be offended if my questioning is in pursuit of the truth, as this is necessarily the pursuit of God. Spiritually mature persons are not afraid of questioning because they are not afraid of what is true. The means that we are always growing, always revising, always seeking the more. Constant questioning can be obnoxious; we have to rest in things we can trust. But fear of questioning or the refusal to question is tantamount to stopping inner growth. Questioning is not the opposite of confidence; it is an expression of it.

Realistic

As we saw in Cannon's assessment criteria of ways of being religious, religion becomes unbalanced when it is utterly idealistic. We also saw this in chapter 6 with the very human Jewish understanding of the "two impulses." Idealism imagines the spiritual life as existing in some pure Platonic spiritual plane of existence. But the reality is that humans are complex, relationships are complex, and the world is complex. To imagine striving for a seemingly impossible ideal may appear spiritually skillful, since it *seems* as though one is shooting for high holiness even if one may never make it. In truth, it is a fool's errand. Wise souls realize another way to be as devout as they can without falling into an idealistic trap. I recall that many years ago, one of my cousins was pregnant before marriage. There was great alarm at the *scandal* and the *sin* of it all. My grandmother said, scowling, "Let go of your egos now, and get on with supporting the kids."

Holistic

A spiritually mature person looks to the whole of her or his life as the field of growth. One does not compartmentalize business from family from faith, and so on. Everything in one's life and every part of one's psyche must be included in the pursuit of wisdom and truth. There ought to be no part of us that gets a pass; the spiritual life is about how we carry ourselves in every part of our life. Our spiritual life matters when we wash the dishes as much as when we share our faith. Anglican theologian John Macquarrie taught that spirituality "has to do with becoming a person in the fullest sense."[5] Perhaps the great task for us could be restated: it is not how to become a holy person, but how to become a human person. Holism in the spiritual life means to be truly integrated within oneself and wholly engaged in the world outside oneself.

Comfortable with Ambiguity

Jack Kornfield, a psychologist and renowned Buddhist teacher, once noted that "spiritual maturity is that of *embracing opposites*, a capacity to hold the contradictions of life in our heart."[6] A developed spirit has a sense of irony, of metaphor, of humor, and the capacity to embrace the whole with all its beauty and outrageousness. In John Tarrant's book on Zen koans, *Bring Me the Rhinoceros*, he interprets a particular koan known as *The Red Thread*. It is very short: "Songyuan asked, 'Why can't clear-eyed Bodhisattvas sever the red thread?'" Tarrant observes that red is "the color of blood, of fire, of sex, of intimacy." He goes on to describe a Zen teacher who was dying of AIDS. He had also been a drag queen in San Francisco—all this at the same time. "It was the red thread of time, when desire and kindness and death were intimately twined together, and the puritans had very little to contribute. . . . Someone had told him that they thought AIDS terribly unfair. 'You get what you deserve,' he replied, 'whether you deserve it or not.'"[7]

Personal and Unique

Recall the quote by C. S. Lewis in chapter 8 that included: "The more we get what we now call 'ourselves' out of the way and let Him take us over, the more truly ourselves we become."[8] What Lewis is getting at is that, in the Divine, our very uniqueness shines. This is not the uniqueness of the particular affectations we express to define ourselves in some artificial way. That is simply a version of "Look at me! See how interesting I am." Rather, we shine with our own truth, our own particular soul. We shine with our own creativity only when we are not trying to advance a *persona*. Then creativity becomes the natural expression of ourselves. Then the real person comes out, comes alive. One of the dangers of the spiritual path is to take some model, whether it be a saint or other kind of hero, and strive to replicate their holiness. The story goes that Leo, a friend of St. Francis of Assisi, was bemoaning that he could never be like Francis. Francis replied, "Leo, on the last day God will not ask, 'Have you been a good Francis?' but rather, 'Have you been a good Leo?'"

Equanimous

We saw in chapter 6 that equanimity is one of the divine abiding meditations. Recall that its *near enemy* is indifference. This is perhaps the greatest of sins; to stop caring is to stop living. The equanimity of spiritual maturity is balanced and even flexible. Consider it a kind of flexible-stability, whereby one stands stably for the deepest self and yet engages in life with skillful fluidity. Equanimity is open to the moment, sensitive to the present, and available to it. It is non-reactive and thus free. The wizened soul tries less to control the moment than to act skillfully within it. Equanimity represents a heart and soul that is spacious enough to hold a great deal and to live calmly and collectively therein. It is in this space that one responds to the world most freely and most fully.

Deeply Embedded in a Tradition

When I was going through my doctoral program's defense of my five comprehensive exams, one of the examiners asked me a question rather out of the blue: "Do you think someone can be holy without belonging to a religion?" I paused long to think. My answer was, "Yes, but I have never met someone I imagine holy who was not deeply involved in a spiritual tradition." I fear that ours is an age of spiritual dilettantes, those seeking *cheap grace*. One can sign up for a weekend retreat and imagine learning tantric esoterica or shamanic rites. One can mess around with such things and imagine much. But real transformation requires a long haul. Spiritual development is painstaking work, and I believe that it succeeds best when it is done within the care of authentic leaders and a supportive faith group. One's spirituality would be limited in some ways. Religions are specific, and they provide a lens that heightens a vision and facilitates experiences within that vision. This, of course, then is somewhat limiting. There are other lenses of spiritual imagination that would have to be set aside. One cannot deeply practice anything and everything. The purpose of this book is to inspire and to highlight insights from some of the world's great traditions. Some of these perspectives might be able to be integrated into one's path, others less so. At the end of the day, if you want to be holy or at least spiritually mature, pick a path and walk it. This is my advice.

Notes

1. John Hick, *An Interpretation of Religion: Human Responses to the Transcendent*, 2nd ed. (New Haven, CT: Yale University Press, 2004), 11.

2. *Udana* 6.4.

3. Robert Kennedy, *Zen Spirit, Christian Spirit* (New York: Continuum, 1995), 13–14.

4. Dale Cannon, *Six Ways of Being Religious: A Framework for Comparative Studies in Religion* (Belmont, CA: Wadsworth, 1996).

5. John Macquarrie, *Paths in Spirituality* (New York: Harper & Row, 1972), 40.

6. Jack Kornfield, *A Path with a Heart: A Guide through the Perils and Promises of Spiritual Life* (New York: Bantam, 1993), 317.

7. John Tarrant, *Bring Me the Rhinoceros: And Other Zen Koans That Will Save Your Life* (Boston: Shambhala, 2008), 77–81.

8. C. S. Lewis, *Mere Christianity* (New York: Harper and Collins, 1952, 2001), 223.

Bibliography

Buddhism

Anguttara Nikaya: The Numerical Discourses of the Buddha. Translated by Bhikkhu Bodhi. Somerville, MA: Wisdom Publications, 2012.

Buddhaghosa, Bhadantacariya. *The Path of Purification* [*Visuddhimagga*]. 5th ed. Translated by Bhikkhu Nanamoli. Kandy, Sri Lanka: Buddhist Publication Society, 1991.

Burtt, E. A., ed. *The Teachings of the Compassionate Buddha: Early Discourses, the Dhammapada, and Later Basic Writings*. New York: New American Library, 2000.

Conze, Edward, ed. *Buddhist Scriptures*. New York: Penguin, 1959.

Digha Nikaya: The Long Discourses of the Buddha. Translated by Maurice Walshe. Somerville, MA: Wisdom Publications, 1987.

Feldmeier, Peter. *Dhammapada: The Way of Truth*. Kandy: Buddhist Publication Society, 2013.

Gunaratana, Mahathera. *Bhavana Vandana: Book of Devotion*. Taipei, Taiwan: Bhavana Society, 1990.

Kornfield, Jack. *A Path with Heart: A Guide through the Perils and Promises of Spiritual Life*. New York: Bantam, 1993.

Majjhima Nikaya: The Middle Length Discourses of the Buddha. Translated by Bhikkhu Nanamoli and Bhikkhu Bodhi. Somerville, MA: Wisdom Publications, 1995.

Robinson, Richard, et al. *Buddhist Religions: A Historical Introduction.*
     5th ed. Belmont, CA: Wadsworth, 2005.
Samyutta Nikaya: The Connected Discourses of the Buddha. Trans-
     lated by Bhikkhu Bodhi. Somerville, MA: Wisdom Publica-
     tions, 2000.
Shantideva. *Bodhicaryavatara.* Translated by Kate Crosby and Andrew
     Skilton. Oxford: Oxford University Press, 1995.
———. *Shantideva's Bodhicaryavatara.* Translated by Padmakara Trans-
     lation Group. Boston: Shambhala, 2003.
Suzuki, D. T. *Essays in Zen Buddhism.* London: Rider, 1973.
Tarrant, John. *Bring Me the Rhinoceros: And Other Zen Koans That
     Will Save Your Life.* Boston: Shambhala, 2008.
———. *The Light Inside the Dark: Zen, Soul, and the Spiritual Life.*
     New York: Harper Perennial, 1998.
Thurman, Robert. *The Tibetan Book of the Dead: Liberation through
     Understanding in the Between.* New York: Bantam, 1994.
Udana and Itivuttaka. Translated by John Ireland. Kandy: Buddhist
     Publication Society, 1997.
Victoria, Brian. *Zen at War.* New York: Rowman & Littlefield, 2005.
———. *Zen War Stories.* London: Routledge/Curzon, 2003.
Watson, Burton, trans. *The Lotus Sutra.* New York: Columbia Univer-
     sity Press, 1993.
Williams, Paul. *Mahayana Buddhism: The Doctrinal Foundations.* 2nd
     ed. London: Routledge, 2009.
Wright, Dale. *What Is Buddhist Enlightenment?* Oxford: Oxford Uni-
     versity Press, 2016.

Christianity

Athanasius. *The Life of Antony and the Letter to Marcellinus.* Trans-
     lated by Robert C. Gregg. New York: Paulist Press, 1980.
Augustine, Saint. *The Confessions.* Translated by Henry Chadwick.
     Oxford: Oxford University Press, 1991.
Barton, John, and John Muddiman, eds. *The Oxford Bible Commen-
     tary.* Oxford: Oxford University Press, 2001.
Basil the Great. *St. Basil: Ascetical Works.* Translated by Monica Wag-
     ner. New York: Fathers of the Church, 1950.
Benedict XVI, Pope. *Caritas in Veritate.* 51 ASS 101 (2009).
Bernard of Clairvaux. *Bernard of Clairvaux: Selected Works.* Translated
     by G. S. Evans. Mahwah, NJ: Paulist Press, 1987.

Brown, Raymond E., et al. eds. *The New Jerome Biblical Commentary*. Englewood Cliffs, NJ: Prentice Hall, 1990.

Feldmeier, Peter. *Encounters in Faith: Christianity in Interreligious Dialogue*. Winona, MN: Anselm Academic, 2011.

———. *Christian Spirituality: Lived Expressions in the Life of the Church*. Winona, MN: Anselm Academic, 2015.

———. *The Christian Tradition: A Historical and Theological Introduction*. New York: Oxford University Press, 2017.

———. *Experiments in Buddhist-Christian Encounter: From Buddha-Nature to the Divine Nature*. Maryknoll, NY: Orbis Books, 2019.

Flannery, Austin, ed. *Vatican II: The Conciliar and Post Conciliar Documents*. Rev. ed. Vol. 1. Northport, NY: Costello, 1975.

Francis I, Pope. *Laudate Si'*. Vatican City: Libraria Vaticana, 2015.

Francis of Assisi. *St. Francis of Assisi: Writings and Early Biographies*. 4th ed. Edited by Marion Habig. Chicago: Franciscan Herald Press, 1983.

Gavrilyuk, Paul, and Sarah Coakley, eds. *The Spiritual Senses: Perceiving God in Western Christianity*. Cambridge: Cambridge University Press, 2012.

Gutiérrez, Gustavo. *We Drink from Our Own Wells*. Translated by Matthew O'Connell. Maryknoll, NY: Orbis Books, 1972.

Haight, Roger. *Jesus, Symbol of God*. Maryknoll, NY: Orbis Books, 1999.

Howells, Edward, and Mark McIntosh, eds. *The Oxford Handbook on Mystical Theology*. Oxford: Oxford University Press, 2020.

John of the Cross. *The Collected Works of John of the Cross*. Rev. ed. Translated by Kieran Kavanaugh and Otilio Rodriguez. Washington, DC: ICS Publications, 1991.

John Paul II, Pope. *Redemptor Hominis*. 15 ASS 71 (1979).

Kennedy, Robert. *Zen Spirit, Christian Spirit*. New York: Continuum, 1995.

Lane, Dermot. *Christ at the Centre: Selected Issues in Christology*. New York: Paulist Press, 1991.

Lewis, C. S. *Mere Christianity*. New York: Harper and Collins, 1952, 2001.

Lohfink, Gerhard. *Jesus of Nazareth: What He Wanted, Who He Was*. Translated by Linda Maloney. Collegeville, MN: Liturgical Press, 2012.

———. *No Irrelevant Jesus: On Jesus and the Church Today*. Translated by Linda Maloney. Collegeville, MN: Michael Glazier, 2014.

Lossky, Vladimir. *The Mystical Theology of the Eastern Church*. Crestwood, NY: St. Vladimir's Seminary Press, 1976.

Louth, Andrew. *The Origins of the Christian Mystical Tradition: From Plato to Denys*. 2nd ed. Oxford: Oxford University Press, 2007.

Macquarrie, John. *Paths in Spirituality*. New York: Harper & Row, 1972.

Merton, Thomas. *Conjectures of a Guilty Bystander*. New York: Image Books, 1968.

———. *New Seeds of Contemplation*. New York: New Directions, 1961.

Paul VI, Pope. *Octogesima Adveniens*. 21 AAS 63 (1971).

Pizzuto, Vincent. *Contemplating Christ: The Gospels and the Interior Life*. Collegeville, MN: Liturgical Press, 2018.

Rahner, Karl. *The Spirit in the Church*. New York: Seabury, 1979.

Smith, Mark. *How Human Is God?* Collegeville, MN: Liturgical Press, 2014.

Ware, Kallistos. *The Orthodox Way*. Rev. ed. Crestwood, NY: St. Vladimir's Seminary Press, 1979.

Watson, Francis. *The Fourfold Gospel: A Theological Reading of the New Testament Portraits of Jesus*. Grand Rapids, MI: Baker Academic, 2016.

Daoism

Ames, Roger T., and David L. Hall. *Daodejing: Making This Life Significant—A Philosophical Translation*. New York: Ballantine Books, 2003.

Brook, Timothy. "Rethinking Syncretism: The Unity of the Three Teachings and Their Joint Worship in Late-Imperial China." *Journal of Chinese Religions* 21 (Fall 1993): 13–44.

Chan, Wing-tsit, trans. and ed. *A Source Book in Chinese Philosophy*. Princeton, NJ: Princeton University Press, 1963.

Chuang Tzu [Zhuangzi]. *Chuang Tzu: Basic Writings*. Translated by Burton Watson. New York: Columbia University Press, 1964.

Kohn, Livia. *Readings in Daoist Mysticism*. Magdalena, NM: Three Pine Press, 2009.

Lao Tzu [Laozi]. *Tao Te Ching*. Translated by D. C. Lau. New York: Penguin Books, 1963.

Lao Tsu [Laozi]. *Tao Te Ching*. Translated by Gia-Fu Feng and Jane English. New York: Vintage, 1972.

Laozi. *Daodejing*. Translated by Edmund Ryden. Oxford: Oxford University Press, 2008.

Li, Puqun. *A Guide to Asian Philosophy Classics*. Peterborough, ON: Broadview Press, 2012.

Zhuangzi. *Zhuangzi*. Translated by Hyun Hochsmann and Yang Guorong. New York: Pearson, 2007.

Hinduism

Ayyangar, T. R. Srinivasa. *The Yoga Upanishads*. Madrass: Vedanta Press, 1938.

Bhagavad-Gita. Translated by Barbara Stoler Miller with Introduction by Huston Smith. New York: Quality Paperback Book Club, 1998.

Clooney, Francis X. *Hindu Wisdom for All God's Children*. Maryknoll, NY: Orbis Books, 1998.

Cornille, Catherine, ed. *Song Divine: Christian Commentaries on the Bhagavad-Gita*. Leuven: Peters, 2006.

Hopkins, Thomas. *The Hindu Religious Tradition*. Encino, CA: Dickenson Publishing, 1971. All citations from the *Rig-Vedas* come from this volume, unless otherwise noted.

Klostermaier, Klaus K. *A Survey of Hinduism*. 2nd ed. Albany: State University of New York, 1994.

Radhakrishnan, Sarvelpalli, trans. and ed. *The Principal Upanishads*. London: George Allen Unwin, 1953. All citations of the Upanishads come from this volume, unless otherwise noted.

Ramakrishna, Sri. *The Gospel of Sri Ramakrishna*. Translated by and with an Introduction by Swami Nikhilananda. New York: Ramakrishna-Vivekananda Center, 1942.

———. *The Life of Ramakrishna Compiled from Various Authentic Sources*. 2nd ed. Calcutta: Advaita Ashrama, 1964.

Saradananda, Swami. *Sri Ramakrishna the Great Master*. 3rd ed. Translated by Swami Jagadananda. Madras: Sri Ramakrishna Math, 1963.

Shantideva. *The Bodhicaryavatara*. Translated by Kate Crosby and Andrew Skiilton. Oxford University Press, 1995.

Sivaraman, Krishna, ed. *Hindu Spirituality: Vedas through Vedanta*. Delhi: Motilal Banarsidass, 1995.

Sundararajan, K. R., and Bithika Mukerji, eds. *Hindu Spirituality: Postclassical and Modern*. New York: Crossroad, 1997.

Thomas, Edward, trans. and ed. *Vedic Hymns*. London: J. Murray, 1923.

Zaehner, R. C. *Hindu and Muslim Mysticism*. Oxford: Oneworld, 1960.

Islam

Dawood, N. J., ed. *The Koran*. 5th ed. New York: Penguin Books, 1990.

Esack, Farid. *On Being a Muslim: Finding a Religious Path in the World Today*. Oxford: Oneworld, 1999.

Jeffery, Arthur, ed. *A Reader on Islam: Passages from Standard Arabic Writing Illustrative of the Beliefs and Practices of Muslims*. The Hague: Mouton, 1962.

Nasr, Seyyed Hossein, ed. *Islamic Spirituality: Foundations*. New York: Crossroad, 1987.

———, ed. *The Study Quran: A New Translation and Commentary* (New York: HarperOne, 2015.

Rahman, Jamal. *The Fragrance of Faith: The Enlightened Mind of Islam*. Bath, UK: Book Foundation, 2004.

Rumi, Jalal ad-Din. *The Essential Rumi*. Translated by Coleman Banks. New York: HarperSanFrancisco, 1995.

———. *Jewels of Remembrance*. Edited by Camille Helminski and Kabir Helminski. Putney, VT: Threshold Books, 1996.

Zaehner, R. C. *Hindu and Muslim Mysticism*. Oxford: Oneworld, 1960.

Judaism

Biale, David, et al., eds. *Hasidism: A New History*. Princeton, NJ: Princeton University Press, 2020.

Bokser, Ben Zion, and Baruch M. Bokser, eds. and trans. *The Talmud: Selected Writings*. New York: Paulist Press, 1989.

Buber, Martin. *Hasidism and Modern Man*. New York: Horizon Press, 1958.

———. *The Way of Man According to the Teachings of Hasidism*. New York: Carol Publishing Group, 1995.

Diale, David, et al. *Hasidism: A New History*. Princeton, NJ: Princeton University Press, 2018.

Feldmeier, Peter. "Interrelatedness and Spiritual Masters: Why Martin Buber Still Matters." *The Way* 51, no. 3 (2014): 63–75.

Green, Arthur, ed. *Jewish Spirituality: From the Bible through the Middle Ages*. New York: Crossroad, 1996.

Heschel, Abraham Joshua. *I Asked for Wonder: A Spiritual Anthology.* Edited by Samuel H. Dresner. New York: Crossroad, 1986.

———. *The Sabbath: Its Meaning for Modern Man.* New York: Farrar, Straus and Giroux. 1951.

———. *Who Is Man?* Stanford, CA: Stanford University Press, 1965.

Holtz, Barry W., ed. *Back to the Sources: Reading the Classic Jewish Texts.* New York: Touchstone, 1984.

Idel, Moshe, and Bernard McGinn. *Mystical Union in Judaism, Christianity, and Islam: An Ecumenical Dialogue.* New York: Continuum, 1996.

Kushner, Lawrence. *God Was in This Place and I, I Did Not Know.* Woodstock, VT: Jewish Lights, 1998.

———. *Honey from the Rock: An Introduction to Jewish Mysticism.* Woodstock, VT: Jewish Lights, 2000.

———. *Jewish Spirituality: A Brief Introduction for Christians.* Woodstock, VT: Jewish Lights, 2001.

Merkle, John. *The Genesis of Faith: The Depth Theology of Abraham Joshua Heschel.* New York: Macmillan, 1985.

Montefiore, C. G., and H. Loewe, eds. *A Rabbinic Anthology.* New York: Schocken Books, 1974.

Petuchowski, Jakob J. *Our Masters Taught: Rabbinic Stories and Sayings.* New York: Crossroad, 1982.

Scheindlin, Raymond P. *The Gazelle: Medieval Hebrew Poems on God, Israel, and the Soul.* New York: Oxford University Press, 1991.

———. *Wine, Women, and Death: Medieval Hebrew Poems on the Good Life.* New York: Oxford University Press, 1986.

Steinsaltz, Adin. *The Thirteen Petalled Rose: A Discourse on the Essence of Jewish Existence and Belief.* Rev. ed. Translated by Yehuda Hanegbi. New York: Basic Books, 2006.

Telushkin, Joseph. *Jewish Literacy.* New York: Image Books, 1982.

Wiesel, Elie. *Four Hasidic Masters and Their Struggle against Melancholy.* Notre Dame, IN: University of Notre Dame Press, 1978.

Native American

Black Elk, Nicholas. *Black Elk Speaks.* Edited by John G. Neihardt. Lincoln: University of Nebraska Press, 1979.

———. *The Sacred Pipe: Black Elk's Account of the Seven Rites of the Oglala Sioux*. Edite by Joseph Epes Brown. Norman: University of Oklahoma Press, 1953.

Costello, Damian. *Black Elk: Colonialism and Lakota Catholicism*. Maryknoll, NY: Orbis Books, 2005.

Notes, Akwesasne, ed. *Basic Call to Consciousness*. Summertown, TN: Native Voices, 1978.

General

Cannon, Dale. *Six Ways of Being Religious: A Framework for Comparative Studies in Religion*. Belmont, CA: Wadsworth, 1996.

D'Aquili, Eugene, and Andrew Newberg. *The Mystical Mind: Probing the Biology of Religious Experience*. Minneapolis: Fortress Press, 1999.

Harley, Trevor. *The Science of Consciousness: Waking, Sleeping and Dreaming*. Cambridge: Cambridge University Press, 2021.

Hick, John. *The Fifth Dimension*. Oxford: Oneworld, 1999.

———. *An Interpretation of Religion: Human Responses to the Transcendent*. 2nd ed. New Haven, CT: Yale University Press, 2004.

Katz, Steven, ed. *Comparative Mysticism: An Anthology of Original Sources*. Oxford: Oxford University Press, 2013.

Newberg, Andrew, Eugene D'Aquili, and Vince Rause. *Why God Won't Go Away: Brain Science and the Biology of Belief*. New York: Ballantine Books, 2002.

Paper, Jordan. *The Mystical Experience: A Descriptive and Comparative Analysis*. Albany: State University of New York Press, 2004.

Plantinga, Alvin. "Dennett's Dangerous Idea: Evolution and the Meanings of Life." *Books and Culture* 2 (May/June 1996): 16–18.

Plotinus. *The Enneads*. Translated by Stephen MacKenna. New York: Penguin, 1991.

Putman, Robert, and David Campbell. *American Grace: How Religion Divides and Unites Us*. New York: Simon & Schuster, 2010.

Smith, Christian. *Soul Searching: The Religious Lives of American Teenagers*. New York: Oxford University Press, 2005.

Vaughn, Lewis, ed. *Anthology of World Religions: Sacred Texts and Contemporary Perspectives*. New York: Oxford University Press, 2017.

Index